ESSAYS ON EDUCATION

ESSAYS ON EDUCATION
(1830-1862)

BY

AMOS BRONSON ALCOTT

TOGETHER WITH THE
TOWN REPORTS FOR 1859-1861
AND THE
SCHOOL REPORTS FOR 1861-1862
OF
CONCORD, MASSACHUSETTS

FACSIMILE REPRODUCTIONS
WITH AN INTRODUCTION

BY

WALTER HARDING
State University Teachers College
Geneseo, New York

GAINESVILLE, FLORIDA
SCHOLARS' FACSIMILES & REPRINTS
1960

SCHOLARS' FACSIMILES & REPRINTS
118 N.W. 26TH STREET
GAINESVILLE, FLORIDA, U.S.A.
HARRY R. WARFEL, GENERAL EDITOR

FOR

CARL BODE

L.C. CATALOG CARD NUMBER 60-5072

MANUFACTURED IN THE U.S.A.
LETTERPRESS BY J. N. ANZEL, INC.
PHOTOLITHOGRAPHY BY EDWARDS BROTHERS
BINDING BY UNIVERSAL-DIXIE BINDERY

TABLE OF CONTENTS

ACKNOWLEDGMENTS

I am particularly indebted to Mrs. Ruth Wheeler of Concord, Massachusetts, for calling my attention to the Concord Town and School Reports and suggesting the value of bringing them back into print; to Mrs. Wheeler and Mrs. Gladys Hosmer, also of Concord, for permitting me to use their personal copies of the reports for reproduction in this volume, and to Mrs. Hosmer for searching the archives in Concord Town Hall and the office of the superintendent of schools in Concord in an unsuccessful attempt to uncover Alcott's original manuscript reports.

The two Alcott pamphlets are reproduced from copies in the Library of Congress.

INTRODUCTION

Amos Bronson Alcott (1799-1888) has been a force in American public education for well over a century. The schools he conducted as a young man were among the most frequently visited and widely discussed of their time. His reports as superintendent of schools in Concord, Massachusetts, achieved circulation well beyond that town's borders. He wrote for the educational journals of his day, appeared on lecture platforms, and conducted what he liked to call "conversations" on education up and down the East Coast and throughout the Middle West. His influence on the educational theories of his fellow Transcendentalists — men such as Emerson and Thoreau — was marked; through Emerson in particular he undoubtedly had an influence on the thinking of John Dewey. His most devoted disciple, William Torrey Harris, for seventeen years (1889-1906) the United States Commissioner of Education, gave his theories a direct influence on national educational practices.

Yet, despite his unquestionable importance in American education, Bronson Alcott has been almost completely forgotten by modern historians of education. Ellwood P. Cubberley's *Public Education in the United States*, long considered one of the standard histories, does not even mention Alcott's name. Other accounts of American education give little more than a passing reference to him.

Why has he been forgotten? Part of the fault lies with Alcott himself. He was always more ready to talk than to write, so that comparatively little of his philosophy of education got written. When he did write his ideas down, they were usually published in pamphlet form so ephemeral that now a century later it requires long search to find copies. And, unfortunately, chiefly because of his "Orphic Sayings" in the pages of the Transcendentalist periodical *The Dial*, he acquired a reputation for windy vapidness that does not at all apply to his writings on education.

It is the purpose of this volume, therefore, to bring back into print and make more readily available some of the more significant of Bronson Alcott's writings on education. His reports are presented in the larger context of the complete town and school reports, so that something of the spirit of the community and of its leading citizens may help define Alcott's contribution to Concord.

Although Alcott had comparatively little formal schooling, and most of that in a one-room rural school, his interest in education was life-long. In 1822, while wandering through the South as a peddler, he stopped long enough in Warrenton, Virginia, to conduct a "Writing School" for a few months. A year later he taught the winter term in a rural school in Bristol, near his native Wolcott, Connecticut, and for the next four years taught here and there in neighboring schools. But despite his youth and his lack of formal training, his methods aroused attention; one of his schools was described in Connecticut and Massachusetts newspapers of the time as "the best common school in the state, perhaps in the United States" (Dorothy McCuskey, *Bronson Alcott, Teacher,* New York, 1940, p. 28).

In 1828 Alcott moved to Boston; for the next ten years (except for an interlude in Germantown, Pennsylvania, from 1831 to 1833) he conducted various schools there. His methods continued to attract attention, particularly

when Elizabeth Peabody, who had for a time acted as
his assistant, published a 208-page *Record of a School*
(Boston, 1835), detailing his methods of instruction. But
the publication of Alcott's *Conversations with Children
on the Gospels* (2 vols., Boston, 1836, 1837), a transcript
of his discussions of the life of Jesus with his pupils,
brought down a storm upon his head. The book was de-
nounced as both blasphemous and obscene. Although a
number of outstanding men, among them Ralph Waldo
Emerson, came to his defense, most of the parents with-
drew their children from his school. When he then en-
rolled a Negro child as a pupil, the few remaining children were withdrawn, and he had to abandon his school.
This was his last formal experience as a teacher.

Alcott's interest in education did not disappear. He tu-
tored all his own children and occasionally those of
friends and neighbors. Then, in 1859, came an opportunity to return to active work in the field of education. He
was offered appointment as superintendent of schools in
Concord, Massachusetts, and quickly accepted. For the
next six years Alcott visited every school in Concord at
least once a month, conducted examinations, led teachers' meetings, sponsored parent-teacher discussions, and
wrote annual reports on his activities. Unfortunately in
1865, thanks to what was apparently some undercover
political maneuvering, he was not reappointed. But he
never lost interest in the schools. In 1875-1876 when Edward Emerson, the son of Ralph Waldo, was made superintendent, Alcott voluntarily resumed his rounds of
the Concord schools.

One more of his experiments in education should be
mentioned. In 1879, with the help of William Torrey Harris, Frank Sanborn, and others, he established the Concord School of Philosophy, an informal adult summer

school conducted in a specially constructed hall on the grounds of his home in Concord. Alcott was, by this time, too feeble to bear the brunt of the labors, so that others attended to the mechanics of administration. But he was unquestionably the focal point of the school, and the school closed with his death in 1888. Educational theory was not the sole topic there, but it was never far from the center of attention. Harris, in particular, used the school as a sounding board for an exposition of the theories of education he had learned from Alcott.

From Alcott's various essays on education I have chosen five as the most significant. All five achieved but ephemeral publication in his lifetime and are now extremely difficult to find.

Observations on the Principles and Methods of Infant Instruction (1830) was published in pamphlet form, in an edition of one thousand copies, at the author's own expense by Carter and Hendee of Boston. Alcott was then a "teacher of an elementary school [in] Boston." It is believed that he wrote the essay to compete for a prize of $100 offered by the Controllers of the Public Schools of the First School District of Pennsylvania for the best "system of school discipline, lessons, and other means adapted to the instruction of children under five years of age, which shall embrace economy, efficiency, and simplicity of details." Although the essay did not win the prize, it attracted the attention of Roberts Vaux, president of the Board of Controllers, who wrote Alcott, urging that he publish the essay: "Thy essay I have attentively read; it afforded me more pleasure and instruction than anything of the kind which has come under my notice. It is strongly marked by practical wisdom and pure Christian philosophy, and is worthy a place in every family in our country. . . . I will use every means to aid in the diffusion of such doctrines as thy communication teaches, assured that their adoption by parents and teachers would administer incalculable blessings to the rising generation" (Quoted in McCuskey, pp. 55-56).

It cost Alcott $250 (half of his average annual income at the time) to print. But it served a purpose, for it called Alcott's theories to the attention of Reuben Haines, a wealthy Pennsylvania Quaker, who invited Alcott to come to Germantown to conduct a school. Unfortunately Haines died shortly after the school was established, and it had to be abandoned through lack of funds. Alcott then returned to Boston where he opened his Temple School.

The Doctrine and Discipline of Human Culture (1836), issued as a pamphlet by J. Munroe and Co. of Boston and later included as an introduction to Alcott's *Conversations with Children on the Gospels* (1837), was a direct result of Alcott's work at the Temple School and an exposition of the theories he practiced therein. In the furore that followed the publication of *Conversations*, *The Doctrine and Discipline* was almost completely ignored. Yet as a statement of Alcott's theories it is far more important than the larger work that it introduced.

In New England it was (and is) the custom for each town to publish annual reports of its officials as the basis for discussion of the town's affairs at its annual meeting. Among these reports was usually one from the school committee, devoted for the most part to an enumeration of the teachers' salaries and other expenses of school-keeping. Notable exceptions to these reports are those for the schools of Concord during the first three years that Bronson Alcott was superintendent. The school committee in each of those years submitted the usual rather mundane and prosaic accounting for the funds placed in their trust by the taxpayers, but they appended to their reports the far from mundane and prosaic reports made by their superintendent.

The first Alcott report appeared in the *Reports of the Selectmen and Other Officers of the Town of Concord, from March 7, 1859, to March 5, 1860* (Concord, 1860). It is a condensation of a longer, unpublished report, for, in the words of the school committee, "Mr. Alcott has taken occasion to treat the whole subject [of education] more fully than the limits of a town report allow" (p. 5). The full version apparently has not survived. The published part, even though condensed, is worthy of close attention. Henry Barnard, later the first United States Commissioner of Education, praised it as the best ever compiled and suggested that the next year's report be printed in full and that arrangements be made for its wide distribution. The suggestion was accepted, and the 1861 report (in *Reports of the Selectmen . . . from March 5, 1860, to March 4, 1861*) was nearly triple the size of the first report. In 1862 Yankee economy apparently caught up with Transcendental idealism, and the report that year (in *Reports of the School Committee and Superintendent of the Schools, of the Town of Concord, Mass., 1862*) was cut back to half the length of the first report, the school committee commenting: "He [Alcott] has worked, not only for the town, but for the State and the world; for his annual reports, widely circulated and received with appreciation, have done much to advance true ideas of education in other towns, and throughout the land. The town's liberality in publishing such reports has been well bestowed; but this year it has not been thought best to occupy so much space in this way" (p. 8).

In 1863 the wave of economy hit even harder. No separate report of the superintendent was printed, but instead in the school committee report it was stated, "Your Superintendent, having given his views fully in past years, has not desired to make a separate report this year" (*Annual Report of the School Committee of the Town of Concord, Mass.*, 1863, p. 7). It is hard to believe that Alcott would ever have refused an opportunity to expound his views. Indeed, in the very next sentence of its report the school committee speaks of Alcott's "account of the condition of the schools" and throughout the remainder of its report quotes brief extracts of a factual nature. This same policy of excerpting Alcott's reports was followed for the remaining years of his tenure as superintendent.

Was Alcott's work as superintendent appreciated within his own community? The town printed only one of his reports in full, and in 1865, through a devious political maneuver, he was put out of office. On the other hand, the members of the school committee unquestionably recognized and appreciated his services. In their report at the end of his first year they stated, "The superintendent has discharged his delicate and responsible duties, we believe, to the eminent satisfaction of all with whom he has been brought in contact, and the year's work has thus been harmonious and efficient. ... The general condition of our schools may be set down as very good; apparently better than for several years past. This we may ascribe to ... the zealous and judicious exertions of the superintendent" (pp. 2-3).

In 1861 they spoke of "the Superintendent, who has performed with extraordinary ability, enthusiasm and diligence the labors imposed by his office" (p. 6). In 1862 they commended "the services of a Superintendent of Schools, whose zeal, ability and devotion have proved his eminent fitness for the office. He has brought to his work extraordinary endowments and long experience, and he has doubled or trebled the labor required of him by the terms of his office" (p. 8). In 1863 they said, "Your Superintendent has given to the schools a more constant care and attention, and this with an interest, fidelity, and expenditure of time and strength far beyond any legal requirements of his office. And the Committee rejoice to say that they believe that the schools were never in a better condition than they are at the present time" (p. 3). In 1864 and 1865 the superintendent was not singled out for praise; I do not know if there is any significance in that fact. But in 1866, *after a year without Alcott's services,* the committee reported that "The results of teaching ... have not been as brilliant and striking as in some past years, and ... certainly the supervision has not been as constant and vigilant as could have been desired" (p. 3).

It is not my purpose in this brief introduction to discuss Bronson Alcott's theories of education — their sources, their values, their weaknesses, nor their influence. Those topics have been thoroughly covered in Dorothy McCuskey's *Bronson Alcott, Teacher* and in George Heafner's *A Critical Estimate of the Educational Theories and Practices of A. Bronson Alcott* (New York, 1937). I would like to suggest, however, that there is room for further study of the interest of the Transcendentalists as a group in their local schools and their influence there.

The three Concord school reports included in this volume are an indication of Alcott's interest, but they also at least hint at the interest of some of the other Concord writers. It will be noted in the "school exhibition supplements" which Alcott appended to his reports that Ralph Waldo Emerson not only attended these annual exhibitions but usually took an active part in them. Thoreau planned to take part at least once, though illness finally

prevented him. It is also to be noted that the secretary
of the school committee through much of Alcott's tenure
was Frank Sanborn, one of the younger generation of
Transcendentalists who had moved to Concord specifical-
ly to be near Emerson.

But a far more significant indication of their interest
lies in the "Concord Book" or "Atlas of Concord" that
Alcott discusses in each of the three reports. In the last
years of his life Henry David Thoreau often spoke of his
intention to compile an atlas of Concord, a yearbook of
the natural history of the locale. It is not so widely known
that this book was intended for use in the Concord schools
and that Thoreau was urged on to the work by Alcott.
In the 1860 school report Alcott wrote: "They [the school
committee] have . . . suggested to the citizen of our town
best able to perform the work, the preparation of a small
text book, for the schools, comprising the geography, history and antiquities of Concord" (p. 11). That "the citizen" was Thoreau and the suggestion Alcott's rather than
the committee's is indicated in the entry of February 4,
1861, in Alcott's *Journals:* "I wish him [Thoreau] to compile his Atlas of Concord, for which he has rich material,
and the genius" (Boston, 1938, p. 334). In the 1861 report Alcott adds: "Happily we have a sort of resident Surveyor-General of the town's farms, farmers, animals, and
everything else it contains, — who makes more of it than
most persons with a continent at their call. Will he just
set his ten senses at work upon an illustrated Atlas for
the citizens, giving such account of the world they inhabit, with such hints concerning the one he lives in, as
he pleases? Such a book would suit us all, and become
a model text book for studies out of doors, and a gift to
our children for which they could not be too grateful. —
The town should find ways of using its best men" (p. 26).

It was not a lack of willingness on Thoreau's part that prevented completion of the Atlas. There are still extant among Thoreau's manuscripts, in particular those in the Berg Collection in The New York Public Library, many charts and catalogs of natural phenomena of Concord that he had obviously prepared as preliminary drafts for the atlas project. But by 1861 Thoreau was a sick man. He had not the strength to complete his labors. He died in 1862. Alcott found no one else capable of carrying on the project, so that it was regretfully abandoned. Had Alcott's career as superintendent begun earlier or had Thoreau's health been better, we might have had a revolutionary type of textbook for our grammar schools, a textbook that would have anticipated some of our most recent developments in elementary education.

Bronson Alcott's greatest difficulty was that he was a century ahead of his time. Only a few of his more perceptive contemporaries recognized his value. Even now we are only beginning to realize the truth of Thoreau's words about him in *Walden:* "I think that he must be the man of the most faith of any alive. His words and attitudes always suppose a better state of things than other men are acquainted with, and he will be the last man to be disappointed as the ages revolve. He has no venture in the present. But though comparatively disregarded now, when his day comes, laws unsuspected by most will take effect, and masters of families and rulers will come to him for advice. ... He is perhaps the sanest man and has the fewest crotchets of any I chance to know. ... I do not see how he can ever die; Nature cannot spare him."

WALTER HARDING

State University Teachers College
Geneseo, New York

OBSERVATIONS

ON THE

PRINCIPLES AND METHODS

OF

INFANT INSTRUCTION.

BY A. B. ALCOTT,

TEACHER OF AN ELEMENTARY SCHOOL, BOSTON.

BOSTON:

PUBLISHED BY CARTER AND HENDEE.

1830.

2

PRINTED BY I. R. BUTTS....BOSTON.

INFANT INSTRUCTION.

THE tendency of the public mind, arising from the comparatively free spirit of our institutions in this country, towards the
study and improvement of human nature, constitutes a feature
of the present day, interesting in the highest degree to the
christian philosopher and philanthropist. The study of man is, of
all others, a study of the first and highest importance. Character,
natural and acquired, modified by temperament, by education,
by society, government, and religion, is a subject worthy of all
attention and analysis. All that affects its formation and its re-
formation; all that mysterious process by which the human mind
accomplishes its great purposes — the perfecting of its nature,
and the elevation of its hopes, should be regarded with a deep
and scrutinizing attention, by all those entrusted with its high
capacities and lofty destinies. To the teacher, the guardian,
and the friend of man, all subjects involving in any degree his
welfare, his improvement, and his happiness, present their claims
for unbiassed inquiry and deep-felt interest.

Of the many methods, by which the wise and good of the

present day, are contributing to the best interests of the mind, redeeming it from the slavery of ignorance and vice, to the liberty of intelligence, virtue, and happiness, the institutions of Infant Schools, now so generally established among us, are full of much promise and hope. Their present and increasing popularity; the amount of misery and vice which they relieve and prevent; the happiness and virtue which they create and encourage; their reception of children from all classes of society, at an age when every impression so much determines their future habits, motives, principles, and whole character, places them among the wisest and happiest agents of christian beneficence. Cooperating with the influences of the nursery, in the formation of infant character, their benefits must be as great, as their principles are correct, and their methods successful.

The early influences operating upon infancy, embrace a variety of subjects, principles, and methods. Early education, involving the expansion, direction, and perfecting of the faculties of infant nature, is a subject wide and intricate. All the elements of this nature are embraced as its objects; in its principles and methods a discipline is required, adapted to the order in which these faculties appear, to their relative importance as aids in life, and to their gradual and harmonious developement by a wise selection of exercises and means. The animal nature, the affections, the conscience, and the intellect, present their united claims for distinct and systematic attention. The whole being of the child asks for expansion and guidance. In the constitution of his nature, shall we, therefore, find the principles of infant cultivation.

If we observe the habits of infancy in a physiological point of view, its active propensities cannot fail to meet our notice. The child is essentially an active being. His chief enjoyment consists in the free and natural exercise of his material frame. The quickening instinct of his nature urges him to the exertion of all its functions and to seek in this, every means for their varied and happy activity. A reverential respect for the author of so benevolent a law of its animal economy, will suggest a faithful obedience to its requisitions. The claims of animal nature in infancy, are primary and paramount to all others; and it is not till these are anticipated and relieved by unrestrained movement, that the intellect can be successfully addressed. By encouraging the free and natural activity of the body, the functions on which intellectual energy and happiness depend, are invigorated and most effectually prepared for the lessons of instruction. Play is the appointed dispensation of childhood; and a beneficent wisdom consists in turning this to its designed purpose. When the force of animal impulse has expended itself by free and natural recreation, and left the physical system in a state of tranquillity, the mind imbibes the influence, and forgetting the scenes and activities of its previous joys, yields itself to the loftier claims of its nature, and asks the sympathy and guidance of instruction; and it is by creating, and applying these states of the animal and intellectual nature, for the advancement of the child, that successful results are chiefly produced in early instruction.

The primary want of infancy is enjoyment. In seeking to supply this want from the variety of surrounding objects, the child often fails of his purpose, from the want of reflection and experience. His mind thus becomes saddened by disappoint-

6

ment, his temper impaired, his reason sophisticated and weakened. He needs the hand of friendly guidance and aid. The means employed by the infant system, should guide him to the true and lasting sources of enjoyment. Respecting all the laws of his animal economy, they should associate pleasure with the action of all his faculties, investing all his instructions with an interest, a certainty, and a love, which future experience shall not diminish, nor maturer reason disapprove. By yielding a more intelligent homage to the active propensities of infancy, furnishing a greater proportion, and a more intellectual kind of recreation, than is permitted by other forms of discipline, the infant system diffuses over the young mind the benign and improving influences of happiness, and thus imparts intellectual and moral life to the infant spirit.

The provision which is thus made for the exercise of the animal functions, extends its influence beyond their developement, to the affectionate nature of the child. Associating with minds like his own in the common purposes of amusement and happiness, his affections find free and spontaneous action to multiply and elevate the joys of his existence, to connect him in ties of sympathy and love with his infant friends, and thus to unseal within him the fountains of future felicity. By multiplying and purifying the sensations of his nature, an experienced wisdom is acquired by the child, which, under more restrained and unsocial influences, it would be impossible to impart. A play-room thus becomes an important aid both to intellectual improvement and happiness. An attentive instructer will see in its amusements the true results of his labors ; for it is in the freedom of these, that infant character is most clearly revealed. As in the theatre of adult life, we learn the true characters of men by friendly intercommunication, and frequent collision of purposes and interests ; so in the amusements of the play-room, the arena of infant activity and impulse, will a wise instructer obtain a just knowledge of infant character. Instruction, unless connected with active duty, and expressed in character, can be at best but a doubtful good. For the improvement of the animal and the affectionate nature, the play-room thus becomes an indispensable appendage to the Infant School. In its unpremeditated sports, and under careful superintendence, without restraint or interdiction, except in cases of obvious wrong, the child is happily employed, and most effectually prepared for the more formal lessons of the school-room.

In the general culture resulting from the play-room, it would be as unwise as impracticable to attempt systematic exercises, or descend into positive detail. It is in the school-room that the faculties of infancy are to be separately addressed, and that systematic attention becomes a necessary requisite. And in proceeding to more systematic labors, the intelligent teacher will seek, as before, his chief guidance in the principles pervading the intellectual and moral constitution of the child. By these will he shape out his system, and on these will he raise the fabric of infant character.

The affections will claim his first attention. On the cultivation and direction of these, much of infant happiness depends. A beneficent wisdom will not fail to discern in their early strength and prominence, the obvious intentions of nature, and yield a religious obedience to her unerring requisitions. Affectionate and familiar conversation is the chief avenue to the infant mind.

8

This will invariably reach its recesses, and reflect its influences, in corresponding tones and emotions. This is the powerful spring which puts the young heart in action, and unfolds all its faculties in the sweetest harmony and perfection. What only is felt by the teacher can become effectual in its purpose, or happy in its influence upon the taught; for all truly efficient results must come from the heart.

In an institution so purely moral in its purpose as the Infant School, much depends upon the character of the teacher. Moral results can come only from moral means; and of these the teachers agency is the chief. In him the infant mind should find the object of its imitation and its love. To a pure and affectionate heart, an unsophisticated conscience, and elevated principles of action, the teacher should unite an amiableness of temper, a simplicity of manner, and a devotion to his work, which shall associate with it his happiness and his duty. His mind should be well disciplined by various experience; beautified and adorned by the cultivation of its moral attributes, and purified and elevated by the faith and hopes of Christianity. To these should be added, as an indispensable requisite, a familiar acquaintance with the infant mind, and a deep reverence for its author. He should possess the power of reaching the infant understanding in the simplest and happiest forms; of investing truth in the loveliest attributes, associating liberty and delight with all the means of its pursuit. Free from prejudices and partialities, he should impart instructions from the pure fountains of truth and love alone. Taking a benevolent view of the works of nature and the ways of Providence, his piety should diffuse itself through all his teachings, and with a silent, quickening power, draw wisdom and improvement from every event. Of mere learning he may have little or much ; an intelligent philanthropy, a desire to be useful, are more important requisites, and without which his other attainments will be of little avail. Of patience and self-control, he should be a thorough and constant disciple.

Intimately connected with the cultivation of the affections, is the diviner nature of the child ; the conscience. This fundamental principle of all virtue early reveals itself as a subject of attention and culture. To train and elevate this by frequent appeals to the unerring laws of reason, rectitude, and benevolence, is an all-important work. It is on this portion of infant nature, that the purest influences should fall, and from which the noblest results should be anticipated. Conscientiousness is the parent of all the noblest virtues, and forms the primary attribute of a pure and lofty character. It is by its wise and happy cultivation that the infant mind finds within, the sources of self-dependence, and self-control, and by its divine suggestions is led to the knowledge and worship of its author, and to the divine truths of the christian revelation. An unrelaxing attention should, therefore, be given to all instruction that affects motive, since it is this which lays the permanent foundations of character, and constitutes the true glory of the soul.

The union of these influences, operating upon the animal, the affectionate, and the spiritual nature, like the quickening and expanding airs of spring upon the material world, reaches the intellectual portion of the child, and prepares the way for direct intellectual culture. Every mental faculty should be effectually

2

addressed, and be made to operate in the independent acquisition of knowledge. Formal precepts, abstract reasonings, and
unintelligible instructions, should here find no place ; but interesting incidents, familiar descriptions, approaching as nearly as
possible to the circumstances and relations of life, should embody
no inconsiderable portion of the lessons of infancy. All that
connects the child with the pure, the good, and the happy
around him, should be impressed deeply in his mind. From
the opened volume of nature, always perused with delight by
childhood ; from the varied records of life and experience, and
from the deeper fountains of the mind, and of revelation, illustrations of truth and love may be drawn to expand the infant soul,
to elevate and enrich it with knowledge and piety, for the coming years of its existence. Truth alone, in its divine unity and
beauty, should be presented. All lessons should reach the mind
in an intelligible and visible form. In this way alone can
they find a response in the heart, operate in conscience, and impart energy and life to knowledge and duty.

The work of the infant teacher, simple and attainable as it
may seem, involves, however, in its methods and details, resources of the purest and happiest character ; imposes responsibili-
ties of the deepest kind. But these considerations will never
deter the true friend of infancy, from the prosecution of his work.
In the simple desire to bless, in the consciousness that of all
others, his are labors of usefulness and love, dwells both the
principle and the means, that shall lead him in time to reward
and success. Patience and experience will become his sure
and confiding friends. Acquainted with the constitution of the
infant mind, and knowing that immediate and apparent results

are not to come from his labors, his anxiety will not prematurely hasten their approach. The mind, he knows, is not to be perfected in a day; nor is truth to reach it, and stamp its permanent impression; nor character attain its symmetry, and reveal its strength and perfection, at once. These are the slow product of time and labor : they are the united results of nature and art : they come from providence and instruction. It is the imperceptible and gentle influence of the dews of heaven that gradually expands the opening flower into all its beauty, fragrance and perfection; and so must it be with the opening mind of infancy. And much early labor will consist in shielding this from noxious influences, ere habit, and conscience, and principle have reached their full strength and activity. A religious reverence for the infant mind as the image of its author, will not wantonly pervert its powers by premature temptation, dim its joys by the regrets of disappointment, nor corrode its nature by the restraints of distrust and fear. Infant happiness should be but another name for infant progress; nature, and providence, and instruction, cooperating in their influences to elevate and to bless the infant spirit.

The methods by which the principles and purposes of early culture are applied in the exercise of the school-room, are of the most simple and unpretending character. They preserve all the primary habits of infancy, as expressed in the nursery, and under the observation and affection of a judicious and devoted mother at home. Instruction drawn from common circumstances and objects, assumes all the freedom and simplicity of domestic conversation; and so far as consistent with common order and discipline, follows the unpremeditated thoughts and feelings of every child. The teacher comes as much in direct contact with each as he can ; avoiding all general instructions, except for the purpose of mental relaxation, or of improving the faculties of sympathy, and imitation. Much systematic instruction is repulsive to the habits and feelings of infancy. Order and system, when carried into minute detail, often become to the child, but other names for restraint and unhappiness, and whatever associates these with the operations of the mind, or the impulses of duty, claims no place among early influences. The more direct, therefore, and individual the methods of instruction become in their influence, the more efficient and happy will be their results. The growth and energy of the mind depend upon the freedom and happiness of its movements, and the restraints imposed by system for its action with others, cannot essentially conduce to its benefit. Instruction should refer to the circumstances of coming life and duty. In these, general movements are seldom required. It is through individual channels that the purest and most efficient influences reach the mind, and from tl 's, connect themselves, in the same way, with duty and impr vement.

There is no attainment of the teacher more difficult to possess, and at the same time more indispensable, than the power of making himself understood ; of conversing intelligibly with children. The range of the infant mind is comparatively confined ; all its operations are within a narrow circle. With the fleeting and varied impressions made by the objects within this circle upon its perceptive power, through the medium of the senses, it is the work of the instructer to become acquainted, and to give the image of permanence and truth, by the terms of language. And he is besides this to bring up from the fountains of love and thought, the more refined and evanescent objects within, and give them their true expression and beauty. The language of the teacher, and all his methods of intellectual communion, to be intelligent, must, therefore, descend to the scanty vocabulary of infant thought, drawn from the circle of its observation and experience. It must find a response and an interpreter within, or to the infant ear, he utters instructions in an unknown tongue, and converses only with himself. From whatever source the lessons of the infant school are drawn, the truths they contain should be invested in the simplest and purest forms of language, and associated with nature and happiness. Early impressions, whether true or false, derive their chief power over the mind, and exert their influence upon life and happiness, through association ; and this is the result of education. How important is it therefore in infant instruction, that the distinctions between truth and error, should be religiously preserved, and correctly associated with intelligence and duty. Of this associating power, language is the chief instrument to be used ; the connecting link between material and intellectual nature ; the channel through which thought and feeling, truth and love, are to pass between the teacher and the child. Let him be careful of perverting this power. Let him be sure that he well understands what he presents to their minds ; and that they understand what he presents : for in all misapprehension on the part of either, there is perversion, there is error ; and who shall answer for the consequence ! There is no principle in infant instruction, in yielding obedience to which, the responsibility and the success of the teacher, are more involved than in this.

14

In seeking the primary methods indicated by nature for the instruction of infancy, the faithful observer will recognise in the universal fondness of children for stories and pictures, a ready and happy means of influence. From these no inconsiderable portion of their lessons may be drawn. Next to the free and natural expansion of their powers in play, in the observation of nature and of life, the story and the picture offer them the greatest charms; and by addressing all their moral and intellectual sympathies, contribute most effectually to their culture. To them the story is intellectual play. It is amusement in which their own enjoyments, their pleasures and their pains, are continued and represented in the persons of others. Their willing attention is consequently secured. The incidents, the thoughts, and the feelings thus drawn from subjects so interesting and familiar to their minds, and presented in the simplest tones and language of affection, cannot but delight them. When embodying the purest attributes of truth, connecting motive and principle with action, the story thus becomes a ready channel for moral instruction to reach the mind. Virtue, wisdom, and goodness, in this way, assume a visible and tangible form; and are delineated to the young mind, with a clearness and vividness which more preceptive methods could never impart. And the picture, still more impressively brings the images of the imagination in connexion with the understanding, and subserves the same important purpose.

Stories and prints, being thus important to the success of infant cultivation, should be selected with much discrimination and care. On the fidelity and beauty of their execution, much of their influence will depend. A pure and simple morality, adapted to the circumstances, apprehensions, and wants of infancy, should pervade them.—In supplying the existing wants in this department of infant literature, the highest intellectual and moral attainments might be usefully employed. The writings of Mrs Barbauld, Mr Day, and Miss Edgeworth, may be mentioned as models for imitation ; and without which the library of the infant school would be incomplete. Mrs Crabb's ' Familiar Tales ' are also excellent. The simple and beautiful illustrations of virtue in the parables of the New-Testament, and some portions of the Old, will always interest, and, when presented in language adapted to its apprehensions and tastes, improve and elevate the infant mind. There are few books in our language, so far simplified in thought, subject, and expression, that under the perusal of the teacher, further explanation will not be required : and the teacher will always bear in mind, that misapprehension on the part of the child, is perversion and error, of which he is chiefly the cause.

There is no class of writing more happy in its influence upon children, than that which embodies the lives of children. Well written biography carries with it to the young mind, the simplicity and the force of truth and certainty ; and conveys instruction in the happiest form. The library of the infant school should contain many books of this character. It is much to be regretted that so few have been written ; and that those few have chiefly embodied the lives of children remarkable for some great excellence, or great defect ; while the simple, the beautiful, and at the same time, the elevated character of genuine childhood, has been left almost entirely untouched. In everything presented to the infant mind, the true proportions of character

should be preserved, and constitute the moral. To make dis‑
torted virtue, influence happily the young mind, is both difficult
and dangerous. In the story, and in biography, both real and
ideal beings are introduced, and whenever the romance of ad‑
miration is associated with the imperfections of either, both the
moral and influence are false. Unless used in the service of
truth, the biography and the tale are equally injurious ; but thus
used, they become its happiest auxiliaries.

On the influence of fiction upon the mind in early life, Dugald
Stewart makes the following remarks ; —‘ The attention of young
persons may be seduced, by well selected works of fiction from
the present objects of the senses, and the thoughts accustomed
to dwell on the past, the distant and the future ; and in the same
proportion in which this effect is in any instance accomplished,
the man is exalted in the scale of intellectual being. The tale
of fiction will probably be soon laid aside with the toys and
rattles of infancy ; but the habits which it has contributed to fix,
and the powers which it has brought into a state of activity, will
remai᾿ with the possessor permanent and inestimable treasures
to the latest hour.’ How much then may be done for children,
by embodying in the tale, the active manifestations of those
purer and nobler attributes of humanity, which do not exist in the
best specimens of character around them : thus bringing virtue
from the skies, to dwell in their presence.

Of the same interesting and improving nature with pictures
and stories, are descriptions and specimens of nature and art.
By these the young mind is brought in contact with material
nature, and through its natural, and always intelligible language,
imbibes the unadulterated truths written upon its pages. It

cannot range through its vast departments to behold and define
its varied imagery and beauty ; selections, therefore, from so
inexhaustible a cabinet, presented in the picture, the specimen,
and the description, supply this inability, in part, and excite
much of the enthusiasm of actual observation.   Natural history
is of itself a world of instruction to the young, and is always
studied by them with avidity and happiness.   Accurate representations, by cuts, by simple descriptions, and by anecdotes
embodying the character of various animals, insects, &c., are
important in early education.   Botanical, and geological specimens may likewise be used to much benefit in giving elementary ideas of the subjects which they illustrate.

Besides specimens of nature and art, a few articles of apparatus for illustrating the few principles of science attempted in
the infant school, can be used to advantage.   Of these, the
numeral frame, and a few cubes for illustrating the elements of
numbers, manuscript and roman letters, slates and pencils,
black boards, are the chief.   An addition of pictures representing scenes in history, of the arts, of life, manners, customs,
and natural scenery, might be made of much service.   The
decoration and internal arrangement of the play-room, and the
school-room, might likewise be made to exert a happy and improving influence upon the infant imagination and feelings.   A
few hundred wooden bricks — a few wheelbarrows — and other
articles of amusement in the play-room might also be added.

In applying the principles and methods of the infant system
to the developement and discipline of the intellectual faculties,
to the formation of just habits of thought, feeling, and action,
and to the inculcation of knowledge, it will be important to

3

keep the varied elements of infant nature distinctly in view, and to adapt instructions to the improvement of each. On the ability with which this is done, the harmony and perfection of future character chiefly depends.

Provision is made for the general culture of the animal faculties in the amusements and exercises of the play-room. The eye, the hand, the ear, and the voice, become, however, the subjects of discipline in the school-room. Exercises, among others, favorable for the cultivation of the eye, and hand, are writing and drawing — or what might be more simply expressed, perhaps, by the term, marking. On the slates and black board, the children may delineate in the roman character, letters, figures, lessons in spelling, in defining, and in arithmetic. In these exercises, both the hand and the eye become associated with the operations of the mind, giving the mechanical facility to the one, and the elementary notions of form and connexion to the other, that will essentially aid the child in his more advanced stages of penmanship. Of himself, he will gradually supply the manuscript character in the expressing of his lessons, and ultimately attain that original style of penmanship suited to his taste and genius, without much formal assistance. And the task of transferring his efforts from the slate to paper, will become comparatively slight. Children are fond of using the pencil and the chalk, and this fondness applied in the exercises of the school, may be made a ready and happy means of employment, and at the same time, prepare them for the more systematic applications of the hand and eye in coming years. An ingenious teacher will not fail of adding a variety of exercises of this nature, to those here mentioned.

In the cultivation of the ear and the voice, vocal and instrumental music, reading, and pronunciation, will form favorable exercises. The instrumental music may be confined to the teacher. Singing is always delightful to children; and the infant school offers a happy means for its attainment. As a moral influence its effect is always happy. How many a rising passion, an unhappy association, may be modified by its influence. In connexion with music, the exercise of marching and the simultaneous movements of the hand accompanying the general exercises of the school, conduce to the improvement of the ear.

Occasions might sometimes, perhaps, occur, when systematic amusements, in the play-room for the discipline of the senses, might be agreeable to the children. Liberty and happiness are, however, so intimately associated in the infant mind, that the interference, would be as unwise as unwished for. *Let us alone in our amusements,* is the true instinct of childhood: and a wise instructer, while he provides careful superintendence, and removes the causes of obvious danger and perversion, will yield obedience to the dictate.

To awaken and to elevate the nobler affections and pure sympathies of infancy, and to check and give habits of self-control to the passions, is an interesting and important feature of the infant system. It is on the state of the affections and passions that infant happiness chiefly depends. The issues of life should, therefore, be guarded with unremitted diligence and care; and the infant heart enshrine in its temple, the objects alone worthy its devotion and its love.

20

The methods by which these results are chiefly to be produced are involved in the very character of the teacher. From
this, and its consequent influence in the discipline and internal
management of the school, must they be chiefly anticipated.
Sympathy and imitation, adaptation to surrounding influences,
are prominent tendencies of the infant mind. Whatever the
character of these, such will that of the children insensibly
become; and on the teacher the chief responsibility rests.
Kindness and affection must form a primary element of his character. It is these which will awaken kindred emotions in the
children, and become the chief power of his influence. Love
and love only' can be with him 'the loan for love.' Cheerfulness, complacency, hope and happiness, dwelling in his bosom,
will find way, and, in time, take residence in theirs. By the expression of these, in conversation, by voice, manner, countenance;
by frequent appeals to the best affections, drawn from the lessons
and incidents of the school-room, from stories, and descriptions'
without exciting the passions, the teacher will awaken and
purify the infant faculties, and form those habits and dispositions,
which prepare the heart for the reception of virtue and happiness. The affectionate nature, thus kept in a state of activity,
becomes invigorated, elevated, and improved.

The methods for the developement and illumination of conscience, like those for the cultivation of the affections, are chiefly
involved in the character of the teacher. Of all principles of
infant nature, the conscience demands the most careful cultivation. On this rest the strong foundations of character : from
this come the moral habits of truth, ingenuousness, obedience,
approbation, confidence, forbearance, fortitude, justice, gene-

rosity, and all those attributes of character, which spread themselves throughout the relations of society and of duty. To
awaken and moralise these is an important portion of the teacher's labors. Neglect here, is perversion of all the other powers;
for however cultivated the affections and the intellect may be,
the want of moral principle, of an awakened and intelligent
conscience, will distort the symmetry, and dim the perfections
of the soul.

In all things the teacher should strive to be, what to the
apprehension of the children, they ought to become. By the
kindness of his manner ; his love of truth and right above all
things ; by his obedience to the rules of action which he presents ;
by appeals to the dictates of conscience, principle, and revelation ; by patient, constant forbearance ; by the desire in all
things to improve and bless ; by illustrations of virtue, in stories,
in pictures, in descriptions ; by remarks on infant character,
motives, habits, the teacher will endeavor to reach their minds,
impress duty on their conscience, and lead them to its practice.
No incident of the play-room, or the school-room, from which
profitable instruction can be drawn, will he suffer to pass
unused : improvement will come from every influence. What
the children thus see the teacher to love and respect, to feel an
interest in, they will, in time, come to love and respect, and be
interested in themselves. The reflection of his character will
open the deeper fountains of their nature, and prepare them
for the knowledge of themselves. Taught to look within for
the dictates of duty, they will be led to the exercise of self-
knowledge, and of self-control — the safeguards of virtue and
happiness.

The prevalence of the kind affections, the absence of irritating circumstances, combining with the illuminations of conscience, and the aids of self-knowledge and of self-control, render the government of the infant school, exceedingly simple and unimposing. The preventive influences which are thus kept in action, place correction and punishment mostly out of sight. The infant mind is sustained in its progressive course chiefly from within itself; here it finds its impulses to duty, and progress; or when these become powerless or erroneous, the direct influence of the teacher's voice, presence, and character, prevents frequent transgression : the voice of conscience is heard and obeyed. Few laws are, therefore, required, and few punishments and rewards. The child becomes a law to himself.

Sympathy and imitation, the moral action of the teacher upon the children, of the children on him, and on each other, form the common government of the school, and the chief agents of coercive discipline. The teacher cooperates with the children in creating and in diffusing throughout the internal arrangements and exercises of the school, those principles of order and of right, of which all feel the propriety and the need. Of the common conscience of the school, which is thus brought in action, he forms but a part ; and it is only when the dictates of this, are inoperative or erroneous, that his personal authority is recognised by the children. Harshness and restraint, fear, and interdiction, arbitrary reward and punishment, where the laws of affection, order, and conscience, generally prevail, will not be often required. The formalities of government may be mostly dispensed with.

To all that affects motive, the teacher will pay particular attention. It is not what hurries the infant mind along the path of knowledge alone with the greatest celerity, that claims so much his attention, as the impulse which prompts, and the means which direct its activity. In operating upon it, therefore, the teacher will be careful in the selection of his means. He will not impair its perceptions of virtue, by too frequently associating with it arbitrary rewards; nor degrade its nature, by recurring too often to arbitrary punishments. These are but the associated supports of the erring and the weak; and a system of government founded chiefly on these, must of necessity, create the very error and weakness, which it aims to correct. It is only the ' pure in heart that shall see God ; ' and the infant mind, of all others, should early receive, and act from this impression.

All the essential forms of influencing infancy are expressed and defined, in their purest characteristics, in the nursery. This is the Infant School instituted by creating Wisdom ; and all its original relations should be preserved in its extension to numbers, and to the details of their systematic discipline. A faithful observer will not, therefore, defeat his purpose by an essential departure from its requisitions. In its benign and unobtrusive operations, he will recognise its power ; and to these will he lend his cooperation and confidence. Familiar and affectionate conversation will become the medium through which he will diffuse his instructions. Encouragement, and approbation, not emulation and reproach, will be made the happiest impulses to duty and progress.

By methods equally simple and maternal, should the intellectual faculties of infancy be addressed. The mere communication of knowledge, though an important, is, by no means, the essential purpose of infant discipline. This is chiefly, the awakening and exciting the mind; the formation of its habits; the preliminary discipline of its faculties for the independent search and acquisition of truth. What, therefore, is presented, refers to its prospective as well as present good; and to accomplish its purpose, must reach the mind, become the subject of its action, and incorporate itself with all its thoughts and habits. Mechanical recitations, wordy lessons, dissociated from the intellect, are to be wholly avoided. That only is worthy of the infant mind, which it can understand and feel. Nature has associated interest, pleasure, and progress, with perception alone; and from mystery and error, the infant mind, of all others, should be scrupulously kept free.

The intellectual faculties, which, among others, should become subjects of cultivation in the school-room, are imagination, association, attention, taste, memory, judgment, reflection, and reason. Of these, the imagination, in infancy, should receive special attention, since, before the dawning of reason, and the exercise of reflection, in connexion with the affections, infant happiness depends much upon its activity and guidance. Early associations of ideas and affections, link themselves so vividly with the prevailing habits of infant thought and feeling, and affect so powerfully and permanently the character of children, that the benevolent teacher will guard this avenue to their minds with the nicest care. The amusements, the government, the stories, the pictures, poetry, and descriptions which he employs for the cultivation and guidance of the imagination, will be selected with the discrimination which belongs to their important influence. They will be accurate representations of the transactions, objects, and duties of coming years. Natural and moral taste will be chiefly dependent on these, for their developement and purity.

In the more individual exercises of the school-room, foi the cultivation of memory, judgment, reason, and reflection, the elements of the simplest sciences, and arts, may be happily applied. Attempts, however, should not be made to compel, for any length of time, a strictly scientific application. This is opposed to the prevailing habits of the infant mind. A few elementary facts, spread through the lessons of the school, and wrought up with incident and affection, is all that should be attempted in the way of formal tuition.

Enunciation, spelling the simplest names of familiar objects, actions, and qualities, defining their thoughts, writing, the elements of morality, and natural history, may constitute the chief portion of the children's lessons. During the intervals of more direct influence from the teacher, they may delineate their lessons on the slate and black board. When once interested in the employment of their hands in this way, an ingenious teacher will find in this, an unfailing means of employing their minds. In the succession of their lessons due reference should be had to contrast and variety. Employment is the great safeguard to infant improvement and happiness ; and the attempt to associate this with what is unintelligible to the child, should of all things be avoided. During the early years of infancy, we must be

4

26

satisfied with making desultory impressions upon the mind; the conclusions of science belong to maturer years.

In the views of infant nature and instruction which have been presented, it has been a primary object to designate those faculties, which from their early prominence, seem designed as subjects of early culture; to present the principles by which these faculties may be effectually addressed and improved; to guard the happiness and true progress of infancy from formal and unintelligible influences; and to lead to the perception of the great and noble objects which infant education contemplates — the formation of a pure, and happy, and elevated character.

These views, principles, and objects, appreciated, and felt, by an intelligent and devoted teacher, may direct and assist him in his work. To him their practical application to the details of the school-room must be chiefly left. His acquaintance with the infant mind; his interest in its progress and happiness, will guide him to the best methods. By him no system will be strictly imitated; but from all systems, he will draw instructions to aid him in the course best suited to his circumstances and location. He who cannot do this, is engaged in a work for which he is unfitted, and his influence must be ineffectual and unhappy. The formation of infant character is a work too great to be entrusted to hands unwise and unskilful. He who operates upon it from imitation alone, has imbibed neither the true spirit of duty nor of success; he can do little for its improvement and happiness. He who has low and imperfect views of the infant mind, cannot fail to pervert and degrade its nature; and of all others will be slow, in forming the conclusion, hat '*infant education when adapted to the human being, is founded on the great principle, that every infant is already in possession of the faculties and apparatus required for his instruction, and, that, by a law of his constitution, he uses these to a great extent himself; that the office of instruction is chiefly to facilitate this process, and to accompany the child in his progress, rather than to drive or even to lead him.'*

DOCTRINE AND DISCIPLINE

OF

HUMAN CULTURE.

BY

A. BRONSON ALCOTT.

The wind bloweth where it listeth, and ye hear the sound thereof; but ye cannot tell whence it cometh nor whither it goeth; so is every one that is born of the Spirit.

Jesus in Conversation with Nicodemus.

BOSTON:

JAMES MUNROE AND COMPANY.

1836.

HUMAN CULTURE.

Idea of Man. MAN is the noblest of the Creator's works.
He is the most richly gifted of all his
creatures. His sphere of action is the broadest; his
influence the widest; and to him is given Nature and
Life for his heritage and his possession. He holds
dominion over the Outward. He is the rightful Sove-
reign of the Earth, fitted to subdue all things to himself, and to know of no superior, save God. And yet
he enters upon the scene of his labors, a feeble and
wailing Babe, at first unconscious of the place assigned him, and needs years of tutelage and discipline
to fit him for the high and austere duties that await
him.

Idea of Edu-
cation. The Art, which fits such a being to fulfil
his high destiny, is the first and noblest
of arts. Human Culture is the art of revealing to a
man the true Idea of his Being — his endowments —

31

his possessions — and of fitting him to use th. ... for
the growth, renewal, and perfection of his Spiri· It
is the art of completing a man. It includes all those
influences, and disciplines, by which his faculties are
unfolded and perfected. It is that agency which
takes the helpless and pleading Infant from the hands
of its Creator ; and, apprehending its entire nature,
tempts it forth — now by austere, and now by kindly
influences and disciplines — and thus moulds it at last
into the Image of a Perfect Man ; armed at all points,
to use the Body, Nature, and Life, for its growth and
renewal, and to hold dominion over the fluctuating
things of the Outward. It seeks to realize in the Soul
the Image of the Creator. — Its end is a perfect man.
Its aim, through every stage of influence and discipline, is self-renewal. The body, nature, and life are
its instruments and materials. Jesus is its worthiest
Ideal. Christianity its purest Organ. The Gospels
its fullest Text-Book. Genius its Inspiration. Holiness its Law. Temperance its Discipline. Immortality its Reward.

History and
Type of this
Idea.
This divine Art, including all others, or
subordinating them to its Idea, was never
apprehended, in all its breadth and depth of significance, till the era of Jesus of Nazareth. He it was
that first revealed it. Over his Divine Intellect first

flitted the Idea of man's endowments and **destiny.**
He set no limits to the growth of our nature. " **Be**
Ye Perfect even as my Father in Heaven is **Perfect,"**
was the high aim which he placed before his disciples ;
and in this he was true to our nature, for the sentiment lives in every faculty and function of our **being.**
It is the ever-sounding Trump of Duty, urging us to
the perpetual work of self-renewal. It is the deep
instinct of the spirit. And his Life gives us the promise of its realization. In his attributes and endowments he is a Type of our common nature. His
achievements are a glimpse of the Apotheosis of
Humanity. They are a glorious unfolding of the
Godlike in man. They disclose the Idea of Spirit.
And if he was not, in himself, the complete fulfilment
of Spirit, he apprehended its law, and set forth its
conditions. He bequeathed to us the phenomena of
its manifestation ; for in the Gospels we have the history of Spirit accomplishing its mission on the earth.
We behold the Incarnate One, dealing with flesh
and blood — tempted, and suffering — yet baffling
and overcoming the ministries of Evil and of Pain.

Idea and Type   Still this Idea, so clearly announced,
misapprehended.   and so fully demonstrated in the being
and life of Jesus, has made but little advance in
the minds of men. Men have not subdued it to

1*

themselves. It has not become the ground and
law of human consciousness. They have not married their nature to it by a living Faith. Nearly two
millenniums have elapsed since its announcement,
and yet, so slow of apprehension have been the successors of this Divine Genius, that even at this day,
the deep and universal significance of his Idea has
not been fully taken in. It has been restricted to
himself alone. He stands in the minds of this generation, as a Phenomenon, which God, in the inscruta-
ble designs of his Providence, saw fit to present,
to the gaze and wonder of mankind, yet as a being
of unsettled rank in the universe, whom men may
venture to imitate, but dare not approach. In him,
the Human Nature is feebly apprehended, while
the Divine is lifted out of sight, and lost in the
ineffable light of the Godhead. Men do not deem
him as the harmonious unfolding of Spirit into the
Image of a Perfect Man — as a worthy Symbol of the
Divinity, wherein Human Nature is revealed in its
Fulness. Yet, as if by an inward and irresistible
Instinct, all men have been drawn to him ; and, while
diverse in their opinions; explaining his Idea in different types, they have given him the full and unre-
served homage of their hearts. They have gathered
around the altars, inscribed with his perfections, and,
through his name, delighted to address the God and

Father of Spirits. Disowning him in their minds,
unable to grasp his Idea, they have deified him
in their hearts. They have worshipped the Holiness
which they could not define.

Era of its It is the mission of this Age, to revive his
Revival.
Idea, give it currency, and reinstate it in
the faith of men. By its quickening agency, it is to
fructify our common nature, and reproduce its like.
It is to unfold our being into the same divine likeness. It is to reproduce Perfect Men. The faded
Image of Humanity is to be restored, and man reappear in his original brightness. It is to mould anew
our Institutions, our Manners, our Men. It is to
restore Nature to its rightful use ; purify Life ; hallow
the functions of the Human Body, and regenerate
Philosophy, Literature, Art, Society. The Divine
Idea of a Man is to be formed in the common consciousness of this age, and genius mould all its products in accordance with it.

Means of its The means for reinstating this Idea in the
Revival.
common mind, in order to conduce to
these results, are many. Yet all are simple. And
the most direct and effectual are by apprehending the
Genius of this Divine Man, from the study of those
Records wherein his career is delineated with so much

fidelity, simplicity, and truth. Therein have we a manifestation of Spirit, while undergoing the temptations of this corporeal life ; yet faithful to the laws of its renovation and its end. The Divine Idea of Humanity gleams forth through every circumstance of his terrestrial career. The fearful agencies of the Spirit assert their power. In him Nature and Life are subordinated to the spiritual force. The Son of God appears on Earth, enrobed in Flesh, and looks forth serenely upon Man. We feel the significance of the Incarnation ; the grandeur of our nature. We associate Jesus with our holiest aspirations, our deepest affections ; and thus does he become a fit Mediator between the last age and the new era, of which he was the herald and the pledge. He is to us the Prophet of two millenniums. He is the brightest Symbol of a Man that history affords, and points us to yet fuller manifestations of the Godhead.

Ideal of a Teacher. And the Gospels are not only a fit Text-Book for the study of Spirit, in its corporeal relations, but they are a specimen also of the true method of imparting instruction. They give us the practice of Jesus himself. They unfold the means of addressing human nature. Jesus was a Teacher ; he sought to renovate Humanity. His method commends itself to us. It is a beautiful

exhibition of his Genius, bearing the stamp of natu-
ralness, force, and directness. It is popular. Instead
of seeking formal and austere means, he rested his
influence chiefly on the living word, rising spontane-
ously in the soul, and clothing itself at once, in the
simplest, yet most commanding forms. He was a
finished extemporaneous speaker. His manner and
style are models. In these, his Ideas became like the
beautiful, yet majestic Nature, whose images he wove
so skilfully into his diction. He was an Artist of
the highest order. More perfect specimens of address do not elsewhere exist. View him in his
conversation with his disciples. Hear him in his
simple colloquies with the people. Listen to him
when seated at the well-side discoursing with the
Samaritan woman, on the IDEA OF WORSHIP ; and at
night with Nicodemus, on SPIRITUAL RENEWAL. From
facts and objects the most familiar, he slid easily and
simply into the highest and holiest themes, and, in this
unimposing guise, disclosed the great Doctrines, and
stated the Divine Ideas, that it was his mission to
bequeath to his race. Conversation was the form of
utterance that he sought. Of formal discourse but
one specimen is given, in his Sermon on the Mount ;
yet in this the inspiration bursts all forms, and he rises
to the highest efforts of genius, at its close.

Organ of
Instruction

This preference of Jesus for Conversation, as the fittest organ of utterance, is a striking proof of his comprehensive Idea of Education. He knew what was in man, and the means of perfecting his being. He saw the superiority of this exercise over others for quickening the Spirit. For, in this all the instincts and faculties of our being are touched. They find full and fair scope. It tempts forth all the powers. Man faces his fellow man. He holds a living intercourse. He feels the quickening life and light. The social affections are addressed; and these bring all the faculties in train. Speech comes unbidden. Nature lends her images. Imagination sends abroad her winged words. We see thought as it springs from the soul, and in the very process of growth and utterance. Reason plays under the mellow light of fancy. The Genius of the Soul is waked, and eloquence sits on her tuneful lip. Wisdom finds an organ worthy her serene, yet imposing products. Ideas stand in beauty and majesty before the Soul.

Organ of
Genius.

And Genius has ever sought this organ of utterance. It has given us full testimony in its favor. Socrates — a name that Christians can see coupled with that of their Divine Sage — descanted thus on the profound themes in which he delighted. The market-place; the workshop; the public streets were

his favorite haunts of instruction. And the divine
Plato has added his testimony, also, in those enduring
works, wherein he sought to embalm for posterity,
both the wisdom of his master and the genius that
was his own. Rich text-books these for the study of
philosophic genius. They rank next in finish and
beauty, to the specimens of Jesus as recorded by his
own beloved John.

Genius alone   It is by such organs that Human Nature is
Renews.   to be unfolded into the Idea of its fulness.
Yet to do this, teachers must be men in pos*ession
of their Idea. They must be men of their kind;
men inspired with great and living Ideas, as was
Jesus. Such alone are worthy. They alone can
pierce the customs and conventions that hide the Soul
from itself. They alone can release it from the
slavery of the corporeal life, and give it back to
itself. And such are ever sent at the call of Humanity. Some God, instinct with the Idea that is to
regenerate his era, is ever vouchsafed. As a flaming
Herald he appears in his time, and sends abroad the
Idea which it is the mission of the age to organize
in institutions, and quicken into manners. Such
mould the Genius of the time. They r vive in Humanity the lost idea of its destiny, and reveal its
fearful endowments. They vindicate the divinity of

12

man's nature, and foreshadow on the coming Time the conquests that await it. An Age preëxists in them; and History is but the manifestation and issue of their Wisdom and Will. They are the Prophets of the Future.

Genius mis-
apprehended. At this day, men need some revelation of Genius, to arouse them to a sense of their nature; for the Divine Idea of a Man seems to have died out of our consciousness. Encumbered by the gluts of the appetites, sunk in the corporeal senses, men know not the divine life that stirs within them, yet hidden and enchained. They revere not their own nature. And when the phenomenon of Genius appears, they marvel at its advent. They cannot own it. Laden with the gifts of the Divinity it touches their orb. At intervals of a century it appears. Some Nature, struggling with vicissitude, tempts forth the Idea of Spirit from within, and unlooses the Promethean God to roam free over the earth. He possesses his Idea and brings it as a blessed gift to his race. With awe-struck visage, the tribes of semi-unfolded beings survey it from below, deeming it a partial or preternatural gift of the Divinity, into whose life and being they are forbidden, by a decree of the Eternal, from entering; whose law they must obey, yet cannot apprehend.

They dream not, that this phenomenon is but the complement of their common nature ; and that in this admiration and obedience, which they proffer, is both the promise and the pledge of the same powers in themselves ; that this is but their fellow-creature in the flesh. And thus the mystery remains sealed, till at last it is revealed, that this is but the unfolding of human nature in its fulness ; working free of every incumbrance, by possessing itself.

Idea of Genius.
For Genius is but the free and harmonious play of all the faculties of a human being. It is a Man possessing his Idea and working with it. It is the Whole Man — the central Will — working worthily, subordinating all else to itself; and reaching its end by the simplest and readiest means. It is human nature rising superior to things and events, and transfiguring these into the image of its own Spiritual Ideal. It is the Spirit working in its own way, through its own organs and instruments, and on its own materials. It is the Inspiration of all the faculties of a Man by a life conformed to his Idea. It is not indebted to others for its manifestation. It draws its life from within. It is self-subsistent. It feeds on Holiness ; lives in the open vision of Truth ; enrobes itself in the light of Beauty ; and bathes its powers in the fount of Temperance. It aspires after the

2

Perfect. It loves Freedom. It dwells in Unity. All men have it, yet it does not appear in all men. It is obscured by ignorance ; quenched by evil ; discipline does not reach it ; nor opportunity cherish it. Yet there it is — an original, indestructible element of every spirit ; and sooner or later, in this corporeal, or in the spiritual era — at some period of the Soul's developement — it shall be tempted forth, and assert its claims in the life of the Spirit. It is the province of education to wake it, and discipline it into the perfection which is its end, and for which it ever thirsts. Yet Genius alone can wake it. Genius alone inspire it. It comes not at the incantation of mere talent. It respects itself. It is strange to all save its kind. It shrinks from vulgar gaze, and lives in its own world. None but the eye of Genius can discern it, and it obeys the call of none else.

Wane of Genius. Yet among us Genius is at its wane. Human Nature appears shorn of her beams. We estimate man too low to hope for bright manifestations. And our views create the imperfection that mocks us. We have neither great men, nor good institutions. Genius visits us but seldom. The results of our culture are slender. Thirsting for life and light, Genius is blessed with neither. It cannot free itself from the in-

cumbrance that it inherits. The Idea of a Man
does not shine upon it from any external Image.
Such Corporeal Types it seeks in vain. It cries for
instruction, and none satisfies its wants. There is
little genius in our schoolrooms. Those who enter
yearly upon the stage of life, bearing the impress of
our choicest culture, and most watchful discipline,
are often unworthy specimens of our nature. Holiness attends not their steps. Genius adorns not their
brow. Many a parent among us — having lavished
upon his child his best affections, and spared no
pains which money and solicitude could supply, to
command the best influences within his reach — sees
him return, destitute of that high principle, and those
simple aims, that alone ennoble human nature, and
satisfy the parental heart. Or, should the child return with his young simplicity and truth, yet how
unarmed is his intellect with the quiver of genius, to
achieve a worthy name, and bless his race. The
Soul is spilt out in lust; buried in appetite; or
wasted in vulgar toils; and retreats, at last, ignobly
from the scene of life's temptations; despoiled of its
innocence; bereft of its hopes, and sets in the dark
night of disquietude, lost to the race.

Cause of
Declension.
Yet not all depravity nor ignorance is to
be laid at the door of our Institutions.

The evil has two faces. It is deeper in its origin. It springs from our low estimate of human nature, and consequent want of reverence and regard for it. It is to be divided between parents and institutions. The young but too often enter our institutions of learning, despoiled of their virtue, and are of course disabled from running an honorable intellectual career. Our systems of nursery discipline are built on shallow or false principles; the young repeat the vices and reproduce the opinions of parents; and parents have little cause to complain. They cannot expect fruits of institutions, for which they have taken so little pains to sow the seeds. They reap as they sow. Aiming at little they attain but little. They cast their own horoscope, and determine by their aim the fate of the coming generation. They are the organized Opportunity of their era.

Faith of Genius. To work worthily, man must aspire worthily. His theory of human attainment must be lofty. It must ever be lifting him above the low plain of custom and convention, in which the senses confine him, into the high mount of vision, and of renovating ideas. To a divine nature, the sun ever rises over the mountains of hope, and brings promises on its wings; nor does he linger around the dark and depressing valley of distrust and

of fear. The magnificent bow of promise ever gilds
his purpose, and he pursues his way steadily, and in
faith to the end. For Faith is the soul of all improvement. It is the Will of an Idea. It is an Idea seeking to embody and reproduce itself. It is the All-
Proceeding Word going forth, as in the beginning of
things, to incarnate itself, and become flesh and blood
to the senses. Without this faith an Idea works no
good. It is this which animates and quickens it into
life. And this must come from living men.

And such Faith is the possession of all
Genius alone
Inspires. who apprehend Ideas. Such faith had
Jesus, and this it was that empowered him to do the
mighty works of which we read. It was this which
inspired his genius. And Genius alone can inspire
others. To nurse the young spirit as it puts forth its
pinions in the fair and hopeful morning of life, it
must be placed under the kindly and sympathising
agency of Genius — heaven-inspired and hallowed —
or there is no certainty that its aspirations will not
die away in the routine of formal tuition, or spend
themselves in the animal propensities that coexist
with it. Teachers must be men of genius. They
must be men inspired. The Divine Idea of a Man
must have been unfolded from their being, and be a
living presence. Philosophers, and Sages, and Seers,

2*

— the only real men — must come as of old, to the holy vocation of unfolding human nature. Socrates, and Plato, and the Diviner Jesus, must be raised up to us, to breathe their wisdom and will into the genius of our era, to recast our institutions, remould our manners, and regenerate our men. Philosophy and Religion, descending from the regions of cloudy speculation, must thus become denizens of our common earth, known among us as friends, and uttering their saving truths through the mouths of our little ones. Thus shall our being be unfolded. Thus the Idea of a man be reinstated in our consciousness. Thus Jesus be honored among us. And thus shall Man grow up, as the tree of the primeval woods, luxuriant, vigorous — armed at all points, to brave the winds and the storms of the finite and the mutable — bearing his Fruit in due season.

Idea of Inspiration.   To fulfil its end, Instruction must be an Inspiration. The true Teacher, like Jesus, must inspire in order to unfold. He must know that instruction is something more than mere impression on the understanding. He must feel it to be a kindling influence; that, in himself alone, is the quickening, informing energy ; that the life and growth of his charge preëxist in him. He is to hallow and refine as he tempts forth the soul. He is to inform the understanding, by chastening the appetites, allaying the passions, softening the affections, vivifying the imagination, illuminating the reason, giving pliancy and force to the will; for a true understanding is the issue of these powers, working freely and in harmony with the Genius of the soul, conformed to the law of Duty. He is to put all the springs of Being in motion. And to do this, he must be the personation and exampler of what he would unfold in his charge. Wisdom, Truth, Holiness, must have preëxistence in him, or they will not appear in his pupils. These influence alone in the concrete. They must be made flesh and blood in him, to reappear to the senses, and reproduce their like. — And thus shall his Genius subordinate all to its own force. Thus shall all be constrained to yield to its influence; and this too, without violating any Law, spiritual, intellectual, corporeal — but in obedience to the highest Agency, co-working with God. Under the melting force of his Genius, thus employed, Mind shall become fluid, and he shall mould it into Types of Heavenly Beauty. His agency is that of mind leaping to meet mind; not of force acting on opposing force. The Soul is touched by the live coal of his lips. A kindling influence goes forth to inspire; making the mind think; the heart feel; the pulse throb with his own. He arouses every faculty.

He awakens the Godlike. He images the fair and
full features of a Man. And thus doth he drive at will
the drowsy Brute, that the Eternal hath yoked to
the chariot of Life, to urge man across the Finite!

Hallowed
Genius.
To work worthily in the ministry of Instruction, requires not only the highest
Gifts, but that these should be refined by Holiness.
This is the condition of spiritual and intellectual
clearness. This alone unfolds Genius, and puts Nature and Life to their fit uses. " If any man will know
of the Doctrine, let him do the will of my Father,"
said Jesus; and he, who does not yield this obedience,
shall never shine forth in the true and full glory of his
nature.

Quenching of
Genius.
Yet this truth seems to have been lost
sight of in our measures of Human
Culture. We incumber the body by the gluts of the
appetites; dim the senses by self-indulgence; abuse
nature and life in all manner of ways, and yet dream
of unfolding Genius amidst all these diverse agencies and influences. We train Children amidst all
these evils. We surround them by temptations,
which stagger their feeble virtue, and they fall too
easily into the snare which we have spread. Con-
cupiscence defiles their functions; blunts the edge

of their faculties; obstructs the passages of the soul
to the outward, and blocks it up. The human body,
the soul's implement for acting on Nature, in the
ministry of life, is thus depraved; and the soul falls
an easy prey to the Tempter. Self-Indulgence too
soon rings the knell of the spiritual life, as the omen
of its interment in the flesh. It wastes the corporeal
functions; mars the Divine Image in the human form;
estranges the affections; paralyzes the will; clouds
the intellect; dims the fire of genius; seals conscience, and corrupts the whole being. Lusts en-
trench themselves in the Soul; unclean spirits and
demons nestle therein. Self-subjection, self-sacrifice,
self-renewal are not made its habitual exercises, and
it becomes the vassal of the Body. The Idea of
Spirit dies out of the Consciousness; and Man is
shorn of his glories. Nature grows over him. He
mistakes Images for Ideas, and thus becomes an Idol-
ater. He deserts the Sanctuary of the Indwelling
Spirit, and worships at the throne of the Outward.

Means of
Reform.
Our plans of influence, to be successful,
must become more practical. We must
be more faithful. We must deal less in abstractions;
depend less on precepts and rules. We must fit the
soul for duty by the practice of duty. We must
watch and enforce. Like unsleeping Providence, we

must accompany the young into the scenes of temptation and trial, and aid them in the needful hour. Duty must sally forth an attending Presence into the work-day world, and organize to itself a living body. It must learn the art of uses. It must incorporate itself with Nature. To its sentiments we must give a Heart. Its Ideas we must arm with Hands. For it ever longs to become flesh and blood. The Son of God delights to take the Son of Man as a co-mate, and to bring flesh and blood even to the very gates of the Spiritual Kingdom. It would make the word Flesh, that it shall be seen and handled and felt.

Spiritual Culture. The Culture, that is alone worthy of Man, and which unfolds his Being into the Image of its fulness, casts its agencies over all things. It uses Nature and Life as means for the Soul's growth and renewal. It never deserts its charge, but follows it into all the relations of Duty; at the table it seats itself, and fills the cup for the Soul; caters for it; decides when it has enough; and heeds not the clamor of appetite and desire. It lifts the body from the drowsy couch; opens the eyes upon the rising sun; tempts it forth to breathe the invigorating air; plunges it into the purifying bath; and thus whets all its functions for the duties of the coming day. And when toil and amusement have

brought weariness over it, and the drowsed senses
claim rest and renewal, it remands it to the restor-
ing couch again, to feed it on dreams. Nor does it
desert the Soul in seasons of labor, of amusement,
of study. To the place of occupation it attends it,
guides the corporeal members with skill and faith-
fulness; prompts the mind to diligence; the heart to
gentleness and love; directs to the virtuous associate;
the pure place of recreation; the innocent pastime.
It protects the eye from the foul image; the vicious
act; the ear from the vulgar or profane word; the
hand from theft; the tongue from guile; — urges to
cheerfulness and purity; to forbearance and meek-
ness; to self-subjection and self-sacrifice; order and
decorum; and points, amid all the relations of duty,
to the Law of Temperance, of Genius, of Holiness,
which God hath established in the depths of the
Spirit, and guarded by the unsleeping sentinel of
Conscience, from violation and defilement. It renews the Soul day by day.

Self-Appre-
hension.
Man's mission is to subdue Nature; to
hold dominion over his own Body; and
use both these, and the ministries of Life, for the
growth, renewal, and perfection of his Being. As
did Jesus, he must overcome the World, by passing
through its temptations, and vanquishing the Tempter.

But before he shall attain this mastery he must apprehend himself. In his Nature is wrapt up the problem of all Power reduced to a simple unity. The knowledge of his own being includes, in its endless circuit, the Alphabet of all else. It is a Universe, wherein all else is imaged. God — Nature — are the extremes, of which he is the middle term, and through his Being flow these mighty Forces, if, perchance, he shall stay them as they pass over his Consciousness, apprehend their significance — their use — and then conforming his being to the one; he shall again conform the other to himself.

Childhood a Type of the Godhead. Yet, dimmed as is the Divine Image in Man, it reflects not the full and fair Image of the Godhead. We seek it alone in Jesus in its fulness; yet sigh to behold it with our corporeal senses. And this privilege God ever vouchsafes to the pure and undefiled in heart; for he ever sends it upon the earth in the form of the Child. Herein have we a Type of the Divinity. Herein is our Nature yet despoiled of none of its glory. In flesh and blood he reveals his Presence to our senses, and pleads with us to worship and revere.

Misapprehension of Childhood. Yet few there are who apprehend the significance of the Divine Type. Child-

hood is yet a problem that we have scarce studied.
It has been and still is a mystery to us. Its pure
and simple nature; its faith and its hope, are all
unknown to us. It stands friendless and alone, pleading in vain for sympathy and aid. And, though
wronged and slighted, it still retains its trustingness;
still does it cling to the Adult for renovation and
light. — But thus shall it not be always. It shall be
apprehended. It shall not be a mystery and made
to offend. "Light is springing up, and the day-
spring from on high is again visiting us." And,
as in times sacred to our associations, the Star led
the Wise Men to the Infant Jesus, to present their
reverent gifts, and was, at once, both the herald and
the pledge of the advent of the Son of God on the
earth; even so is the hour approaching, and it lingers not on its errand, when the Wise and the
Gifted, shall again surround the cradles of the New
Born Babe, and there proffer, as did the Magi,
their gifts of reverence and of love to the Holiness
that hath visited the earth, and shines forth with a
celestial glory around their heads; — and these, pon-
dering well, as did Mary, the Divine Significance,
shall steal from it the Art — so long lost in our Consciousness — of unfolding its powers into the fulness
of the God.

Renovation of
Nature.
And thus Man, repossessing his Idea, shall conform Nature to himself. Institutions shall bear the fruits of his regenerate being. They shall flourish in vigor and beauty. They shall circulate his Genius through Nature and Life, and repeat the story of his renewal.

Human
Renewal.
Say not that this Era is distant. Verily, it is near. Even at this moment, the heralds of the time are announcing its approach. Omens of Good hover over us. A deeper and holier Faith is quickening the Genius of our Time. Humanity awaits the hour of its renewal. The renovating Fiat has gone forth, to revive our Institutions, and remould our Men. Faith is lifting her voice, and, like Jesus near the Tomb of Lazarus, is uttering the living words, "I am the Resurrection and the Life, and he that Believeth, though dead in doubts and sins, shall be reassured of his Immortality, and shall flourish in unfading Youth! I will mould Nature and Man according to my Will. I will transfigure all things into the Image of my Ideal." — And by such Faith, and such Vision, shall Education work its mission on the Earth. Apprehending the Divine Significance of Jesus — yet filled with the assurance of coming Messiahs to meet the growing nature of Man — shall inspired Genius go forth to

renovate his Era; casting out the unclean spirits and
the demons that yet afflict the Soul. And then shall
Humanity, leaving her infirmities, her wrongs, her
sufferings, and her sins, in the corrupting grave, reappear in the consciousness of Physical Purity;
Inspired Genius; and Spotless Holiness. Men shall
be one with God, as was the Man of Nazareth.

OF THE

SELECTMEN AND OTHER OFFICERS

OF THE

TOWN OF CONCORD,

FROM MARCH 7, 1859, TO MARCH 5, 1860.

INCLUDING

The Marriages, Births and Deaths in Town, in 1859.

ALSO,

THE REPORT OF THE SCHOOL COMMITTEE

FOR THE YEAR ENDING APRIL 1, 1860.

CONCORD:
BENJAMIN TOLMAN, PRINTER.
1860.

State of the Treasury, March 5th, 1860.

RECEIPTS.

Balance in Treasury, March 7th, 1859,	$2082	81
Of Joseph Holbrook, Collector, bal. tax, 1857,	296	45
Commonwealth, Military Bounty, 1858,	375	00
" School Fund,	88	83
Trustees Cuming and Beaton Funds,	94	00
Selectmen, rent of Town Hall,	217	00
Chas. B. Davis, pay't in part for Cemetery Meadow,	147	50
J. Hancock Bent, amount given by him to town towards alteration of Turnpike,	50	00
Town Clerk, licenses of dogs,	43	00
License of Circus,	10	00
Sundry persons, Taxes paid under Act of 1852, chap. 169,	7	00
Town, County and State Tax, for 1859, and overlay on same,	13,355	78

$16,767 37

PAYMENTS.

Sundry orders on Treasury paid,	$10,911	68
State Tax, 1859,	642	00
Balance of County Tax, 1858,	305	48

$11,859 16

Balance, $4908 21

JOHN B. MOORE, *Treasurer.*

March 5th, 1860.

There will be due, April 19, 1860, from C. B. Davis, balance for land sold him, $147 50

SELECTMEN'S REPORT.

The usual monotony of the municipal life of this town has been varied the past year by an event of no small moment. It pleased the powers at the head of the affairs of this Commonwealth, to order an encampment of all the volunteer militia of the state, and Concord was selected as the favored spot where it was to be held. The announcement of this determination created almost as much sensation among the citizens of this place, as did the proposed excursion of the troops of George the 3d to Concord in 1775, and the Selectmen on the one hand were besieged by numerous highly respectable citizens, who set forth in the most pathetic manner, the dire calamities that would befall the town if six thousand troops were suffered to cross its boundaries, and take up their abode here for the space of three days,—that rum, riot and gambling would, without molestation, rule at the muster field ; that, in the village, buildings would be broken into and fired, hen roosts robbed and clothes lines stripped ; while, on the other hand, as many and as respectable citizens, set forth in glowing terms the great advantage that the town would derive by so great an addition to its population ; that perhaps there would be a little rum drinking and gambling done on the sly, on the other side of Acton line, but that the encampment was to be a model temperance gathering ; that the ancient military reputation of the town would suffer if a timid policy was pursued, and they urged the Selectmen to give the assent required by the statutes.

There being so great a diversity of opinion upon this subject, it was thought advisable to submit the whole matter to the town. A town meeting was accordingly called, and upon the suggestion, "that as 800 regulars were so easily disposed of in 1775, a few irregulars could be taken care of in 1859," and it was voted by a large majority, that the Selectmen should give their assent, provided the town should be at no expense for police force. Acting upon this vote, the Selectmen began to make arrangements for a requisite police force ; the sum of seven hundred and fifty dollars was raised by parties outside of the town and interested in the encampment, and put into the hands of the Selectmen. Although at first this sum was deemed to be ample, it was found to be wholly inadequate for the purpose, if all the policemen were to be paid their per diem compensation in full. Letters were therefore sent to the mayors of several of the cities of this Commonwealth, requesting them to volunteer a police force for the term of the muster. The cities of Boston, Cambridge, Charlestown, Lowell, Chelsea, Roxbury, New Bedford and Lynn, generously responded to this call, and good officers were sent from each of these places without charge for the same, except for their board, &c., while on duty. For this liberality as evinced by these cities, the undersigned know that every citizen of this place will be grateful ; and on behalf of the town they tender their sincere thanks to them. The above money, and that derived from licenses for exhibitions, was nearly sufficient to settle all police expenses, leaving only a small amount to be paid out of the treasury of the town. And the Selectmen are of the opinion that the unusual quiet and good order observed on that occasion, was attributable in a great measure to the strong police force, and the precautions used to prevent any violation of law or disturbance of the public peace.

By a vote of the town, at the last April meeting, it was determined that the money raised for the support of schools, should be expended under the direction of the School Committee ; orders, therefore, have been drawn for the whole sum raised for the year 1859–60, directly to the School Committee. The details of the expenditure of the same will appear in their report. The special amounts paid teachers, &c., as by the following report, were for the unexpired term of the year 1858–9, and have been taken from the general balances in the treasury to which it was transferred in 1857, when, by a vote of the town, the wages per week of teachers was fixed by the town.

It is found by an examination of the bridges, that a larger sum than usual will be required for the support of same. Somewhat extensive repairs must be made upon the Powder Mill bridge, and the bridge near Damon's factory, involving an outlay of from two to three hundred dollars for each bridge. The Nine Acre Corner bridge, near the residence of Isaac S. Lee, must be repaired at an expense of from fifty to seventy-five dollars. Most of the other bridges are believed to be safe and in fair repair, and will not require a large appropriation to keep them in good condition.

The following sums are recommended to be raised by the town for the ensuing year :

Support of Schools,	$3300 00
Payment of Town House debt and interest,	1780 00
Repairs of Highways,	1000 00
Support of Poor,	800 00
Fire Department,	350 00
Repairs of Bridges,	700 00
Town Library,	287 00
Improvement of Public Grounds,	100 00
General Expenses,	1500 00

The following statement of the Receipts and Expenditures of the town for the year ending March 5, 1860, is herewith submitted.

GEORGE M. BROOKS, ⎫ Selectmen
B. N. HUDSON, ⎬ of
JULIUS M. SMITH, ⎭ Concord.

Concord, March 5, 1860.

Appropriations and Receipts.

APPROPRIATIONS.

For Support of Schools,	$3300	00
" Payment of Town House debt and interest,	1840	00
" Support of Poor,	1000	00
" Repairs of Highways,	1000	00
" General Expenses,	1500	00
" Alteration of Turnpike,	700	00
" Fire Department,	350	00
" Repairs of Bridges,	300	00
" Repair of Bedford Road,	300	00
" Town Library,	293	00
" Improvement of Public Grounds,	100	00
" Repair of Sluice near Emeline Barrett's,	100	00
" County Tax,	1475	97
" State Tax,	642	00

——— $12,900 97

RECEIPTS FROM OTHER SOURCES.

Overlay on Taxes,	$454	81
Rent of Town Hall,	217	00
Commonwealth School Fund,	88	83
" Military Bounty, for 1858,	375	00
Income Cuming and Beaton Funds,	94	00
" Silent Poor Donations,	253	83
Of J. Hancock Bent, towards altering turnpike,	50	00
Licenses of Dogs,	43	00
C. B. Davis, payment in part for land purchased,	147	50
License for Circus,	10	00
For Taxes paid by persons under act of 1852,	7	00

——— $1740 97

Expenditures.

SUPPORT OF SCHOOLS.

Appropriation for 1859–60,	$3300 00	
Income Cuming and Beaton Funds,	94 00	
" State School Fund,	88 83	
		$3482 83

Paid orders of School Committee,	$3317 75	
" John Garrison, care of School rooms,	73 00	
" Proportion of fuel charged to Dist.	92 08	
		$3482 83

The following amounts due to teachers and for school expenses for the year 1858–9, have been drawn against the general balance in the Treasury, a portion of which belonged to the schools.

Paid Mary H. Davis, N. Centre School, teaching,	$80 00	
" Jane Hosmer, E. Centre, School, do.,	80 00	
" Harriette Buttrick, W. Centre School, do.,	80 00	
" John Brown, Jr., Dist. No. 1, care &c.,	24 73	
" Mary H. Wood, Dist. No. 2, teaching,	90 00	
" E. W. Bull, Dist. No. 2, wood, care &c.,	34 76	
" Mary Lee, Dist. No. 3, teaching,	84 00	
" Gardner Wheeler, Dist. No. 3, wood, care, &c.,	15 19	
" Martha Farmer, Dist. No. 4, teaching,	108 00	
" Augusta H. Barrett, Dist. No. 5, do.,	80 00	
" Wm. G. Barrett, Dist. No. 5, care, &c.,	14 97	
" Sarah P. Bean, Dist. No. 6, teaching,	114 00	
" Wm. Melvin, Dist. No. 6, care and wood,	6 46	
" Caroline E. Hosmer, Dist. No. 7, teaching,	38 50	
" Francis Hunt, Dist. No. 7, care, &c.,	7 96	
		$858 57

PAYMENT OF TOWN HOUSE DEBT.

Appropriation,	$1840 00
Paid Middlesex Institution for Savings,	840 00
Balance unpaid,	$1000 00

SUPPORT OF POOR.

Appropriation,		$1000 00
Paid Jabez Reynolds, Chairman Overseers of Poor,		1000 00

REPAIRS OF HIGHWAYS.

Appropriation,		$1000 00
Paid N. B. Stow, District No. 1,	$265 07	
" Wm. S. Rice, " No. 2,	83 05	
" Wm. Wheeler, " No. 3,	126 87	
" Jas. P. Brown, " No. 4,	134 42	
" E. Wood, Jr., " No. 5,	99 50	
" Jos. D. Brown, " No. 6,	114 80	
" Silas Conant, " No. 7,	124 73	
" W. H. Adams, " No. 8,	49 63	
		$998 07
Unexpended balance,		$1 93

ALTERATION OF TURNPIKE.

Appropriation,	$700 00	
Rec. from J. Hancock Bent, (a gift to town,)	50 00	
		$750 00
Paid J. B. Moore, work on 204 1-2 rods road,	$255 63	
" Geo. L. Prescott, posts and lumber for railing,	20 21	
		$275 84
Unpaid balance,		$474 16
Of which there is due the contractor but held by the trustee process,		$350 00

FIRE DEPARTMENT.

Appropriation,		$350 00
Paid Geo. L. Prescott, Chief Engineer, May 31, 1859,	$264 27	
" Geo. L. Prescott, " " March 5, 1860,	157 46	
		$421 73
Deficiency,		71 73

CEMETERY.

Unexpended balance in Treasury,		$75 18
Paid John S. Keyes, Chairman Committee,		75 18

REPAIRS OF BRIDGES.

Appropriation,		$300 00
Paid Geo. L. Prescott, lumber and plank,	$185 47	
" Joseph P. George, labor and materials,	103 77	
" Horton Hall & Co., spikes, nails, &c.,	37 50	
		$326 74
Deficiency,		$26 74

REPAIR OF BEDFORD ROAD.

Appropriation,		$300 00
Paid Enoch Garfield, as per contract,	$249 00	
" " " for work since,	11 76	
" H. D. Thoreau, surveying, &c.,	10 00	
		$270 76
Unexpended balance,		$29 24

TOWN LIBRARY.

Appropriation,	$293 00
Paid E. R. Hoar, Chairman Library Committee,	293 00

IMPROVEMENT OF PUBLIC GROUNDS.

Unexpended balance,	$54 87	
Appropriation,	100 00	
		$154 87
Paid Samuel Staples, Superintendent,		145 44
Unexpended balance,		$9 43

REPAIR OF SLUICE NEAR EMELINE BARRETT'S.

Appropriation,		$100 00
Paid Cyrus Pierce, work on sluice and paving gutter,	$78 25	
" for stone for same,	10 00	
		$88 25
Unexpended balance,		$11 75

SILENT POOR.

Unexpended balance,	$25 32	
Income from Donations,	253 83	
		$279 15

2

Paid sundry persons, as appears by Selectmen's
  book, $247 00

   Unexpended balance, $32 15

State Tax, $642 00

County Tax, $1475 97

GENERAL EXPENSES.

Appropriation,	$1500	00
Overlay on Taxes,	454	81
Commonwealth, Military Bounty,	375	00
Rent of Town Hall,	217	00
License of Circus,	10	00
Taxes of sundry persons, in 1858,	7	00
		$2563 81

EXPENSE OF TOWN HOUSE.

Paid Geo. L. Prescott, for coal,	$101	13
John Garrison, care of school rooms,	73	00
" " " hall and moving seats,	67	30
" " " library room,	10	00
Walcott & Holden, fluid, oil, candles, &c.,	59	53
For oil, and express on same,	25	50
E. Stowell & Co., cleaning stoves, and		
pipe, and work on furnace,	26	26
G. Chilson & Co., new grate for furnace,	6	10
Sundry repairs on house, fence, &c.,	18	65
Wood and cutting, and charcoal,	17	00
		$404 47
Deduct am't charged Dist. No. 1, for fuel, care, &c.,		165 08
Leaves expense of Hall and rooms,		$239 39

REPAIRS OF SCHOOL HOUSES.

Paid J. M. Smith, painting and setting glass in		
District No. 1,	$18	89
M. Hobson, work on houses in do.,	15	20
E. W. Bull, repairs on fence and work on		
grounds, District No. 2,	42	26
J. M. Smith, setting glass in do.,	1	00
H. H. Buttrick, whitewashing, and repairs		
of plastering in do.,	10	50
J. M. Smith, painting house, and repairing		
blinds in District No. 3,	48	02
J. M. Smith, painting fence, District No. 6,	6	20
J. P. George, repair'g slating on school houses,	5	00
		$147 07

MISCELLANEOUS.

Paid Alvan Pratt, keeping weights and measures, $10 00
Wm. D. Brown, services on School Com., 29 00
Minot Pratt, do., 30 50
Joseph Reynolds, do., 48 50
A. Stacy, stationery for town officers, 6 32
Concord Artillery, bounty, 345 00
F. Buttrick, work railing on highways, 15 50
Geo. L. Prescott, posts and rails for do., 69 78
H. Newton, entertainment of town officers, 27 37
Robert H. Logan, work on highway near
    muster field, 9 00
Eben Wild, salary as librarian, 50 00
Richard Barrett, services as Assessor and cash
    paid tax book, 93 50
John B. Moore,   "   " use of team, 45 00
S. H. Rhoades,   "   " 35 00
Jos. Holbrook, sundry abatements of taxes,
    1857, 7 92
John B. Moore,   do.,   do., 1858, 43 75
    do.,   do., salary as Town Treasurer, 10 00
    do.,   do., serving warrants, 2 00
    do.,   do., collecting tax, 1858, 163 39
F. Stowell, care of clocks on church and
    school houses, 25 38
Geo. Heywood, services as Clerk, 20 00
    " recording and returning marriages,
    births, and deaths, 13 86
Geo Heywood, going to Lincoln to count
    votes for representative, 2 00
Moses Hobson, repair of liberty pole, 4 50
J. M. Smith, painting of do., 12 68
    "   " fences, 11 25
C. Pierce, work and material on Mill Dam
    sluices, 15 52
Policemen, cattle show, 4 00
Derby Brothers, powder for salutes, &c., 31 16
For express and postage, 3 05
Interest on money borrowed, 46 40
Geo. L. Prescott, lumber for muster, 56 83
B. Tolman, printing town reports, warrants,
    dog license book, &c., 88 55
J. P. George, railing highways, 23 81
Jonas Melvin, returning 17 deaths, 1 70
    " repairing sluices, 6 38
J. S. Keyes, damage to sleigh by defect in
    highway, 3 25
S. Staples, services killing dogs, 6 00

Paid tax on land in Carlisle,   2 21
   Sundry small bills paid by Selectmen,   13 75
   Selectmen, making report,   15 00
                                          ——— $1448 81

        Unexpended balance, $728 54

TABULAR STATEMENT OF

Receipts and Expenditures,

FROM MARCH 7TH, 1859, TO MARCH 5TH, 1860.

RECEIPTS.

Unexpended balance as per Treasury Report, March 7, '59, $2082 81
Of Joseph Holbrook, balance of tax, 1857,   296 45
Appropriations for various objects,   12,900 97
Receipts from other sources,   1487 14

                                     $16,767 37

EXPENDITURES.

Support of Schools, 1859–60, $3482 83
   "   "   balance 1858–59,   858 57
Payment Town House Debt and Interest,   840 00
Support of Poor,   1000 00
Repairs of Highways,   998 07
Alteration of Turnpike,   275 84
Fire Department,   421 73
Cemetery,   75 18
Repairs of Bridges,   326 74
Repair of Bedford Road,   270 76
Town Library,   293 00
Improvement of Public Grounds,   145 44
Repair of sluice near Emeline Barrett's,   88 25
General Expenses,   1835 27
County Tax, balance 1858,   305 48
State Tax, 1859,   642 00
                               ———$11,859 16

        Unexpended balance, $4908 21

Eighth Annual Report of the Town Library Committee.

The Library Committee present their Report for the year ending on the first Monday in March, 1860.

The amount of money received by them, is as follows :

The balance of last year's account,	$78 51	
The Town's appropriation for 1859,	293 00	
Fines collected by Librarian in 1859,	8 58	
		$380 09

The amount expended has been :		
For 233 volumes purchased,	$259 12	
For binding and covering books, and stationery,	7 06	
Leaving a balance unexpended, of	113 91	
		$380 09

The whole number of books now belonging to the Library is 2762. The number added the past year has been, by purchase, 233 ; by donation, 26. No book has been lost during the year, and all but four volumes were in the Library room at the time of the annual examination.

The number of ratable polls in Concord in the year 1859, was 574, and the appropriation for the maintenance and increase of the Library which the town is allowed by law, and required by contract to make this year, is $287 00.

A duplicate set of Miss Edgeworth's and of Dickens' works, strongly bound, have been purchased during the year, the sets already in the Library having been nearly read to pieces. The demand for both is so great, that it will be convenient to have two sets as long as the old ones last.

The additions to the Library have been greater during the past, than in any previous year ; and it is now nearly twice as large as it was eight years ago. Another year will probably increase it to three thousand volumes, and it will then fill all the available space in the room which it now occupies. It is perhaps proper, therefore, for the town to begin to consider what accommodations shall be provided for its future growth. The room now occupied by the Intermediate school, while it is not very convenient for a school room, is very well adapted by its size and shape to the requirements of such a library as we hope in a few years to possess. As the question must so soon be presented, we have thought it best to make the suggestion thus seasonably.

E. R. HOAR,
R. W. EMERSON,   } Library
SIMON BROWN,
GEO. HEYWOOD,   } Committee.
G. REYNOLDS,

CONCORD, March 5, 1860.

REPORT OF THE

Superintendent of Public Grounds.

During the past year a strong and substantial fence has been put around the Green in front of the Town Hall, at a cost of about $70, which will be readily seen is of a lasting quality. The usual care of the Burying Grounds have come in course. There have been from 50 to 75 trees planted, and some replaced where others have died ; and an arbor vitæ hedge put in front of the Old Burying Ground, near Mrs. Bigelow's.

I think that the office of Superintendent of Public Grounds, and Superintendent of the Cemetery, might both be in one ; and as Mr. Keyes is a superior man for the place, I hope that the town will choose him, as I must decline the office, on account of other business taking up my time for the present season.

The expenditures of the last year have been as follows :

Paid Cyrus Pierce,	$46	00
George Clark,	1	50
Samuel Pierce,	11	20
Edward Hall,	6	00
E. C. Wetherbee,	4	83
G. Hyde,	27	50
Jerry Nolan,	10	50
Anthony Wright,	19	19
John Gregg,	2	00
For 108 chestnut posts,	9	72
For horse and cart, boards, nails, &c., &c.,	14	00

$152 44

Respectfully submitted.

SAMUEL STAPLES, Superintendent.

Concord, March 5, 1860.

Report of the Cemetery Committee.

The Committee having charge of the Cemetery, report that the operations of the year have consisted chiefly in the regular care of the ground, the planting of the flower border on the side of the main avenue, the making of a new entrance from the road, and of the work on the pond. This has occupied all the time of the superintendent, except when at work for the owners of lots.

The Concord Musical Society contributed the proceeds of a concert given by them, (amounting to over fifty dollars,) in a well selected collection of ornamental trees and shrubs. These were planted in the portion of the ground nearest to the village, and will soon add much to its beauty. The ladies raised nearly $200 by their Fourth of July entertainment, which was expended in excavating the pond. The mud dug out was sold for a fair price, and the amount received has been expended in gravelling the banks of the pond this winter.

For the coming season, the most pressing want is a well to supply water for the ground, and next, a thorough covering of the paths and avenues with gravel. These, with the care of the Cemetery, and the improvement of lots, will furnish work for one man the whole season, and the Committee recommend that the present superintendent be employed another year. Seven lots have been sold this year, for $122, which is probably about the average yearly demand, and the whole number sold to this time is ninety-six, for $1,865. The number of interments the past year is ten, previously one hundred.

The meadow north of the Cemetery, was sold at auction pursuant to the vote of the town, and brought $295, which sum will soon be in the town treasury unappropriated. It affords an opportunity to the town to do something handsome. What shall it be ?

The accounts for the year are as follows :

RECEIPTS.

From Fourth of July entertainment,	$198 27
Receipts from pay for nine lots,	142 00
From labor of superintendent on lots, &c.,	86 92
From wood, and mud, and grass sold,	70 00
From town, unexpended balance of last year,	75 18
	$572 37

Paid J. Wood, for 8 months' labor, at $27,50, $220 50
    J. Wood, work in March, Dec., Jan., Feb., 55 00
    J. Buttrick, for use of wagon, 2 75
    J. M. Smith, for painting summer house, 7 71
    Moses Hobson, for fence and new gate, 22 36
    B. F. Nealey, for wheelbarrow, 6 50
    E. Hall, blacksmith work, 4 67
    H. Newton, use of horse and cart, 7 50
    J. Holbrook, do., do., 2 00
    J. W. Garfield, do., do., 7 50
    G. L. Prescott, lumber for fence, &c., 12 80
    G. Clark, sods and loam, 9 75
    J. B. Moore, for trees, 6 67
    Walcott & Holden, for sundries, 9 26
    C. B. Davis, for rent of tenement, 9 00
    For three ladders, 6 00
    For labor on pond in August and Sept., 162 61
                                     $552 58

        Unexpended balance, $19 79

    There are several sums still due for the work of the superintendent, and for deeds of lots, sufficient, when collected, to pay any outstanding bills, and leave a small balance to begin the new season with.

               J. S. KEYES,
               J. M. CHENEY,
               R. W. EMERSON, } Committee.
               N. BARRETT,
               J. HOLBROOK,

CONCORD, March 5, 1860.

Tenth Annual Report of the Fire Department.

Herewith is submitted to the town a list of the officers of the Fire Department for the year 1859–60, together with a statement of the condition of the property belonging to the town. There have been seven alarms of fire during the year, five of which were caused from fires out of town. The services of the engines have been required but twice ; once at the burning of a shed, owned by Col. Shattuck, and once at the burning of Edward Conner's barn.

The Department is organized as follows :

GEO. L. PRESCOTT, Chief Engineer ;

SAMUEL LEES,   ⎫
JOEL W. WALCOTT, ⎬ Assistant Engineers.
JOHN B. MOORE,   ⎭

Fountain,   ⎧ MOSES HOBSON, Foreman ;
No. 1.   ⎨ FRANCIS STOWELL, Assistant Foreman ;
            ⎩ CHARLES BOWERS, Clerk.
               30 Members.

Factory Boy, ⎧ SAMUEL LEES, Foreman ;
No. 2.   ⎨ W. D. BROWN, Assistant Foreman and Clerk.
            ⎩ 25 Members.

Independence, ⎧ EDWARD STOWELL, Foreman ;
No. 3.   ⎨ JONAS MELVIN, Assistant Foreman ;
            ⎩ JOHN F. WINCH, Clerk.
               45 Members.

Engine No. 1, is in good order ; has 300 feet leading hose, and 35 feet suction hose.

No. 2, is in good order ; has 200 feet leading hose, and 24 feet suction hose, and is well manned by a volunteer company.

No. 3, is also in good order ; has 825 feet leading hose, and 36 feet suction hose.

The expenses for the past year have been as follows :

EXPENSES OF NO. 1.

Paid for wood,	$1 64
Charles D. Tuttle for horse,	1 00
J. M. Smith,	1 69
N. H. Warren, horses,	5 00

3

Paid E. Stowell & Co.'s bill, ... 2 00
 F. E. Bigelow, ... 5 00
 Walcott & Holden, 2 doz. chairs, and 1 table, 10 15
 E. Hall, ... 4 24
 G. W. Todd, horses, ... 9 00
 T. A. Skinner's bill, ... 4 94
 H. C. Watts's bill, ... 20 00
                $64 66

EXPENSES OF NO. 2.

Paid T. A. Skinner, repairing hose, ... $6 65

EXPENSES OF NO. 3.

Paid for wood, ... $1 40
 L. Fay, 9 pulley blocks, ... 5 00
 J. M. Smith, ... 2 17
 C. E. Snell, steward, ... 16 50
 Sweet oil, candles, &c., ... 2 12
 E. Stowell & Co., ... 1 75
 Walcott & Holden, ... 1 04
 E. Hall, ... 6 24
 G. W. Todd, horses, ... 12 00
  " " oiling harness, ... 3 00
 T. A. Skinner, ... 27 04
                $78 26

GENERAL EXPENSES.

Paid Derby Brothers' bill of 1858, ... $2 67
 B. Hastings, refreshments after fire at Lincoln, 5 22
                $7 89

Summary, General Expenses, ... $7 89
Expense of No. 1, ... 64 66
 " " 2, ... 6 65
 " " 3, ... 78 26
Pay of Engine Company No. 1, ... 102 50
 " " " " 3, ... 131 77
Chief Engineer's salary, ... 30 00
                $421 73

       GEO. L. PRESCOTT, Chief Engineer.

CONCORD, March 5, 1860.

Report of the Overseers of the Poor.

RECEIPTS.

By order on Treasury, $1000 00

EXPENDITURES AT THE FARM.

Paid Joseph Dakin, amount due as per last report,	$71 00	
Joseph Dakin, salary in part,	605 00	
M. Hobson's bill for work,	11 85	
J. M. Smith's bill for door and paint,	2 45	
J. H. Bent, bill for fence,	9 60	
" " for wagon cap,	1 50	
" " setting tire on cart,	2 00	
" " whitewashing,	2 50	
There will be due Superintendent, April 1st,	45 00	
		$750 90

EXPENDITURES AWAY FROM THE FARM.

Paid town of Provincetown, support of Haynes' boy,	$7 36	
City of Lowell, support of Mrs. How and 3 children,	70 05	
Mrs. Hayward, support of 3 children,	110 00	
City of Lynn, " Elsey Hook,	8 36	
" Boston, " Martha Fletcher,	19 74	
Eliza H. Gilson, " Mrs. Bailey,	26 00	
Interest on borrowed money,	2 33	
Wood, groceries, &c., to John Goodwin,	8 78	
Groceries to William Haynes,	6 18	
Aid rendered sundry persons,	9 55	
J. Reynolds, journey to Lowell,	2 50	
Postage, stationery, &c.,	1 25	
Dr. Bartlett, services rendered,	5 00	
J. H. Bent, journey and expenses to Lowell,	10 00	
" services as overseer,	7 00	
		$294 10
		$1045 00

From which deduct balance due Superintendent,
    as per last report, $71 00
Repairs in and about the premises,   29 90
Amount due from State,   15 00
                                                ———— $115 90

Will give the cost of supporting the poor for the year, $929 10
    Respectfully submitted.

                          JABEZ REYNOLDS,   } Overseers
                          J. HANCOCK BENT,   } of
                          MOSES HOBSON,   } the Poor.
CONCORD, March 5, 1860.

Marriages, Births and Deaths in Concord, in 1859.

The records of Marriages, Births and Deaths which have occurred in Concord, during the year 1859, show the following facts :

MARRIAGES.—Whole number, 19. Of the parties, 28 were inhabitants of Concord, and 10 of other places ; 7 were born in Concord, 9 in other towns in Massachusetts, and 22 in other places. Of the males, 18 were first marriages, and 1 a second marriage. Of the females, 18 were first marriages, and 1 a second marriage. There were in 1858, 13 marriages ; increase, 6.

BIRTHS.—Whole number, 48, being 7 more than 1858. Males, 29, females, 19. Of these, 24 were born of Irish parents, being one-half of the whole number. Still-born, 3 ; illegitimate, 1.

DEATHS.—Whole number, 17. Males, 7, females, 10. Of the males, 2 were married, 3 unmarried, and 2 were widowers. Of the females, 4 were married, 4 unmarried, and 2 widows.

The whole number of deaths is less for the year 1859, than in any year since 1791.

Of these persons, 6 were born in Concord, 5 in other towns in the State, and 6 in other places.

Of the males over 15 years of age, 2 were farmers, 1 a trader, 1 a pencil manufacturer, 1 a laborer, and 1 a pauper.

Deaths between						males,		females,
Deaths between	80	and	90	years of age—	males,	1	—females,	0
"	"	70	"	80	"	"	" 2	"	3
"	"	60	"	70	"	"	" 0	"	2
"	"	50	"	60	"	"	" 2	"	1
"	"	40	"	50	"	"	" 0	"	1
"	"	30	"	40	"	"	" 1	"	0
"	"	20	"	30	"	"	" 0	"	2
"	"	10	"	20	"	"	" 0	"	0
"	"	5	"	10	"	"	" 0	"	0
"	"	1	"	5	"	"	" 0	"	0
"	under	1 year,				1	"	1

Average length of life, 50 1-4 years.

Deaths by Consumption,	9	Deaths by Asthma,	1
" " Old age,	2	" " Schirrus of stomach,	1
" " Typhoid fever,	2	" " Infantile,	2

Of the persons who died of Consumption, 5 were between 50 and 70 years of age.

The names and ages of the persons who died in 1859, are as follows, viz :

John Thoreau, 71 yrs.	Hannah Whiting, 71 yrs.
William Tarbell, 81 yrs.	Lucia H. Simmons, 71 yrs.
Tilly Buttrick, 75 yrs.	Abel B. Heywood, 54 yrs.
Sarah R. Barrett, 63 yrs.	Amos Wheeler, 51 yrs.
Margaret Mahoney, 52 yrs.	Crista Thompson, 43 yrs.
Caroline Vance, 62 yrs.	William Wood, 31 y., 7 m. 26 d.
Rebecca Prescott, 74 yrs.	Sarah A. Ball, 27 yrs.
Helen Auty, 27 yrs.	Margaret Fahan, 2 m.

John Appleton, 1 day.

The deaths in 1859, were, according to the United States Census for 1850, as 1 to every 132 1-3.

GEO. HEYWOOD, Town Clerk.

Concord, Jan. 1st, 1860.

Town Officers, for 1860, '61.

Town Clerk,—GEORGE HEYWOOD.

Selectmen,—EPHRAIM W. BULL, BARZILLAI N. HUDSON,
JULIUS M. SMITH.

Assessors,—RICHARD BARRETT, GEO. HEYWOOD,
JOHN B. MOORE.

School Committee,—F. B. SANBORN, J. S. KEYES, JOSEPH
REYNOLDS, E. W. BULL, EDWIN WHEELER, WM.
D. BROWN, JACOB B. FARMER, L. W. BEAN,
NATHAN BARRETT.

Treasurer,—GEO. HEYWOOD.

Overseers of the Poor,—JABEZ REYNOLDS, JAMES P.
BROWN, MOSES HOBSON.

Collector of Taxes,—JONAS MELVIN.

Constables,—MOSES PRICHARD, SAMUEL STAPLES, JOHN B. MOORE.

Library Committee, ⟨ E. R. HOAR,   R. WALDO EMERSON,
SIMON BROWN,   GRINDALL REYNOLDS,
GEO. HEYWOOD.

Surveyors of Highways,—
Dist. No. 1, NATHAN B. STOW,   Dist. No. 5, ELIJAH WOOD, Jr.,
"   2, JOHN B. MOORE,   "   6, JOSEPH D. BROWN,
"   3, GARDNER WHEELER,   "   7, SILAS CONANT,
"   4, CYRUS HOSMER,   "   8, THOS. M. BALCOM.

Fence Viewers,—SAMUEL STAPLES, SAMUEL H. RHOADES,
SAMUEL BARRETT.

Surveyors of Lumber,—JAMES ADAMS, GEO. L. PRESCOTT,
WILLIAM WHITING.

Measurers of Wood and Bark,—
JAMES ADAMS, N. W. BROOKS, WILLIAM D. BROWN, CHARLES
B. DAVIS, JOSEPH P. GEORGE, JONATHAN HILDRETH, SILAS
M. HOLDEN, GEORGE L. PRESCOTT, MICAJAH RICE,
WILLIAM WHITING, ANTHONY WRIGHT.

Field Drivers,—JAMES M. BILLINGS, J. HANCOCK BENT, PETER HUTCHINSON, JOSEPH A. MELVIN.

Cemetery Committee,—JOHN S. KEYES, JOHN M. CHENEY, R. WALDO EMERSON, NATHAN BARRETT, JOSEPH HOLBROOK.

Superintendent of Public Grounds,—SAMUEL STAPLES.

Sealer of Weights and Measures,—ALVAN PRATT.

Pound Keeper,—JOHN WHEELER.

Engineers of Fire Department,—GEO. L. PRESCOTT, J. W. WALCOTT, SAMUEL LEES, JOHN B. MOORE.—(Appointed by Selectmen.)

Auctioneer,—SAMUEL STAPLES.—(Appointed by Selectmen.)

Weigher,—GEORGE L. PRESCOTT.—(Appointed by Selectmen.)

Liquor Agent,—JOSEPH REYNOLDS.—(Appointed by Selectmen.)

Sexton,—JONAS MELVIN.—(Appointed by Selectmen.)

REPORT OF THE

SCHOOL COMMITTEE OF CONCORD,

FOR THE YEAR ENDING APRIL 2, 1860.

The attempted repeal of the District System, which, in a modified form, has been so tenaciously adhered to by this town, furnished last year the occasion for a new organization of the committee, that possessed sufficient novelty and has been found to work so well practically, as to merit a brief description in our report.

This town has always owned its school houses, and raised its money for schools in the town meeting; but it has entrusted the selection of teachers and the immediate care and management of the schools to the Prudential Committees of the several districts. The school meetings that have thus been held in each of the districts, have tended strongly to keep up and increase the interest in the schools, and have proved that if those more directly interested in the welfare and usefulness of the schools have not always managed them discreetly, those less immediately connected cannot if they would. The argument for the abolition of the District System, has been all on one side. The general School Committee set forth their views of the expediency of abolishing the system, in all their printed reports, and the other side has no such means of reaching the public ear. The Prudential Committee man, if he make a report, must necessarily do so to the smaller audience of a district meeting. His views and opinions, however sound and able, do not reach much beyond the walls of his school house, as he has no power or authority to print, and no machinery of a department of the government to spread his reports through the community. His side of the question has been, therefore, but seldom if ever heard; and its real strength is only manifested, when, by some such legislation as that of last winter, every one of these little democracies, the districts, finds

4

its very existence imperilled. Then, with a voice that makes itself heard above the cries of party, and the din of business, and the tumult of society, they thunder out a *No* that compels a pause and a retracing of steps, however awkward or unwilling. "We are competent, and we will manage our childrens' schools in our own way," swells up from a thousand districts in a roar, like that of the mingled rivulets united in a mighty cataract.

To secure the favorable eddies, not to attempt to stem such a current, was the effort of our citizens, and they effected their purpose by a plan which combines the advantages of both systems.

Enlarging their School Committee so that it would consist of three members from the centre district, and one from each of the six outer districts, the town authorized them to employ a Superintendent, at a salary of $100, and recommended them to hold regular monthly meetings, and to appoint a sub-committee on each school, of not less than two members, and voted to pay each member for his attendance at any meeting or examination of a school out of his district, thus securing to each member a compensation for the expense the proper discharge of his duties would create. Thus enlarged and empowered, the committee organized by the choice of John S. Keyes, Chairman, F. B. Sanborn, Secretary, and A. Bronson Alcott, Superintendent, and have endeavored faithfully to carry out the other votes and wishes of the town. By this plan each district has been represented, its local wants and views made known, its interests protected, and its coöperation secured. The meetings of the committee have been more formal and methodical, than when only two or three met together. The sub-committees have felt more responsibility for their own schools, have watched them closer, and kept up an acquaintance more intimate with them, than if they were not expected to report on them at each monthly meeting. The superintendent has discharged his delicate and responsible duties, we believe, to the eminent satisfaction of all with whom he has been brought in contact, and the year's work has thus been harmonious and efficient. The revision of the regulations, and the list of text books, and the classification of our schools, have furnished abundant work for even the enlarged committee, and our meetings have never failed of interest for want of matter. The whole financial system has likewise been revised, and a better economy introduced into all its departments. The teachers have got their pay when they have done their work, and the schools have never suffered for want of proper attention and apparatus.

Besides their regular monthly meetings, the committee have held nine special meetings, and ten meetings of the committee and teachers; they have also caused to be held, under the direction of the superintendent and one or more of the committee, public evening meetings in all the district school houses, and in the Town Hall, and close their year with a meeting of all the schools, teachers, committee, parents, and the public generally in the Town Hall; an account of which will appear as an appendix to this report.

It was voted by the committee that the chairman and secretary prepare the annual report, after receiving the superintendent's report, which in whole or part was to be annexed. We will, therefore, present a brief statement of the school affairs, before coming to the remarks of our superintendent. Our financial statement, together with the tables usually printed, will appear at the end of the report.

The general condition of our schools may be set down as very good; apparently better than for several years past. This we may ascribe to two causes : 1st, A fortunate selection of teachers ; 2nd, An increased interest among the children and parents, awakened by the labors of the committee, but more especially by the zealous and judicious exertions of the superintendent. Whether our teachers have been more permanent this year than usual, we cannot say ; but it has been the purpose of the committee to continue the same teacher in the same school as long as possible. Of the eleven schools, six have had no change of teachers, and another school received its teacher in December from the eleven appointed in April. Still it would be very much for the good of all, if we could keep the whole eleven from one year's end to the other, and even for a course of years. A school always suffers from a change of teachers, even where the change is, in some respects, beneficial. But it may be doubted if we can secure this desirable object without increasing the pay of our teachers, which we would accordingly recommend.

The High and Intermediate Schools have been more particularly under charge of the three members from the centre of the town. The High School is established and supported at an expense far greater than the other schools of the town, though by no means too great, for the purpose of carrying forth the education of such pupils as have graduated at the lower schools. In it are taught the Greek, Latin, and French tongues, together with the higher English studies ; and it is desirable that as many as possible should share in its advantages. It appears, however, that this school is only about half as large as it was seven or eight years ago, and that of those who attend, a considerable portion study neither of the foreign tongues, nor any more advanced studies than are pursued in the district schools. Some have ascribed the small number in the High School to the fact, that the standard of admission is so low; probably it is due to several causes combined; but it is a misfortune to the town, and an inconvenience to the teacher. It seems wrong that a teacher of superior qualifications, capable of instructing thoroughly in three foreign languages, and in such English branches as Algebra, Geometry, Book-Keeping, Chemistry, Botany and Zoology, should have his time taken up with classes half-way through their Arithmetic and Elementary Grammar. These can be as well or better taught in the Intermediate and District Schools, and the High School might be filled, perhaps, by more advanced pupils than now attend there.

The committee were pained to notice at the November examination, that the French pupils were more numerous than those in Latin, and took occasion to remark upon it; since when the number of those studying Latin has considerably increased. It is much to be wished that as many pupils as can be induced to study the classic authors, should have every facility to do so; for in our hurrying and practical country they are apt to be too much neglected, and the importance of the study of any foreign tongue to be overlooked. Therefore, without neglecting the so-called practical studies, we should give what aid we can to the study of Language and Literature, not only in our High Schools, but in all the rest. We will not anticipate what the superintendent has to say on this point, further than to express the opinion that much may be done, even in the Primary Schools, to cultivate the Imagination, Thought and Form of Expression of young pupils, by careful choice of reading books, and by such artful and stimulating questions as develope the powers of thought and fancy in young persons.

The Intermediate School suffers from two inconveniences: 1st, An ill-shaped room, too small for the number of pupils; 2nd, From the occasional presence, (for they are absent at least half the time,) of half-a-dozen vicious, idle, and dull boys and girls, who get little or no benefit from the school, but are a serious injury to it. Nearly all the difficulty which a female teacher finds in this school, which ought always to be taught by a woman, comes from this class of children. Without them, the school would be easy to control and apt to learn, and the committee would not need twice a year to be seeking for a teacher to manage it. It would seem best, therefore, that these truant and idle pupils be removed altogether from the school; but as they are in especial need of school discipline, the town should provide some other teaching for them, if possible. A Town Reform School, if successful, might do much for a portion of these children; others must be continued in the common schools till some better way offers.

As the town will soon need a part of the Intermediate School room for the library, a plan has been discussed among the committee for uniting the two schools in the Town House, under the supervision of the High School master, with the other teacher as assistant. There are many advantages in this, and some obvious disadvantages; on the whole, it seems the best way of removing most of the difficulties in the way of the lower school; whether it would be of equal service to the High School is more doubtful. The High School teacher might then classify more strictly, and the assistant teacher would be relieved of some of the burdens of discipline. We therefore recommend this union as a measure to be acted on by the town.

Mr. Allen has given many extra hours to the work of his school; and by his experiments in Chemistry especially, during the last winter, has done much to promote a knowledge of that science among his pupils. Miss Dillingham deserves great praise for the care and good judgment shown in her school.

Of the other schools, and of the general subject of education in Concord, we will add nothing here; but subjoin extracts from the report of the superintendent. Mr. Alcott has taken occasion to treat the whole subject more fully than the limits of a town report allow; but we understand and hope he may in some other form publish the result of his valuable labors, and his experienced suggestions on this great topic.

The committee are of opinion that the suggestions of the superintendent are worthy of careful attention; especially his remarks on the study of Grammar and Geography, and the necessity of some new discipline for truants and idle scholars. They also agree in his criticism of the several schools, and offer his report as a part of their own.

JOHN S. KEYES,   ⎫
JOSEPH REYNOLDS, ⎬ No. 1,
F. B. SANBORN,   ⎭
E. W. BULL,   No 2,
EDWIN WHEELER, No. 3,

WILLIAM D. BROWN, No. 4,
JACOB B. FARMER, No. 5,
L. W. BEAN,   No. 6,
NATHAN BARRETT,   No. 7.

SUPERINTENDENT'S REPORT.

Gentlemen of the School Committee:

I find my duties as Superintendent of the Schools defined as follows :

I. VISITS.—The Superintendent shall make all the visits required by law, and such others as may be necessary from time to time.

II. REPORTS.—He shall make a report to the committee at their regular monthly meetings of the condition \and wants of the several schools, and shall attend said meetings for the purpose of affording the committee information ; and he shall also at the end of the school year make to them in writing a detailed report of the condition and operation of the several schools, with suggestions for their improvement.

III. POWERS.—He shall have and exercise in concert with the sub-committee for each school all the powers and duties of the general committee over the admission, classification and discipline of the scholars in said schools.

IV. GENERAL OVERSIGHT.—The aim and object of the Superintendent shall be to elevate the standard of the schools, increase the average attendance and awaken the interest of the pupils, improve the methods of teaching, and promote a better understanding between the different teachers, and between the teachers and the parents of the pupils.

These aims and objects I have had steadily in mind during the school year which closes to-day, and I now present to you some account of the several schools, of my intentions and services since they came under my supervision ; adding some views and suggestions thereto, concerning particular branches of study, and education generally considered.

The school is the primary interest of the community. Every parent naturally desires a better education for his children than he received himself ; and spends liberally of his substance for this pleasure ; wisely hoping to make up his deficiencies in that way, and to complement himself in their better attainments ; esteeming these the richest estate he can leave, and the fairest ornaments of his family name.

So thought the founders of these excellent institutions which we now enjoy. Very wise they were, and discerning of the roots and

87

grounds of culture and intelligence for the country they came to settle and adorn. And we shall see how convictions thus conservative and just were planted fast and still flourish here in this offshoot and earliest inland settlement of the colony.

The sentiment of neighborhood once centered itself in the school, and was bounded by the district lines. These little territories were so many jurisdictions of their own, and the school house was the common gathering place. Owing to the prevalence of local causes and of larger interests, our affairs are losing something of the social and family character they once had. But the old names served to mark the new things,—in some cases the old divisions. We cannot let them pass away. They sound as then, and have a puritanic accent still. They connect us with the venerable names of Bulkley and Winthrop, and Buttrick and Merriam, and Conant and Hosmer, and Barrett and Melvin, and many more; with their descendants and the living population, and the landscape we know so well.

Our School Districts are named :—

     I.   The Centre   District.
    II.   East Quarter   "
   III.   Nine-Acre Corner "
   IV.   Factory Village   "
    V.   Barrett's Mill   "
   VI.   Bateman's Pond   "
  VII.   North Quarter   "

MONTHLY VISITS.

My visits have been rare opportunities for becoming acquainted with the children in the several districts. The privilege has been esteemed a pleasure, and I have wished I had more than the half-day's time to give to each school. A whole day is little time for the work. Sometimes I have been indulged with the privilege of giving examples of teaching the simplest, or some of the more difficult and abstruse studies. Especially have I wished to introduce them to the study of their minds, the love of thinking; often giving examples of lessons in analysis and classification of their faculties. I think I may say that these exercises have given much pleasure, and have been found profitable alike to the teacher and the children. In most instances I have closed my visits by reading some interesting story or parable. These have never failed of gaining attention, and in most cases, prompt responses. I consider these readings and colloquies as among the most profitable and instructive of the superintendent's labors. There are a few books suitable for use in this way, but the library is scanty. Krummacher's Parables, Æsop's Fables, parts of the Fairy Queen, Pilgrim's Progress, Flower Fables, with some of the popular stories known to most teachers, may be named. Each teacher has her favorites, and should read only what interests her at the moment. All depends on the teacher ; on her power to touch the fancy and move the mind.

School Exercises.

The graceful exercise of singing has been introduced into some of the schools. It should prevail in all of them, to break the monotony and tedium of the daily routine of things. It is an accomplishment in itself. It softens the manners, cultivates the voice, and purifies the taste of the children. Even the youngest can catch the air and join with the rest. It promotes harmony and good feelings. The old masters thought much of it as a discipline, and used it to advantage and happily. I think singing is a proper qualification of a teacher, and a cordial gift, indispensable in our primary, and desirable in all of our schools ; since making melody in the heart soonest brightens the wits and kindles the desire for excellence. " Let us sing," has the welcome sound of " Let us play,"—and is perhaps the child's prettiest translation of " Let us pray,"—admitting him soonest to the intimacy he seeks.

Grammar and the Study of Languages.

This something called Grammar, and taught under that name in our schools ; is a waste study, for the most part worthless. Children dislike it and avoid it if they can ; very few comprehend the sense of it or find any use for it afterwards. Their teaching should begin from the lips of the teacher ; first by correcting any slips of the tongue on their part, and then conforming their practice to the true standards in every one's mind, with the aid of the dictionary and the style of the best writers. Conversations on words,—paraphrases and translations of sentences, are the natural methods of opening this study. The study of words from the columns of a good dictionary, including the spell-

5

ing, defining and derivation, is the basis of any sound acquirement in the use of language, and the first step to the arts of composition, conversation and public speaking. A vocabulary of the English tongue, freed from any pedantry of learning, but laying open to the mind the roots and substance of the language is needed for our schools. A book of synonyms should be used also. A child should never be suffered to lose sight of the prime fact that he is studying the realities of nature and of the mind through the picture books of language. Any teaching falling short of this is hollow and a wrong done to the mind.

For composition, let a boy keep his diary, write his letters, try his hand at defining from the dictionary, and paraphrasing, and he will find ways of expressing himself simply as boys and men did before the grammars were invented. Not that I would see the technical study of English Grammar entirely abandoned, but deferred to a riper age and made as real as possible to the child.

ARITHMETIC.

Arithmetic, or the reasoning upon the relations of numbers by the clear methods of Pestalozzi, has been taught as it should be in our schools since Colburn's books came into general use. This method is an example of pure teaching. It involves the necessity of thinking and calls the reasoning faculties into exercise. Its general introduction into the schools has been the best thing done for them since the opening of the century. Arithmetic is the only thing yet taught at all as a master would teach, and it is taught perfectly. Even the youngest children have the profit of it and come early to the perception of its principles. In several of our schools, from the natural manner in which it is presented, it is the favorite study, and the children are never tired of solving the problems.

GEOGRAPHY AND HISTORY.

All studies should begin at home, and Geography especially, to be of any worth or significance. It opens to the child, as his eyes open on the spectacle of the little territory he inhabits, his homestead and district particularly. Here let his studies begin. The natural aspect and productions, the occupations, customs, antiquities and history of his town first attract his notice and are the key to the general atlas and history of the planet on which we live. These should be studied together, since they group themselves so in nature.

Besides its natural attractions, our town offers much to the student of history and of biography, being the earliest of the inland settlements and celebrated for its part in the revolutionary struggle. We have a good town history, which it is much to be regretted is now nearly out of print. The committee have expressed the intention of putting a copy of this in every school, just as each school has been furnished with the map of Concord. They have also suggested to the citizen of our town best able to perform the work, the preparation of a small text book, for the schools, comprising the geography, history and antiquities of Concord. I hope that this suggestion may be carried into effect, and that the town may express its sanction of so desirable a work. It need not go beyond a hundred pages, though it might be much more full in its details. It should be illustrated with maps and cuts.

PENMANSHIP.

I notice in the schools less improvement in writing, than in other things. In one or two of the schools skill and care are bestowed by teacher and pupils, but as a general rule, this important art is too much neglected. Let the child write his words before spelling them from the book ; beginning with printing on his slate, he will run presently into the italic and the script characters. He thus learns to write without much instruction and in a hand of his own.

PARENTS' VISITS.

I am sorry to find by the register so few credits for visits to the schools by the parents ; in some, but the names of the committe-man and two or three others ; nor is it much better in any of the districts. The parent who seldom or never visits the school to see for himself how his children are managed, and to form his opinions from personal observation, cannot reasonably complain of what happens there under the ordinary proceedings. He can know next to nothing about it. Of its merits or demerits, he cannot judge. And he should be slow of taking hearsay from any, least of all from his own children, when they are parties interested.

VILLAGE INFLUENCES.

There have been a few cases of truancy and some troublesome boys for the town, or some one to care for. These cannot be reached, perhaps, by any means known to the committee, nor corrected by the superintendent. Older culprits, and village temptations share the blame,—the town's negligence, or the state's indifference. What older children or grown men do, the youngsters, except the best of them, will be swift to imitate, if they can without being found out, and think themselves wronged, oftentimes if protected from the evil example, or checked from following it. The old truants and sinners have been before them and set the snares.

TEACHERS' INTERCHANGES.

The teachers have availed themselves, to some extent, though not all of them, of the privilege granted by the committee, of visiting each others' schools during the term. It has proved agreeable and of great advantage, as offering a means of comparing their gifts, and of gaining suggestions from each others' practice of improving their modes of management and of teaching. Even a badly taught and ill-managed school is profitable in the way of showing what should be avoided, as a good one is of what may be imitated. Our schools are different, and each reflects the teacher's image ; nor is there a better way of learning the art of teaching and ruling than to observe a school in actual operation. And if the teacher could take her pupils along with her, the pleasure and the profit would be mutual to all concerned ; especially to the children, as a little romance in their school experience, which they enjoy at the time, and which remains a pleasing picture in their memories.

MEETINGS OF TEACHERS AND COMMITTEE.

Our meetings at the houses of the committee, from time to time, have been found pleasant and useful to all parties ; the teachers have been generally present, and most of the committee. They have promoted a better acquaintance among the teachers, and brought them together often for comparing methods of teaching and government, and to learn the views of the committee ; and they have served to make the committee more familiar with the characters and aims of the several teachers. The evenings have been spent in discussing in a conversational way, various questions concerning the schools. Among the topics considered were the following :

The Personal Character of Teachers ;

Teaching and Discipline ;

Motives to Study and Behavior ;

Examinations and Exhibitions ;
Recitation Marks, and Checks ;
English Grammar ;
Definitions and Illustrations.

I hope that these excellent meetings may be continued.

SUNDAY EVENING MEETINGS.

Wishing to carry our purpose fairly into effect, by giving it the broadest advantages, we have held a series of meetings at the school houses on Sunday evenings. They have been well attended, and promise to do good. Our object has been to present the subject of education generally to the consideration of parents, and particularly to press the claims of home culture upon their attention. In this connection, let me suggest that much may be done by visiting families in our neighborhood, and engaging parents as far as we might by such intimacy in the education of their children. It would be beginning very near the beginning certainly, and in good earnest. The office of superintendent includes properly and invites to some intercourse of this sort ; easy access, if possible, to the sources of character and habits, which are forming the children he meets monthly at the schools. He naturally desires to form an acquaintance with their parents. Confidence and the best feelings should grow out of the visits. Discreetly undertaken, and carried out kindly and considerately, they would subserve the best interests of all. Nor should any jealousy of private right or pride of family, oppose objections to a mission so beautiful and benevolent. The civilization that makes it conceivable, should also make it practicable. With these preliminary remarks, I come to a report of the condition of each school.

SCHOOL PORTRAITS.

Our schools are the sunniest spots and the greenest in the landscape ; these little families of families, sparkles of enjoyment outside, of business within ; each a little world of its own ; has its climate, its habits, its physiognomy, its manners, individualities : the neighborhood reflected in the image of the teacher. How difficult to describe them, and how delicately just it should be done if attempted ; painting all,—parents, children, families, neighborhoods,—to the life.

The school embodies the neighborhoods in its group : the district with its families for the background, the teacher its frontispiece. Painting her, painting him, tells the whole. We shall make the circuit of the districts for the originals of our portraits, begging pardon of each, and all of them, for hanging them around our gallery. Ah ! could they know how timidly, how conscientiously we have touched, retouched our sketches : hoping to take them to the life and their deservings. The transitions from one to another, show the different aspects of the lively worlds inside of our school houses ; their varieties of atmosphere, manners of the little people gathered there ; the climates of each one of them ; the teacher properly shedding darkness or the day in the shadow or shine she casts inside.

Let us enter them. We begin with the—

NORTH PRIMARY.

This is a pleasant school and select. The children are comely ; mostly bright, and well behaved. Their knowledge of the rudiments is commendable considering their ages, some of them being scarcely four, and none, I judge, much over ten years or so. They number over forty in all, and their attendance has been generally steady and punctual. The youngest of them print their spelling and other lessons on their slates ; the older ones write handsomely some of them in their copy-books with the pen. All practice more or less on the black-board. (Please look in sometime, and see how delicately they use the pencil.) The mistress has happy expedients for interesting them in the proprieties of behavior, the pleasures of study. They sing prettily. Some of them take kindly to speaking. They are thoughtful too, and prompt at their recitations. I think them under good training ; and forward for children admitted so lately into the mysteries of letters, and of their faculties. They are a happy group, and a benefit to see : a credit to themselves and to the families they come from. If a drawing master. I should be tempted to take some pretty portraits I could name.

Miss Hosmer is mistress of the art of persuasion. She takes a sisterly interest and comfort in her charge. She makes them pains-taking, mannerly ; holding them fast and softly to her wishes by invisible threads,—the sunny countenance, sound sense, the kind regards. It is personal presence, the sway of manners, the power of a mechanism working unseen, for the benefit of giver and receiver.

Everything is favorable to a good school in this attractive neighborhood. It is the chairman's own : the children live near their school room, and are of interesting ages. It would be surprising if under all these advantages, the school were not attractive and successful.

The school appeared well at the examination, which was chiefly conducted by the teacher ; Messrs. Keyes, Dr. Reynolds, and the Superintendent, assisting a little. Mr. Bull was present, and a few of the parents.

I regret to find so few calls noted in the register. I think I may commend such as being very delightful in themselves, besides very good for confession and repentance.

The school houses are ornaments of New England. Great improvements have been made upon the former ones, and there was need of it. Ours are all new. They might have been better placed. But the rooms are convenient generally and comfortable ; ample in all cases, save the one now occupied by the Intermediate school. Most of them have a time-piece. Maps of the hemispheres and of the several countries, and of Concord town, adorn the walls.

Good desks, easy seats, and one to every child, small as he may be. Then to these advantages and facilities for study are added the blackboard, and a slate and pencil to the least. The under classes in the outer districts and the primaries, should have Philbrick's tablets. These are designed to occupy and interest them during the intervals coming between the lessons and out-door pastimes, while they please also and beguile them into some acquaintance with the rudiments ; and spare the penalties and pains incident upon having nothing given them to do. I consider them as a necessary part of the child's outfit ; as a gift and a pleasure he has waited for long and will approve.

His tasks shall seem irksome to him at best, and tedious with every attraction we can lend ; by agreeable apartments, kind manners, lively illustrations, sallies apt, pictures, conversation, the illusions of fable ; by consulting his taste, his aptitudes for study and methods of work. As far as in us lies we should cast around him every allurement to learning and the virtues, varying his studies with pleasures at home and out of doors. Let us catch his fancy and his heart by every lure. We cannot commence too soon, since " those who have the office of education should do most in their first years, for they can do more with half the power. And as some farmers believe their fields prove the most fertile which are sown during a mist, so do we reap more abundantly from what is sown during the first thick mist that crowned the morning of our childhood."

East Primary.

The Centre District includes the best part of our Irish population, which mingles its children with ours, and perhaps to the advantage of both. Of this class, the larger number come to the East Primary. It is a sprightly element, and a spur to the classes, wheresoever it enters. Yankee blood first deliberates, then aims carefully, sure to be mortified at missing its mark. But this foreigner shoots at the venture, hitting or not hitting, it matters not to him; so there is fire and the stroke. We have some sharpers on the seats; the East Primary a good many such.

It is a cunning little company, and has a mistress with a tact, almost a genius at pricking them forward as fast as one could wish; jetting in at fitting moments, the vitalities for quickening the wheels in their revolutions; spirts of animation for running faster, or slackening the gearings for turning off the necessary tasks. It suits the volatile dispositions of the little folk, and works its wonders with them. The drill-mistress pins them for the time; then relaxes to vary the performance; sometimes with a song, sometimes with a march, a little speaking, as the mood may require, the humor suggest. Excellent all of it, and giving a relief to their doings inside and out. It pleases, and profits, and shows how swiftly even dullness may run, if we will let it, and be glorified so. 'Tis not quite imitable, however, nor describable in its details, nor measurable by book nor class, nor individually : the platoons moving out and in so capriciously, wheeling round suddenly, or whisking off and out of sight, as the mixed Celtic Saxondom must.

Perhaps the class of little ready reckoners comes nearest to it, doing shopping and marketing on the Mill-dam, casting their accounts and making right change as fast as the figures fall from the lips of the teacher. Then they sing very prettily. It is a pleasing variety and a relief. All write or print on their slates. They have been pleased with the superintendent's stories, and nothing is easier than a talk with them at any time. They have some outside engagements, also, cultivating and dressing in spring seasons the flowers in the yard, where they have little posy beds, and might have many more.

They are familiar with their teacher, and confiding and mannerly in their ways. Miss Hosmer has had them a good while under her care ; and they show the fruits of her attentions. We see in her case the benefits of long acquaintance with the children and parents. A suitable teacher for any new situation is not found so easily ; and where fortune favors any district as here, the whole town shares the benefit.

The examination was a success. Many persons were present. The reading was spirited, and the scholars proved their familiarity with the maps and with mental arithmetic. The mistress varied the exercises by reliefs of singing, speaking, postures, casting a certain romance about the dullest parts, and so made the occasion telling and attractive. Some questions were asked, and slight parts taken in the way of examining by Dr. Reynolds, and the superintendent. Mr. Bull was present, and paid his compliment at the close.

Our meeting at this school-house was thinly attended and composed mostly of children. It was addressed by Dr. Reynolds. The superintendent held one of his talks with the children on the pleasures of study and the uses of the mind. Mr. Bull, Mr. Channing and Mrs. Emerson were present. Mrs. Emerson has interested herself in this school. The children have received New Year's gifts annually at her house across the street, and the flower-beds were laid out and set by her hands. These out-door pleasures are a part of early culture, and the cheapest part of it; they are so insinuating and available, so consonant to nature's ways, and so wholesome. The play-ground, scooped out of the sand-hill, is already become the school's florist and a study. It may become more than this. The German " Kinder Garten " or childs' garden system, recently introduced into England, is attracting attention with us. It is the happiest play-teaching ever thought of, and the Childs' Paradise Regained for those who have lost theirs. It must prevail with the spread of love, and the kingdom come in sanctified souls.

A teacher is a choice person, since so many gifts have gone to the making of her, and time along with opportunities for trial with the rest. Nor may we hazard our children with every candidate who shows credentials from learned faculties, or school committees. Common sense as the basis, as much uncommon as we can get, with the requisite difference of disposition and candor of judgment—these certainly. Cold sense, rigor, the stiff, the conventional ; brute strength, any lack of delicacy, any selfish stains, are hostile to the art and spoil whatever they touch. An ingenuous, glowing soul, along with the kindliest, the mellowest gifts, are the aptitudes and skills for the task. Gifts and motives are to be considered in our estimate, and correspond with one another. None can teach anything admirably who does not love it and find his reward in it. There are grades of ability as of intention ; and these run up from the ground of plain sense and of self-interest through the intermediate talents and considerations, to enthusiasm and genius. The last are the chosen ones, the masters, the mistresses of the art.

WEST PRIMARY.

A frequent change of teachers is detrimental to any school. For, while the new-comer may be superior in some, it may be in all respects to her predecessor, she stands step-mother to the little family till the new intimaces, the new rules and relations are established. The ties that unite teacher and pupils are knitted by time. If not motherly and sisterly they are but seemings. The heart must inspire the head and so sway the will, or the place is but a factory, the tasked and task-mistress meeting day by day to fulfill the unwilling engagements. Love for the art is but another name for an interest in children, for the enthusiasm that, in imparting itself, communicates information and delight to every child.

This school has felt the disadvantages attending any change of teachers during the year. Miss Buttrick had charge of it during the Summer term. It is a mixed school ; the foreign elements being blended largely with the native and numerically predominant in it. There is great disparity of age, as of attainment, always embarrassing the teacher. Here are some comely children, quite forward for their ages, bright, keen-witted, who will be a serious loss to the school when they leave it. There has been a deficiency of slates for the younger classes, and the consequent temptations to idleness and mischief-doing in school. But the tablets will dispose of such troubles hereafter.

Miss Buttrick brought decided gifts to her task. She was energetic and earnest ; expected promptness and dispatch. She had an enterprising method, and went straight to the business. Her demands were strict. She held her pupils to literal accuracy ; stuck close to the text : for words were words, and should stand out stoutly. She pushed forward her scholars by force of will and personal command ; by the sway of temperament and the check. The school was always orderly and busy when I called. I thought her devoted and careful ; I believe she had the confidence of the parents, and proved herself an efficient school-mistress.

The school has lost nothing of strictness and straight-forwardness under the charge of Miss Richardson, while it has gained something by the softening influence of singing, and a more general use of the slate and writing-book. The children write with more than ordinary freedom, and show an improved facility in other exercises. Miss Richardson shows good sense in not intermeddling with specialities of the children too much, but gives room and time to work out results. Something more of variety, and flexibility of method ; of sympathy and power to meet individual cases, would give point and efficiency to her endeavors. If she could give forth the best she has, there would be great gain for all. She seems feeling anxiously for the teacher's gift ; half persuaded it is hers ; yet timid in assuming all its prerogatives. She seeks access to the children's minds and affections, and needs but time and assurance to approve herself worthy of the vocation, so useful to others, and the best possible opportunity for self-culture.

The examination reflected praise on her pains-taking exertions, and on the school. Standing diffidently, in the back-ground herself, she displayed her scholars very fairly in their several exercises. The speaking, in two or three instances, was a pleasing part of the performances.

Messrs. Keyes, Sanborn, and Brown were present with the Superintendent ; also several of the parents.

East Quarter.

This school consists of good children : for the most part steady attendants and of more than average attainments. One or two of the eldest are advanced in their studies, and would be ornaments of any school they might enter. They serve as fair examples to the rest. Under the care of Miss Wood, who had charge of the school for the Summer term, the proceedings were remarkable for their straight-forward and business-like aspect, and for turning off good work down to the last of them. She kept them busy and secured faithful lessons. Every where Arithmetic is taught as it should be ; calling the reasoning faculties into exercise by right methods. Miss Wood had the gift of reasoning, and it was brought to bear directly and effectually, by every means, upon the minds of her scholars, she persisting in having them understand their lessons thoroughly, and all of them. Her influence in quickening the memory was noticeable also. She expected faithful recitations, but gave them to understand that she comprehended the distinction between saying, and seeing the sense of them. She held them by force of clear sense, by patient dealing with them and impartiality. So she won the respect of the boys, who are wont to wait for feeling the bit, the awfulness of power, as certain proofs of authority. Girls have other ways of minding. The exercises were creditable at my several visits. The Geography seemed to be studied off the map, and outside the school house, and dealing with the world and the parts of it described   The arts of Reading and Spelling await the rational and artistic treatment. The books are mostly at fault and we should amend this matter as soon as possible.

Miss Wood applied her strong sense to teaching Grammar by "Green's Analysis," and redeemed the subject from some of its perplexities. The parsing of some of the oldest was ready, as were their recitations in Chemistry and Physiology, and the history of the United States.

Miss Hubbard was persuaded to become Miss Wood's successor. She took charge of the school reluctantly and with some misgivings. She has taught it during the Winter term. The children seem to have brought down through most of their studies the memory of Miss Wood's methods to prompt and assist in furthering the present teacher's wishes, who, less regardful of orderly details and set methods, has striven by a spirit of moderation, kindness, consistency, and appeals to the moral sentiment, to ensure attention and a regard for right behavior. She has brought them forward in their lessons ; secured the confidence of the scholars, and the good will of the district.

The examination was one of interest. Most of the parents were present, and the children though embarrassed by the novelty and demands of the occasion, showed that they had studied to good profit under the guidance of a faithful and devoted mistress. There was a larger variety of studies than is usual in our district schools ; Algebra and Chemistry having been added to the list.

Messrs. Bull, Keyes, and Sanborn attended, and took part in the examination.

The superintendent took advantage of the occasion to speak of the importance of the sentiment of neighborhood, to the keeping alive an interest in the school and promoting harmony in the district ; and of the benefits arising from visiting the school to parents and families.

The sub-committee man has always taken an active interest in this school district. He has done much in nameless ways from time to time, to promote harmony and prosperity in the affairs of his school and neighborhood. Our Sunday evening meeting was well attended ; it was addressed by the Chairman, also by Messrs. Bull and Farmer, and the Superintendent.

North Quarter.

The attendance at this school has been very irregular. There are but few scholars in all ; and of ages so unequal, and attainments so varied, as to render classification difficult. Several of the classes have consisted of one member only. One or two of the oldest are considerably advanced in their studies. They show some proficiency in transposing sentences ; in paraphrasing ; and parse very well. They have practiced analysing and classifying the parts of speech from the scale on the black-board ; and the spelling lessons have generally been defined. The recitations from Colburn have been ready ; and the Geography well attended to. The reading is not so good ; the current school tones being prevalent. There has been a deficiency of slates for some of the smallest.

Miss Barrett has scarcely had the chance given her for a fair trial. The scholars were few, and their attendance interrupted. She has adhered closely to the letter, rote and routine. I have supposed she did so from necessity of temperament, perhaps more from habit than otherwise ; on longer acquaintance with her methods, I find she has adopted suggestions and improved the general tone of the several studies. The improvement has been marked ; and to the credit of her discernment, good sense and ambition to succeed in her efforts.

I have found the children attentive and well-behaved ; but have been less successful in overcoming their timidity and reserve than in most of the schools. I have thought there might have been some outside pressure on their judgments and apprehension, qualifying their studies and opportunities unfavorably. I may have mistaken the state of matters. I find the parents have seldom called to make themselves familiar with the school proceedings ; they cannot therefore comprehend the disabilities and discouragements under which it has labored from the first.

The old custom of boarding round the district had some advantages ; taking the families in turn it led to a personal acquaintance, if not friendship with the teacher and children as well as intimacy with the wishes of the parents—promoting harmony in the school and neighborhood.

The school, although reduced to less than a dozen, appeared well at the examination. The scholars were less reserved and more lively than usual. The Spelling and Geography were good ; they were familiar with the maps ; and have studied Arithmetic to profit. The committee found evidence of fidelity on the part of their teacher, and a fair progress in the scholars.

Our Sunday evening meeting in this district was full; and there was apparent interest taken in the remarks of the speakers on home influence and its bearings on the schools.

Of the committee, Messrs. Barrett and Bull were present, with the Superintendent.

BATEMAN'S POND.

Everything conspires to render this one of our best schools. It is a good neighborhood; the children are forward in their studies and well-disposed, punctual in their attendance and steady. The classes have made a pleasing appearance always: a class of little girls particularly, who have many acquirements for their years and uncommon fluency in speaking and reciting their lessons together. They read with expression and spell unusually well. An advanced class has shown an aptness in solving problems from Colburn's Arithmetic, and they are good grammarians. They have been interested in the scale of the mind and in conversations on words. One or two of the older girls are agreeable readers. They have also had some studies in the History of the United States and the Latin tongue. A certain carefulness has marked all the studies here and down to the youngest in the school.

The teacher stands in pleasing relations to all and manages to have them waste no time, nor lose any herself. Miss. Bean holds them fast by a motherly interest, by her readiness to consult not only their tastes and wishes, but their opinions concerning their lessons and behaviour. It is an instance of frank interchange of thought and sympathy between mind and heart, and works admirably; taking the place of privileged rights and imposed power, assumed so often by the teacher and so apt to separate and excite jealousy between herself and subjects. How. well it works may be inferred from the fact of her having two foreign young men, laborers, who, desirous of self-improvement, have taken their seats daily beside mere children, adding to the weight of her influence by their gentlemanly behaviour and devotion to their studies. Their example has been prompted, it is safe to say, by their own good sense, and is the reflex in a good measure of their teacher's. It serves to show that the best government consists not in arbitrary rules, imposed by private caprice for one's personal convenience, but in conspiring with the authorities that sway the mind and conduct and to which teacher and taught are held responsible alike and always.

Miss Bean is fortunate also in having been furnished with good materials for composing an excellent school, and she has presented us with a pleasing picture and image of teaching. Her children are of classified ages and attainments, of bright gift and docile dispositions. She is devoted to her charge and has gained a place in the children's affections and parents' regards. How can they discharge better some part of their large indebtedness than by frequent calls on the mistress of so many hearts dear to them, and to which themselves minister, each at their own fire-sides?

The appearance of the school was satisfactory to the committee at examination, though some of the children were embarrassed a little by the presence of so many spectators. The classes in Reading gave great pleasure by their natural tones and fluency of utterance. A Grammar class proved themselves better acquainted with the rules and structure of language than is usual. A paraphrase lesson was specially commended by the committee. They heard recitations in Geometry, History and Latin also.

Messrs. Keyes, Sanborn, Bean and Farmer and the Superintendent were present, also a good many of the parents.

We opened our series of Sunday evening meetings at the schoolhouse in this district. It was largely represented by the parents and families of the neighborhood. The chairman, Messrs. Bean, Sanborn, Farmer, Simon Brown and Superintendent, addressed them on the subject of home influences and the duties of neighborhoods. It was a good meeting.

NINE-ACRE CORNER.

My visits to this school have been always satisfactory and agreeable. Only seventeen children on the list and all generally present ; the room uniformly neat, the scholars orderly and diligent. An easy freedom from undue restraint and an air of happiness has reigned throughout the little company ; no play, listlessness or disobedience to mar the proceedings. The children give unmistakable proofs of capacity and of good habits of study. Their lessons have been well committed and faithfully recited ; their proficiency in Arithmetic is extraordinary. A few have paid some attention to Drawing. The Grammar lessons appear to have been studied to profit and the Geography is commendable, also the Writing. The good fault of overloud Reading needs correcting. But the Spelling is excellent ; and regard is paid to defining the words of the lesson. The teacher aims at thoroughness and favors an agreeable variety in their studies; which, in so small a school, is most desirable and profitable.

Miss Lee loves teaching and holds the magic sway. An enthusiast, she works by sympathy and sound perception ; inspiring pleasure in study and the sense of power. She uses the books, but illuminates the text, illustrating and happily explaining ; thus teaching the uses of books, while showing ways of mastering their contents by insight and thought. She aims at making her pupils independent and self-helpful ; leading them into the sense and reason of things, and so imparting the elements of logic, morals and metaphysics at once. Then she has pleasing ways of anticipating their wishes and meeting their wants, seldom sitting, but moving about and so close at hand to serve any on the spot. Certainly she knows what to do with children and the books and has the educator's gifts. She is fortunate also in outward advantages, being connected with the principal families and a favorite of the district. Her school is a delightful resort for lovers of children and rewards the visitor with good suggestions and happy memories. One seldom finds the duties of the school room performed more gracefully and the family sentiment so well represented in the teacher.

Messrs. Keyes, Sanborn, Brown and Wheeler were present at the examination ; most of the parents also. Miss Lee surprised us by the accuracy and speed with which she conducted the exercises and the flood of information which she had in reserve to communicate, had there been time. She cast about every thing the romance of reality and made it plain that the school room might indeed be an attractive place for all ; for parents as well as children. Even the Arithmetic was dissolved and made fluent by her touch. The black-board exercises were surprising ; she contrived by a few strokes to bring out the fine points of her classes and show what they knew. There was nothing of weariness on the part of the children, the spectators, nor even the committee ; who only wished they had the whole instead of part of the day assigned for the examination. Three things were remarkable : the Arithmetic, the Geography and the Drawing. We heard lessons also in Physiology and History, making a wider variety than is usual in our common schools. The tone of speaking was better than that of the reading, which was over-loud.

Our Sunday evening meeting at the school house was well attended. It was addressed by Dr. Reynolds, Mr. Sanborn and the Superintendent.

Factory Village.

This district reflects the forms of the old system, yet has lost the sentiment of neighborhood that made the old ways effective, if not lovely. There was something venerable, to say the least, in the aspect of the old school house, standing at the cross roads, so gladly pouring the youthful population through its doors and seating them hospitably, inside, with a blazing fire in view, during the winter months, and pleasant prospects spreading around outside. The new building has forfeited those privileges, by straggling away to plant itself along the roadside, there standing exposed to the winds, midway between the cross roads it left, and the village that names it, and from which it receives the largest part of its inmates. Perhaps it so indicates, better, the mixed condition of the district, whose children gathered inside from the scattered farm-houses and factory, appear to be unrelated, the parents wanting the sentiment of neighborhood to unite them. Busy virtues in families are essential to promote its interests. For the whole neighborhood comes inside, parents and all, to keep the school if kept; keep it with or against the teacher, and are apt enough to throw any blame upon her shoulders. A social institution it asks for the sympathy of its families, and the union of all within its district.

Miss Hagar had charge of the school for the Summer term. She brought some accomplishments to her task, with an affection for teaching. She won the regard of the children; personally enforcing good habits of study and of behavior. She was precise, systematic and particular, measuring work carefully by the clock, and proceeding deliberately through the routine of studies. She taught penmanship and reading remarkably well. The recitations were faithful, and she was particular in the matter of definitions. Then she concerned herself in the happiness of the younger children, and found pleasant occupation for them, by giving out little picture-books to look at, and the privilege of marking on the slate, as a reward for their good conduct. True sympathy stoops to the minutest regards, and works out large results, by attention to things seemingly trivial and indifferent.

The school has been under the care of Miss Tincker for the Winter term, and shows marked improvement. Already she has moulded the mixed materials into some shape, and is impressing her wishes upon them. She has the confidence of the scholars, has secured obedience, and good habits of study. The Reading so well taught by her predecessor is a favorite exercise still, and the Penmanship under

7

her own graceful and flowing style, is an improvement upon that. Then she puts soul into the exercises, redeeming them from tameness. Her work is real, thorough, exact; nothing is feebly or half done. Arithmetic becomes a process of linked reasonings, under her promptings, and the steps, as under Miss Lee's genius, are sharply rendered to the ear, as well as mentally taken.

At the examination she did not bring out the strength of her school as could have been wished. The classes labored under much embarassment, at the presence of so much company. Abundant evidence appeared, however, of the teacher's ability and of progress in the several studies. The Reading was better than usual, and the Penmanship was praised by every one. The study of Geography seemed to have been turned to good account, the scholars showing considerable knowledge of the district and town they live in.

At the Sunday evening meeting, Messrs. Brown, Sanborn, and the Superintendent, addressed the company. The meeting was thought a good one.

***

BARRETT'S MILL.

We best describe a school in describing its neighborhood. And where the sentiment of neighborhood is divided or feeble, there is not much to be said. The teacher can do little, however capable or devoted. Outside prejudices cripple her influence, and the concern is a discouragement and failure from beginning to end. The best things are falsely interpreted, and the worst made still worse. Unanimity of feeling is necessary to just judgments on all sides, and a good understanding between parents and teacher, is indispensable to a good one between teacher and pupils. Family prejudices are disinclined to stay at home; they venture abroad and are reflected back through the vision of the children. Any want of sympathy operates as a discouragement. The voice of the district is apt to be raised soon enough concerning the teacher's qualification for managing the little republic over which she presides, and sometimes without looking inside to give the fair verdict of blame or approval. ' Tis safest to be just in our dealings with the word justice and make sure of its standing sponsor for our speech.

Miss Hubbard entered the school in good faith, and with a fair share of learning along with superior gifts of disposition and devotion to her duties. She had taught, it was understood, successfully, and loved teaching. The school was not large, but the children were backward, and some accustomed to feel the strong hand, were a little rough in manner, and not over susceptible to the influence of the meeker virtues. She found some difficulty in reconciling the discordant elements at once; nor did she succeed in her endeavors at last. There was dissatisfaction without, and the difficulties within were so formidable that she declined resuming it after the close of the Summer term. Considering all the circumstances, the wonder is that she continued so long, and turned the time to the profit she did. The only complaint I ever heard from any was, that the government fell so far short of the teaching, and that some of the boys took advantage of her kindness and long forbearance. The girls were all attached to her, and bore testimony to her kind instruction

Miss Prescott succeeded Miss Hubbard, and has proved herself a teacher of skill and ability. She aims at being methodical and thorough, and to put the mind in possession of the subject studied. It appears that she has given satisfaction thus far, and won the confidence of her scholars and the district. She has conducted a somewhat difficult school to manage, with spirit and good judgment. She deserves great credit for the order and discipline which she has established.

Sickness kept a good many of the children away from the examination. Those present gave evidence of having been studious and well taught. A class in Reading won praise from the committee. It seemed that the map of Concord had been studied here, as well as the other maps. Messrs. Keyes and Farmer were present and the Superintendent. Also a good many visitors, some of them parents of the children.

Our Sunday evening meeting in the district was full, and a good one. Rev. Mr. Reynolds, the Superintendent, Mr. Farmer and Dr. Reynolds, spoke on Family Government, and the duties of parents to the schools.

INTERMEDIATE SCHOOL.

Our Intermediate school takes in the children of the village at a pleasing age. It is a spectacle well worth seeing. Ingenuous youngsters, sprightly girls and promising boys, that Plato would have praised. I should like to give portraits of a few of them as I have seen them in the school room reciting sometimes. Here my visits have been seasons always of interest to me. I have reason to believe they have been to the school generally. I wish our conversations may have been as refreshing to the children as they have been to myself.

Miss Farmer had this department under her charge for the Summer term. She brought to her task a clear comprehension of her duties with a reserve of power, sure of working them out alike in principle and particulars. She knew when to help and how ; where help was necessary and when it would be a hindrance ; putting the mind upon its resources whenever she could. She insisted upon having perfect recitations. Her teaching was thorough and faithful. Her rule was strict, but just and generous also. The scholars knew that she was careful to be in the right and would have her way and so did not oppose. She wasted no time in dealing with faults which she had not the skill to correct. Perhaps she needed much time, but if she took it, she came out right and sure at the close. Her plain strength bore honest fruits ; she was every way equal to her work. I thought her an excellent disciplinarian and suitable person for the place she held in the village school, wherein a stronger rule seems necessary than in some others.

Miss Dillingham is her successor. She brings to her business a perfect knowledge of the books, keen common sense, a love of youth, and some experience in teaching. She is an admirable drill-mistress : she adheres strictly to methods and manages to get a good deal of work out of her pupils. In many respects she carries forward and in more varied manners the thoroughness to which they had been accustomed under her predecessor. The children have been cramped and much incommoded for want of space. We hope to better their condition for the coming Summer term by making some changes. The inconveniences were felt very sensibly at the examination and especially at the last one.

The examination was spirited. There was accuracy and speed in the recitations. The children acquitted themselves to good acceptance in Reading, Arithmetic and Spelling ; the last exercise particularly. The Penmanship was better than we have seen in some of the schools.

Of the committee, there were present Messrs. Keyes, Reynolds, Barrett, Bean, Farmer and Sanborn. The examination was conducted by the teacher, assisted by Messrs. Keyes, Sanborn, Reynolds and the Superintendent. Many parents were present, several teachers and others as spectators. Rev. Mr. Reynolds closed the services with prayer.

HIGH SCHOOL.

Mr. Allen has had charge of the High School since the Summer term of 1858. He has been teaching under some disadvantages and discouragements ; many of his pupils entering before being grounded in the common elements ; and wishing to pursue the higher branches without the necessary preparation ; then the variety of studies required has added to his many perplexities. He has done the best he could under the circumstances and brought something like method and classification into the exercises. He has sought to diversify agreeably the lessons with some novelties of method and trials of less formal styles of instructing his classes. Much time has been given to the study of the classics. I have thought favorably of some studies in English literature, which have been lessons on the text of Shakspeare, and Milton ; also of analysis of sentences according to the methods of Mr. Green and Prof. Crosby. He has paid some attention to bettering the deficient Spelling and mending the Reading. Chemistry has been studied also and Geometry. I have availed myself of opportunities for giving some examples of teaching the elements of Grammar by the scale of the parts of speech ; also on the faculties of the mind, illustrated by the poets.

Mr. Allen's methods are scholastic and pains-taking. He has wished to emancipate the memory from the dead letter of the text and to make his teaching less formal and literal. Still, he has not been as successful as might have been expected from his labors.

The young ladies, with the diffidence so native to them, have found it not easy to speak so as to be heard distinctly across the room. It has been a serious inconvenience and troubled the committee a good deal at the examinations. So many young persons, susceptible, intelligent, and alive to the pleasures of conversation, and yet answering so bashfully the gentlest promptings, or not at all.

If devotion to his school, if the giving of much time and thought to it, could insure success, Mr. Allen is deserving the highest commendation. His gentlemanly deportment and good habits have won him the respect of all who knew him. Of scholarly attainments he seems fitted for letters, and as teacher or professor should make good his master's degree.

Many people attended the examination. It was conducted by Mr. Allen, assisted by Dr. Reynolds, Mr. Sanborn, the Superintendent, Messrs. Keyes and Brown. The examination in Greek showed a good knowledge of the Grammar and the principles of construction. The recitation in French showed that much pains had been taken in pronunciation especially. The Latin translations were good. There was some excellent Reading, and a Recitation by the young ladies was given with spirit. The order of the school was especially good and though in so large a room, besides the difficulty of hearing distinctly, it is more difficult to watch closely the behavior of pupils, the committee thought they had nowhere seen a school so orderly and disposed to respect the teacher in his government. There was a disposition to avoid answering questions requiring thought and reasoning, which may have been owing to timidity. The classes appeared to disadvantage; and did not meet the general expectation of the committee. The recitations were timidly delivered and the obvious blemishes became so much the more apparent from the hesitancy and diffidence of the scholars.

It fell to the superintendent to declare the disappointment of the committee at the close of the exercises. This duty, coming upon him by surprise, may have been discharged at the cost of wounding the feelings of the school and perhaps of parents and others. It was not sought by him, nor could it be gracefully declined under the circumstances. He would here speak for himself and say that his judgment would have deferred any censure, if any was to be spoken, to a less public occasion, and that those for whom he spoke should have found a fitter instrument for pronouncing the verdict.

Very choice gifts are requisite to bring out the attainments of a class, to the best advantage. Some scholars can exhibit all they know, all they are, without hesitation or reserve. But such are not aptest usually, nor the best at the best studies. The tender touch is most effective. An examination should not be a dissection but a sympathy, the best things answering best to kindness and coming forth diffidently, because being so fine and tender they shrink from any touch but the most delicate and discriminating. An examiner should know how to save time and make the occasion one of interest and profit to all, to scholars, teachers, and spectators. His object should be to strike out by a few skillful touches and strokes what is known, what is not; showing the teacher's gifts and attainments through the scholar's progress and deportment.

SUNDAY EVENING MEETINGS.

We have had two meetings at the Town Hall on Sunday evenings. At the first of these the speakers were Rev. Charles Brace, of New York City, who described the Ragged Schools : Mr. Simon Brown made some remarks on the Westboro' "Reform School," and the Superintendent on the Powers and Gifts of Teachers. This was our first meeting in the village. It was opened by the Chairman, who explained the general objects and plan of the series.

At a second meeting there was a general attendance. Opening remarks were made by the Chairman of the Committee, followed by the Superintendent, on the subject of Home Culture in its Ideas and Results : by Mr. Emerson, on the Value of Learning and Books ; and by Mr. Sanborn on the Practical Duties and Relations of Parents to their Children and the Schools.

Our Exhibition of all the schools in the Town Hall on Friday, March 30, was a beautiful and brilliant affair. Most of the children with their teachers were present and a crowd of spectators. The schools appeared to advantage, and carried the town by acclamation. We hope to print a full account of this meeting in a supplement.

The town owes its thanks to your former Superintendent and present member of your body, for his labors in former years. I think them deserving of special acknowledgment. They have served as an indication and a basis for what I have attempted since the schools came under my special supervision.

Gentlemen, I owe you my thanks for the confidence that has enabled me to form so agreeable an acquaintance with the children in the several schools, with so many of their parents, with their teachers, and with yourselves particularly. I have esteemed it a privilege, and a graceful way of discharging some debts one owes to his townsmen and to the town in which he lives. I regret not having more time to give to an interest lying so near the hearts of parents and good men everywhere. I have not felt warranted in suggesting every improvement which seemed to me feasible and desirable in the schools. Some such, however, I have in part intimated, in the hope they may commend themselves to your judgments, and be thought worthy to be laid before the town.

Respectfully submitted, by

A. BRONSON ALCOTT.

FINANCIAL STATEMENT.

The amount placed at the disposal of the Committee, by the vote of the Town, consisted of

Appropriation for Schools,	$3300	00
Income of Cuming and Beaton Donation,	94	00
Income of Massachusetts School Fund,	88	83
		$3482 83

Which has been expended as follows :

Mr. C. A. Allen, teaching High School,	$800	00
Proportion of fuel and care, charged by town,	92	08
Books, chemicals and incidentals,	36	79
Total cost of High School, 42 weeks,		$928 87

Miss M. Farmer, teaching Intermediate School,	$78	00
Miss M. A. Dillingham, ditto,	162	00
Proportion of fuel, care, books, and incidentals,	96	60
Total cost of Intermediate School, 40 weeks,		$336 60

Miss L. Hosmer, teaching N'th Primary School,	$200	00
Fuel, care, books, maps and incidentals,	40	59
Total cost of North Primary, 40 weeks,		$240 59

Miss J. Hosmer, teaching East Primary School,	$202	50
Fuel, care, books, and incidentals,	32	32
Total cost of East Primary, 40 1-2 weeks,		$234 82

Miss H. Buttrick, teaching West Primary School,	$112	50
Miss S. C. Richardson, ditto,	90	00
Fuel, care, books, and incidentals,	31	29
Total cost of West Primary, 40 1-2 weeks,		$233 79

Miss M. Wood, teaching East Quarter School,	$110	00
Miss A. F. Hubbard, ditto,	85	00
Fuel, care, books, and incidentals,	34	14
Total cost of East Quarter School, 38 weeks,		$229 14

Miss M. Lee, teaching Nine-Acre Corner School,	$200	00
Fuel, care, books, and incidentals,	46	56
Total cost of Nine-Acre Corner School, 40 weeks,		$246 56

Miss A. E. Hagar, teach'g Fac'y Vill'ge School, $110 00
Miss H. C. Tincker, ditto,   88 00
Fuel, care, books, and incidentals,   44 33

    Total cost of Factory Village School, 38 weeks, $242 33

Miss A. F. Hubbard, teach' Bar't's Mill School, $100 00
Miss M. A. Prescott, ditto,   85 00
Fuel, care, books, maps, and incidentals,   43 40

    Total cost Barrett's Mill School, 37 weeks, $228 40

Miss S. P. Bean, teaching Bateman's Pond School, 195 00
Fuel, care, books, maps, dictionary, and incidentals, 53 77

    Total cost of Bateman's Pond School, 39 weeks, $248 77

Miss A. H. Barrett, teaching N'th Quarter School, 200 00
Fuel, care, books, maps, and incidentals,   40 81

    Total cost of North Quarter School, 40 weeks, $240 81

    Total cost of Schools, $3410 68
    Unexpended balance, $72 15

ERRATA.

A few errors have been overlooked in the hurry of proof-reading and printing: some of these are intimated below:—

Page 4, line 6 from bottom, for "and," after "vicious, idle," read *or*.

Page 8, lines 5 and 6 from bottom, for "wished to introduce them to the study," read *interest them in the study, &c., and the love of thinking.*

Page 9, last paragraph, for "Grammar and the Study of Languages," read *Language.* Omit the semicolon after "schools," 9th line from bottom, same page.

Page 15, line 12 from bottom, omit semicolon after "lend."

Page 17, line 10 from bottom, for "difference," read *diffidence.* After "conventional" omit the semicolon and insert a comma.

Page 19, line 13 from top, omit the comma after "diffidently."

Page 23, line 4 from top, for "gift" read *gifts.*

Page 29, line 17 from top, for "also on the faculties," read *of* the faculties.

SCHOOLS.	TEACHERS.	Whole No.		Average Attend'ce		No. over 15.	No. under 5.	Wages per month	Length in weeks.	SUB-COMMITTEE.
		Summer.	Winter.	Summer.	Winter.					
High School,	Charles A. Allen,	34	33	27 6-100	30	24	0	$800 pr.yr.	42	Joseph Reynolds, F. B. Sanborn.
Intermediate,	Martha Farmer, M. A. Dillingham,	44	54	34 23-62	41 23-85	2	0	$24	40	John S. Keyes, Nathan Barrett.
North Primary.	Lydia Hosmer,	51	54	42 34-47	42 40-88	0	6	20	40	John S. Keyes.
East Primary,	Jane Hosmer,	59	51	45	41	0	0	20	40	E. W. Bull.
West Primary,	Harriette Buttrick, Sarah Richardson,	54	49	48	37	1	2	20	40	F. B. Sanborn, W. D. Brown.
East Quarter,	Mary H. Wood, Abby F. Hubbard,	27	30	24 11-13	23 1-2	3	1	20	38	E. W. Bull, Joseph Reynolds.
Nine-Acre Corner,	Mary Lee,	17	16	13 1-2	14	0	0	20	40	Edwin Wheeler, W. D. Brown.
Factory Village,	Ann E. Hagar, H. C. Tincker,	39	43	31	34	3	0	20	38	W. D. Brown, Edwin Wheeler.
Barrett's Mill,	Abby F. Hubbard, M. E. Prescott,	27	26	22 1-2	20	2	1	20	37	J. B. Farmer, L. W. Bean.
Bateman's Pond,	Sarah P. Bean,	21	23	15 2-3	13 1 2	4	1	20	39	L. W. Bean, J B. Farmer.
North Quarter,	Augusta H. Barrett,	16	16	11 4-10	11	3	1	20	40	Nathan Barrett, John S. Keyes.

SCHOOL EXHIBITION.

Friday, March 30th, the day fixed for the exhibition of all the Public Schools of Concord, in the Town Hall, was a warm and lovely day and crowds of parents and friends, as well as children, were present. The hall has 'seldom been better filled and never with a more interesting assembly. The eleven schools were all represented and all the teachers and committee were present. The average attendance in all the schools this winter has been 313 pupils, and of these 275 pupils took their places on the long benches ; each school with its teacher at its head, a sight worth seeing by all our people and proper to gratify some town pride in its schools and teachers. The Superintendent, Mr. Alcott, prefaced the exercises by saying how much pleasure it gave him to introduce the coming century to the present, which would for this afternoon give place to its juniors and successors. They could speak better for themselves than any one for them and he would therefore stand aside and leave the field to them. Rev. Mr. Reynolds then offered prayer.

ORDER OF EXERCISES.

Introductory Address by the Superintendent of Schools.
Prayer, by Rev. Mr. Reynolds.
Salutatory, by a pupil of the Intermediate School.
Song,—"Brothers, in this place of festive meeting," by High School.

EAST CENTRE PRIMARY SCHOOL,—MISS JANE HOSMER.
Song,—" Come cheerful companions unite in this song."
Recitation,—" Gertrude and her Kittens."

WEST CENTRE PRIMARY SCHOOL,—MISS S. E. RICHARDSON.
Song,—" Oh, we 've come here to see you and sing a little song."
Recitation,—" Who stole the bird's nest?"
Declamation,—"The Child's Prayer."
Recitation,—"The Clock."
Song,—" Will you come with me my school mates?"

NORTH CENTRE PRIMARY SCHOOL,—MISS LYDIA HOSMER.
and
INTERMEDIATE SCHOOL,—MISS M. A. DILLINGHAM.

Song,—" Happy Land," by Intermediate.
Song,—" The Stars," by Intermediate and Primary.
Dialogue,—Primary.
Declamation,—" Long Ago," Intermediate.
Song,—" The Mountain Maid's Invitation," both schools.
Declamation,—" The Hours," Primary.
Recitation,—" The Child's Funeral," Intermediate.
Dialogue,—"Just my Luck," Intermediate.
Declamation,— The Farmer's Boy," Primary.
Declamation,—" Absence of Mind," Intermediate.
Song,—" Come cheerful companions," both schools.
Song,—" Let me kiss him for his mother," Primary.

EAST QUARTER SCHOOL.—MISS ABBIE F. HUBBARD.

Declamation,—" The Sea."
Reading,—" David and Goliath."
Declamation,—" Success alone seen."
Song,—" How beautiful the morning."
Remarks by Dr. Joseph Reynolds.

CHILDREN'S SONG.

The world lies fair about us, and a friendly sky above,
Our lives are full of sunshine, our homes are full of love,
Few cares or sorrows dim the beauty of our day,
We gather simple pleasures, like daisies by the way.

> *Chorus,*—Oh ! sing with cheery voices,
> Like robins on the tree,
> For little lads and lasses,
> As blithe of heart should be !

The village is our fairyland, its good men are our kings,
And wandering thro' its bye-ways, our busy minds find wings.
The school room is our garden, and we the flowers there,
And kind hands tend and water us, that we may blossom fair.

> *Chorus,*—Oh ! dance in airy circles
> Like fairies on the lea,
> For little lads and lasses,
> As light of foot should be !

There's the Shepherd of the sheep-fold, the Father of the vines ;
The Hermit of blue Walden, the Poet of the pines,
And a Friend who comes among us, with counsels wise, and mild,
With snow upon his forehead, yet at heart a very child.

Chorus,—Oh ! smile as smiles the river,
　　　Slow rippling to the sea,
　　　For little lads and lasses,
　　　As full of peace should be !

There's not a cloud in heaven but drops its silent dew,
No violet in the meadow but blesses with its blue ;
No happy child in Concord who may not do its part,
To make the great world better, by innocence of heart.

Chorus,—Oh ! blossom in the sunshine,
　　　Beneath the village tree,
　　　For little lads and lasses,
　　　Are the fairest flowers we see !

———

Remarks, by R. W. Emerson.

———

NINE-ACRE CORNER SCHOOL,—MISS MARY LEE.

Song and Declamation.
Exercise in Arithmetic.

———

FACTORY VILLAGE SCHOOL,—MISS H. C. TINCKER.

Concert exercise in Geography.
Song,—" Old Iron-sides at anchor lay,
In the harbor of Mahon."

———

BARRETT'S MILL SCHOOL,—MISS M. E. PRESCOTT.

Reading. Manual Exercise.
Song. Dialogue. Song.

———

BATEMAN'S POND SCHOOL,—MISS S. P. BEAN.

Exercise in Reading. Concert Reading.

———

NORTH QUARTER SCHOOL,—MISS A. H. BARRETT

Recitation in Geography.

HIGH SCHOOL,—MR. CHARLES A. ALLEN.

Song,—" Up the hills in early morn," by the school.

Extract from the 1st Part of King Henry IV., Act II., Scene IV.

Prince Henry, Nathan Henry Hosmer, Jr. | *Falstaff*, Charles E. Bowers.
Poins, Joseph M. Gleason. | *Francis*, Hersey Brown.

Declamations,—" The Nautilus " from Holmes,—Miss Adelaide E. Adams.
            " The Passage," from Longfellow,—Miss Mary H. Moore.
            " Good-bye," from Emerson,—Miss Mary C. Wheeler.

Songs,—" When in the gloomy midnight deep,"—by Miss Annie E. Hosmer.
      " The Wanderer's Farewell,"—by the school.

Declamation,—Conclusion of Seward's recent Speech in U. S. Senate,—by Charles H.
      Hildreth.

Concluding Remarks, by Rev. Mr. Reynolds and the Superintendent.

At two o'clock the hall was full and the exercises began. A few of the parts were omitted, but others were added and it was nearly six o'clock before they ended Then followed something not set down in the printed programme ; a collation for the children, furnished by the teachers and served to them by zealous and graceful ushers. A little past six the happy children returned home, tired no doubt, but rejoicing in the pleasures of the day and the applause of their elders.

Where all was so good, it seems hardly proper to speak of particular schools and persons ; yet this is perhaps expected and may be done without invidious criticisms.

Miss Jane Hosmer's school opened the performances of the separate schools, after the salutatory so bravely delivered by Master Holbrook and the cheerful song of the High School. The plan was that each teacher should be allowed ten minutes to exhibit her pupils, but this was not strictly followed ; some taking more and others less time. Miss Hosmer's pupils won universal praise for the prettiness of their dress and manners and their ease of singing and reciting. When they left the platform (where each school took its place for its performance) and presented bouquets to different members of the committee, those gentlemen were so surprised and pleased that they forgot to return their thanks to the little messengers, who were half hidden by the flowers they carried. They would now acknowledge their gratitude to the school and its deputies for this graceful testimonial of their regard for their official friends and well-wishers.

Miss Richardson's school made a good appearance and sung and recited with much effect ; particularly in the dramatic recital of the

Bird's Nest song; which we trust impressed its moral on all little boys and girls who heard it. The Child's Prayer was touchingly recited by one of the brightest scholars in the whole town.

Miss Lydia Hosmer and Miss Dillingham united their schools, so that it was hard to distinguish one from the other; which the committee a little regretted; wishing to show each school separately under its teacher. Their songs and declamations were effective and drew forth great applause.

Miss Hubbard brought her pupils forward, each adorned with a badge and motto; giving a pleasing, half-military air to this fine school. They read with spirit and declaimed in loud and clear tones.

After Dr. Reynolds had closed his appropriate remarks to the children, and a short recess had been given to refresh the tired little actors, Miss Alcott's lively and beautiful song was sung by a portion of the pupils. Mr. Emerson then spoke briefly of the pleasure he had taken in observing the pretty spectacle and listening to the singing of the children, which had delighted even his not very musical ear. He thought all the operas and concerts of the city could not please him more. No better art than the musical to soften and civilize children in our schools; they could hardly speak an angry word or cherish bitterness, when such harmony was in the air. He had been pleased too with their reading and declaiming; but wished there had been more reading, since good reading is so rare an accomplishment. The sight of the black-board warned him that arithmetic was soon to have its place in the exercises and he expected much from that. He closed by expressing his hope that this would become a yearly festival for the town.

Miss Lee next marshalled her school and took her place with them on the platform. Singing has not been so common in her school as in some others, but her boys declaimed boldly and their rapid and accurate recitations in arithmetic won great praise.

Miss Tincker pleased the audience by the novel geographical chant, peculiar to her school, and by their general excellence in singing shown by her pupils. One young lady in particular excited much applause by the richness and melody of her voice in the Marseille's Hymn and many expressed the hope that so fine a voice should be carefully cultivated, as has been done this winter by the teacher.

Miss Prescott gave still a new variety to the performances by a spirited dialogue and some exercises in postures. Her school appeared finely; so many fresh, hearty boys, and bright girls, whose singing was tender and pleasing.

Miss Bean and Miss Barrett exhibited their schools together; neither of them being very large. The reading of Miss Bean's scholars, though not quite loud enough, was better than any before, and showed much care in training the voice to follow the meaning of the passage read. This too is a school to delight the eye; so much intelligence and grace in the self-possessed young people of both sexes.

Miss Barrett's pupils recited in Geography with accuracy, but not so as to be very distinctly heard, as indeed in so large a room could hardly be expected.

Mr. Allen's young ladies sung several pieces with great applause, to the music of the piano, skillfully played by Miss Ellen F. Wilson, who, with her usual kindness, consented to take this upon herself. The young men amused us with some genuine acting, and called forth shouts of laughter. At the close of their exercises the school presented Mr. Allen with a set of Mr. Emerson's Works, in testimony of their appreciation of his devoted labors, and the audience joined in hearty cheers for him, proposed by one of his sprightliest pupils.

Rev. Mr. Reynolds then spoke, expressing his satisfaction with the exhibition and hoping that it might become an annual institution; in which the audience seemed to concur.

Mr. Alcott then dismissed the elder people with a few remarks, and invited the children to remain for the collation. This we believe was to the minds of all who shared in it, and the day closed with a general expression of delight at the successful festival.

REPORTS

OF THE

SELECTMEN AND OTHER OFFICERS

OF THE

TOWN OF CONCORD,

FROM MARCH 5, 1860, TO MARCH 4, 1861.

INCLUDING

The Marriages, Births and Deaths in Town in 1860.

ALSO,

THE REPORT OF THE SCHOOL COMMITTEE

FOR THE YEAR ENDING APRIL 1, 1861.

CONCORD:

PRINTED BY BENJAMIN TOLMAN.

1861.

State of the Treasury.

RECEIPTS.

Balance in the Treasury, March 5, 1860,	$4908 21	
Commonwealth, Military Bounty 1859,	345 00	
" " " 1860,	267 00	
" School Fund, 1860,	89 59	
Cumming and Beaton Fund,	94 00	
Selectmen, rent of Town Hall,	261 50	
Town Clerk, license on dogs,	26 10	
License of Menagerie,	10 00	
Town, County and State tax and overlay,	10,962 00	
	——— $16,963 40	

PAYMENTS.

Sundry orders on Treasury paid,	$13,073 31	
County Tax, 1859,	1475 97	
" " 1860, in part,	566 33	
State Tax, 1860,	535 00	
	——— $15,650 61	
Balance,	$1312 79	

JULIUS M. SMITH, Treasurer.

March 4th, 1861.

Selectmen's Report.

The Selectmen of the Town of Concord submit herewith their annual report of the receipts and expenditures of the town for the year ending March 4, 1861.

The town has been put to unusual expense this year for the repairs of its roads and bridges.

The new road to Bedford sunk in some places to the depth of twelve feet, and it cost nearly one thousand dollars to fill up and grade it so as to make it safe for travel. It is believed to be secure now against further sinking.

Two of the bridges — at Damon's factory and the powder mill — were found to be very much decayed, and have been very nearly re-built. The best of lumber has been used in the repairs, and the bridges are all in good order, and it is not probable that any appropriation beyond the usual one for ordinary repairs will be necessary for some years to come. The expense has exceeded the appropriation about two hundred dollars.

Engine No. 1 has also received a thorough repair, in accordance with the vote of the town, at an expense of two hundred dollars.

The Chief Engineer of the Fire Department reports the hose of Engine No. 2 as being in very bad condition, and recommends the purchase of new hose, at a cost of not more than two hundred dollars. We accordingly recommend an appropriation of that sum for that purpose.

The following sums are recommended to be raised by the town for the ensuing year:

Support of Schools,	$3,300 00
Payment of Town House debt and interest,	1,720 00
Repairs of Highways,	1,000 00
Support of Poor,	1,000 00
Fire Department,	400 00
Repairs of Bridges,	300 00
Town Library,	280 00
Improvement of Public Grounds,	100 00
General Expenses,	1,500 00

The following statement of receipts and expenditures of the town for the year ending March 4, 1861, is herewith submitted.

EPHRAIM W. BULL, ⎫ Selectmen
BARZILLAI N. HUDSON, ⎬ of
JULIUS M. SMITH, ⎭ Concord.

CONCORD, March 4, 1861.

Appropriations and Receipts.

APPROPRIATIONS.

For Support of Schools,	$3300	00
Payment of Town House debt and interest,	1780	00
Support of Poor,	1000	00
Repairs of Highways,	1000	00
Repairs of Bridges,	700	00
Fire Department,	350	00
Town Library,	287	00
Improvement of Public Grounds,	50	00
County Tax,	1566	33
State Stax,	535	00
	$10,568	33

RECEIPTS FROM OTHER SOURCES.

Overlay on taxes,	$393	67
Rent of Town Hall,	261	50
Commonwealth, School Fund,	89	59
" Military Bounty,	267	00
Income Cuming and Beaton Funds,	94	00
" Silent Poor Donations,	253	83
Town Clerk, license of dogs,	26	10
" " " menagerie,	10	00
	$1395	69

Expenditures.

Support of Schools,	$3300 00	
Income Cumming and Beaton Fund,	94 00	
" State School Fund,	89 59	
		$3,483 59
Paid orders of School Committee,	3317 89	
John Garrison, care of School rooms,	77 00	
Proportion of fuel charged to District,	88 70	
		$3483 59

PAYMENT OF TOWN HOUSE DEBT AND INTEREST.

Appropriation,		$1780 00
Paid Middlesex Institution for Savings,		$1780 00

SUPPORT OF POOR.

Appropriation,		$1000 00
Paid Jabez Raynolds, Chairman Overseers of Poor,		1000 00

REPAIRS OF HIGHWAYS.

Appropriation,			$1000 00
Paid N. B. Stow, District No. 1,		$289 06	
J. B. Moore, " No. 2,		100 00	
Gardner Wheeler, " No. 3,		136 43	
Cyrus Hosmer, " No. 4,		91 75	
E. Wood, Jr., " No. 5,		99 75	
J. D. Brown, " No. 6,		107 11	
Silas Conant, " No. 7,		125 10	
Thos. M. Balcom, " No. 8,		65 78	
			$1014 98
Deficiency,			$14 98

FIRE DEPARTMENT.

Appropriation,	$350 00
Paid Geo. L. Prescott, Chief Engineer,	$400 62
Deficiency,	$50 62
Repair of Engine No. 1, under direction of Committee appointed for that purpose,	$200 00

REPAIRS OF BRIDGES.

Appropriation,		$700 00
Paid Geo. L. Prescott, lumber,	$692 80	
Jos. P. George, labor, stone and iron work,	189 28	
J. M. Smith, painting and sanding,	22 43	
		$904 51
Deficiency,		204 51

BEDFORD ROAD.

Unexpended balance last year,		$29 24
Paid T. M. Balcom, for filling up and grading said road,	953 79	
Geo. L. Prescott, lumber,	18 02	
		$971 81
Deficiency,		$942 57

TOWN LIBRARY.

Appropriation,	$287 00
Paid E. R. Hoar, Chairman of Library Committee,	287 00

IMPROVEMENT OF PUBLIC GROUNDS.

Appropriation,	$50 00	
Unexpended balance last year,	9 43	
		$59 43
Paid Samuel Staples, Superintendent,	$51 16	
Unexpended balance,	8 27	
		$59 43

SILENT POOR.

Unexpended balance,	$32 15	
Income from Donations,	253 83	
" " fines under the statute prohibiting cattle from feeding in highway,	10 00	
		$295 98
Paid sundry persons as appears by Selectmen's book,	$262 00	
Unexpended balance,	33 98	
		$295 98

State Tax,	$535 00
County Tax,	$1566 33

GENERAL EXPENSES.

Overlay on Taxes,	$393 67	
Commonwealth, Military Bounty,	345 00	
Rent of Town Hall,	261 50	
License of Menagerie,	10 00	
		$1010 17

EXPENSES OF TOWN HOUSE.

Paid G. L. Prescott, for coal,	$119 54	
John Garrison, for care of school rooms,	77 00	
" " " hall and moving seats,	89 50	
" " " library rooms,	10 00	
E. Stowell & Co.'s bills,	10 78	
G. Chilson, for furnace grate,	5 69	
Walcott & Holden's bill for oil, &c.,	136 29	
Repairs and painting,	22 31	
Wood and charcoal,	9 00	
J. Adams' bill,	1 25	
		$481 36
Deduct amount charged Dist. No. 1, for fuel and care,		165 70
Leaves expense of Hall and rooms,		$315 66

REPAIRS ON SCHOOL HOUSES.

Paid Edwin Wheeler, repairs on Dist. No. 3,			$3 75
Francis A. Wheeler, "	" No. 3,		31 80
Wm. D Brown, "	" No. 4,		6 27
E. W. Bull, "	" No. 2,		16 79
J. B. Farmer, "	" No. 5,		12 42
E. Stowell & Co., "	" No. 1,		8 03
" "	" No. 2,		24 27

Paid J. M. Smith, painting　Dist.　No. 5,　　75 16
"　　　"　　　"　　　　"　　No. 2,　　46 36
　　　　　　　　　　　　　　　　　　　　　　　———　$222 85

MISCELLANEOUS.

Paid Alvan Pratt, keeping weights and measures, $10 00
　Wm. D. Brown, services on School Com-
　　mittee, 1860,　　　　　　　　　　　　17 75
　Concord Artillery, bounty,　　　　　　267 00
　H. Newton, entertainment of town officers　66 75
　Eben Wild, salary as Librarian,　　　　50 00
　"　　" moving books to new part,　　10 00
　Richard Barrett, services as Assessor,　125 00
　Geo. Heywood,　　"　　　"　　　　75 00
　J. B. Moore,　　　"　　　"　　　　85 00
　"　　" collecting tax, 1859,　　　133 56
　"　　" posting warrants,　　　　　4 00
　F. Stowell, repairing clocks, and care of
　　town clock, &c.,　　　　　　　　　26 05
　Geo. Heywood, services as clerk,　　　25 00
　"　　" recording and returning
　　　　　　marriages, births and
　　　　　　deaths,　　　　　　　　　18 50
　"　　" express and postage,　　　2 35
　"　　" counting the vote at Lincoln,　2 00
　Moses Hobson, work on alteration of High
　　School,　　　　　　　　　　　　51 44
　Moses Hobson, alteration of Library,　　56 91
　H. H. Buttrick's bill alteration High School,　21 43
　"　　　"　　" on Library,　　　10 25
　E. Stowell & Co., on Library and School,　23 31
　J. M. Smith, on Library, $13 20 ; part
　　High School, $5 12,　　　　　　　18 32
　Policemen at Cattle Show,　　　　　　4 00
　J. Brown, Jr., flannel for cartridges,　　1 75
　F. E. Bigelow, iron work for sidewalks, &c.,　2 73
　S. G. Simpkins & Co., books for Assessors,　7 00
　R. Warner, use of room for the police at
　　State encampment,　　　　　　　12 00
　H. C. Watts, work on armory and firing
　　salutes,　　　　　　　　　　　　9 76
　Geo. Hosmer, flannel for cartridges in 1859,　5 26
　C. B. Davis,　　　"　　"　　"　　2 36
　Richard Barrett, powder, &c.,　　　　18 20
　Derby Bros., powder for salutes,　　　28 00
　B. Tolman, printing town reports, warrants,
　　&c.,　　　　　　　　　　　　　95 79
　Jonas Melvin, returning 30 deaths, 1860,　3 00
　2

E. Stowell & Co., stove, work in library
    committee room,   12 53
Wm. D. Brown, wood furnished at encamp-
    ment,   1 42
G. E. Bigelow, damage to chaise from de-
    fect in the highway,   3 38
Horton, Hall & Co., door springs,   92
H. A. Davis, State sealer weights and mea-
    sures, for sealing same,   6 50
Wm. D. Brown, laying up wall in District
    No. 2,   1 00
Edwin Wheeler, services on School Com-
    mittee, 1859,   9 00
E. W. Bull, services on School Com., 1859, 12 00
    "   "   "   1860, 9 00
    "   expense to Roxbury in the
        matter of engine No. 1,   2 00
    "   cash paid Hunneman for exam-
        ination of do.,   4 00
Dr. J. Reynolds, services on School Com-
    mittee, 1859,   15 75
L. W. Bean, services on School Committee,
    1859,   8 25
J. B. Farmer, services on School Commit-
    tee, 1859,   10 50
J. B. Farmer, services on School Commit-
    tee, 1860,   13 50
Geo. L. Prescott, lumber for Armory,   1 63
    "   "   "   turnpike,   7 49
E. Stowell & Co., on library room,   4 50
H. D. Thoreau, surveying on turnpike,   1 00
Jesse C. Richardson, stone work and filling
    up road near his house,   13 00
J. M. Smith, glazing at Armory,   2 36
    "   "   repairs on hearse and painting
    sign boards,   8 25

                  $1,439 13
    Deficiency, $969 47

Tabular Statement of Receipts and Expenditures

FROM MARCH 5TH, 1860, TO MARCH 4TH, 1861.

RECEIPTS.

Unexpended balance as per Treasurer's Report March 5th, 1860,	$4908	21
Appropriations for various objects,	10,962	00
Receipts from other sources,	1093	19
	$16,963	**40**

EXPENDITURES.

Support of Schools,	$3483	59
Town House Debt and Interest,	1780	00
" " " " for 1859,	1000	00
Repairs of Highways,	1014	98
Support of Poor,	1000	00
Fire Department,	400	62
" " for Repairs on Engine No. 1,	200	00
Repairs Bedford Road,	971	81
Town Library,	287	00
Improvement of Public Grounds,	51	16
General Expenses,	1979	64
County Tax, 1859,	1475	97
" " 1860, in part,	566	33
State Tax, 1860,	535	00
Repairs of Bridges,	904	51
	$15,650	**61**

Unexpended balance,	**$1312**	**79**

Ninth Annual Report of the Town Library Committee.

The Library Committee present their report for the year ending on the first Monday in March, 1861.

The amount of money received by them is as follows:

The balance of last year's account,	$113 91	
The town's appropriation for 1860,	287 00	
Fines collected by the Librarian in 1860,	5 23	
		$406 14

The amount expended has been:		
For 331 volumes purchased,	$348 27	
For binding and covering books, and stationery,	6 95	
Leaving a balance unexpended, of	50 92	
		$406 14

The whole number of books now belonging to the Library is 3,105. The number added during the past year has been, by purchase, 331; by donation, 12. No book has been lost during the year, and all but six volumes were in the Library room at the time of the annual examination.

The number of ratable polls in Concord in the year 1860 was 560; and the appropriation for the maintenance and increase of the Library which the town is allowed by law, and required by contract to make this year, is $280.

More books have been added to the Library during this year than in any previous year; and on an average they have been books of greater value, and better bound. The use made of the Library by the people of the town has also increased from last year.

The alteration in the Library, by extending the room so as to include within it a part of what had been the schoolroom of the Intermediate school, which was suggested in our last report, and authorized by the vote of the town, has been accomplished during the winter; and the town has now a convenient and handsome room, capable of containing eight or ten thousand volumes, and sufficient for the probable increase of the Library for the next fifteen or twenty years.

E. R. HOAR,
SIMON BROWN,
R. WALDO EMERSON,   Library
GEO. HEYWOOD,   Committee.
GRINDALL REYNOLDS,

CONCORD, March 4, 1861.

REPORT OF THE

Superintendent of Public Grounds.

The appropriation for the last year not being as large as usual, no new improvements of any moment have been made upon the Public Grounds, and little else has been done than to re-set trees in place of those that have died or been destroyed, and to keep the grounds in good condition. A row of trees however was set in front of the house of Cyrus Stow, and the Superintendent regrets to state, that through a spirit of vandalism which would better become savages than any residents of Concord, most of these trees were broken down and destroyed (as is believed,) by some rowdy good-for-nothing youths who seem to take delight in such acts of wanton malice, and who, if a speedy change is not made in their conduct of life, will soon come under the more immediate supervision of the subscriber, and have their abode in a place that will insure the safety of trees, gates, signs, &c., from their raids, and be an example to all youths who take pleasure in such senseless pastime.

The Superintendent recommends that the sum of seventy-five dollars be appropriated for the Public Grounds for the ensuing year.

The following has been expended during the last year, to wit : —

Paid Anthony Wright, labor,	$19	69
J. Craig and Patrick McManus,	5	12
For trees,	21	00
" 36 posts, boards and nails,	4	05
" expense of journey to Newton, &c.,		
for trees,	4	50
	$54	36

Respectfully submitted.

SAMUEL STAPLES, Superintendent.

Concord, March 4, 1861.

Report of the Cemetery Committee.

The Cemetery Committee report that during the past season they have employed the Superintendent principally in the general care of the grounds, without undertaking any particular new work. The reason of this was the want of any appropriation from the town to authorize the expenditure necessary, and the need of employing the Superintendent in improving the lots of those who desired this done. The result has been to leave quite a balance on hand for the coming season's work, and there are several things much wanted that can be accomplished with this amount. The making a new avenue, and thus laying out more lots for which there is quite a demand, will be the first of these, and a well of good water, and a thorough coating of the walks and roads with gravel will follow soon.

The Committee renew their recommendation to the ladies of the town to get up in some way a donation to the improvement of the ground; and to the citizens generally, who have not already done so, to each plant a tree therein, on the nineteenth of April, the town's anniversary.

The number of lots sold the past year is ten, for the sum of $137,00, the whole number since the laying out of the Cemetery, one hundred and six, for the sum of $2002,00. The number of interments the past year has been sixteen; previously one hundred and ten.

The receipts and expenses have been as follows:

Balance unexpended last year,	$19 79	
For deeds of lots sold,	159 00	
For labor of Superintendent on lots, &c.,	174 67	
		$353 46
Paid J. Wood, Supt., for 8 months labor,	$220 50	
For day's work in the winter,	38 62	
For rent of tenement 9 months,	30 00	
Jonas Melvin's bill for team, &c.,	18 00	
Printing, scythe, express, pickets, &c.,	6 75	
		$313 87
Unexpended balance,		$39 59

This, with the amount still due for lots and work on them, will more than pay all outstanding bills.

For the Committee.

J. S. KEYES, Chairman.

Concord, March 4, 1861.

Eleventh Annual Report of the Fire Department.

Herewith is submitted to the town a list of the officers of the Fire Department for the year 1860–61, together with a statement of the condition of the property belonging to the town. There have been eight alarms since the last report, three of which have been from fires in the woods, and one from a fire in Wayland. The services of the engines have been required but four times, viz. : at the burning of a barn belonging to Ebenezer Conant ; at the burning of C. B. Davis' barn ; at the burning of John Emerson's house ; and at the slight burning of Mrs. Hoar's house.

The Department is organized as follows :

G. L. PRESCOTT, Chief Engineer ;

SAMUEL LEES,   ⎫ Assistant
J. W. WALCOTT,   ⎬ Engineers.
RICHARD BARRETT, ⎭

Fountain,
No. 1.
  ⎧ FRANCIS STOWELL, Foreman ;
  ⎨ J. G. DEAN, Assistant Foreman ;
  ⎩ C. BOWERS, Clerk.
      Thirty members.

Factory Boy,
No. 2.
  ⎧ SAMUEL LEES, Foreman ;
  ⎨ W. D. BROWN, Assistant Foreman and Clerk ;
  ⎩ Twenty-five men.

Independence,
No. 3.
  ⎧ JONAS MELVIN, Foreman ;
  ⎨ CHAS. E. SNELL, Assistant Foreman ;
  ⎨ J. F. WINCH, Clerk.
  ⎩ Forty-five members.

Engine Company No. 1 is in good order ; has 300 feet leading hose and 32 feet suction. It has been thoroughly repaired and painted the past year, at an expense to the town of $211 47, to pay which there was an appropriation of $200 00, leaving a deficiency of $11 47.

No. 2 is in good order ; has 24 feet suction hose ; but the leading hose is very poor, and an appropriation of two hundred dollars is recommended to purchase new hose for this engine.

No. 3 is in good order ; has 825 feet leading hose, and 34 feet suction hose. The expenses for the past year have been as follows :

No. 1—Repairing engine, $164 50
     J. M. Smith, painting,   45 00

No. 1—Freight to Boston and back,	1 97	
Paid H. C. Watts,	3 13	
One-half cord wood,	1 63	
Fluid, &c.,	3 85	
Sawing wood and piling,	50	
Shoveling snow, &c.,	38	
Fluid and can,	39	
Match safe, &c.,	32	
C. S. Adkins, care of engine,	6 50	
Sponge and towel,	35	
Oil,	1 60	
Repairing pump,	1 50	
E. Hall's bill,	50	
		$232 12
No. 2—Paid T. Skinner,	$2 50	
E. Hosmer for oil,	3 25	
Alcohol,	1 60	
		$7 35
No. 3—Paid T. Skinner's bill,	$12 00	
Tank for washing hose,	10 63	
Paid F. Buttrick and express, sash, &c.,	2 75	
" C. E. Snell's bill,	17 25	
" L. Fay, pump and setting,	5 00	
Pick for engine,	1 00	
Setting glass, sweet oil, &c.,	2 28	
E. Stowell & Co.'s bill,	8 53	
G. W. Todd, horses,	21 00	
Oiling harness,	3 00	
E. Hosmer, for oil,	2 12	
E. Hall's bill,	3 88	
Alcohol,	1 17	
7 1-2 feet pine wood,	3 05	
		$93 66
Summary, General Expenses,	$3 75	
Expense of No. 1, including repairs,	232 12	
" " 2,	7 35	
" " 3,	93 66	
Pay of Engine Company No. 1,	96 50	
" " " " 3,	137 25	
Chief Engineer's salary,	30 00	
		$600 63
Special appropriation for repairs on No. 1,		200 00
Leaving the balance for general expenses of Fire Department,		$400 63

GEORGE L. PRESCOTT, Chief Engineer.

CONCORD, March 26, 1861.

Report of the Overseers of the Poor.

RECEIPTS.

Received of Town Treasurer, $1000 00

EXPENDITURES AWAY FROM FARM.

Paid G. H. Gilson, support of Mrs. Bailey,	$25	00
Mrs. Heywood, support of three children,	96	00
City of Lowell, " " Mrs. How and three children,	66	00
Walcott & Holden, groceries for J. Goodwin,	2	66
" " " " Mrs. Gorman,	1	64
B. Hastings, " " J. Goodwin,	1	58
Dr. Bartlett, professional services,	10	00
Dr. Reynolds, " "	7	50
J. Melvin, burial of J. Hutchinson's daughter,	3	75
J. Adams, coffin for " "	4	50
J. P. Brown, journey and expenses to Lynn,	3	50
" " " " " Cambridge,	3	00
" " " " " Boston,	3	45
" " " " " Tewksbury,	3	50
J. Reynolds, " " " Groton,	3	50
" " " " Lowell and Lawrence,	4	54
Derby Brothers, groceries for Mrs. Gorman,	15	39
" " " " Wm. Haynes,	2	00
J. Heywood, support of Haynes boy,	8	00
Abel Farrar, boarding N. Hosmer,	1	50
A. Tuttle, boarding and nursing B. Welch,	10	00
Reynolds & Derby, meat for Mrs. Gorman,	4	12
City of Cambridge, support Mrs. Batchelder,	31	11
Postage, stationery, &c.,	1	37
Aid rendered sundry persons,	22	15

         $335 76

EXPENSES AT THE FARM.

Paid J. Dakin, balance due as per agreement,	$82	83
" for bed pan,	1	50

3

Paid Walcott & Holden, furniture and crockery,   6 92
    J. Brown, Jr., cotton cloth,   6 91
    E. Stowell & Co., stoves, funnel, &c.,   24 73
    C. Benjamin, for work as per bill,   12 00
    H. Buttrick,   "   "   "   3 62
    C. E. Snell,   "   "   "   14 00
    M. Hobson, for work, lumber, &c.,   41 75
    Derby Brothers, paper, nails, &c.,   3 23
    B. F. Nealy, repairing wagon,   1 75
    W. Fay, salary in part,   465 00
                                          ——— $664 24

                                          $1000 00

There will be due W. Fay, April 1st.,   185 00
Also, J. Reynolds, services,   10 00
                                        $1195 00

From which deduct balance paid J. Dakin,   82 83

We have cost of supporting poor, $1112 17

The expenses away from the farm, together with repairs on the house, having considerably exceeded the appropriation, it will therefore be necessary to raise money enough to pay the deficiency, over and above the ordinary expense, which we think will not be less than last year, as some part of the buildings will need shingling ; we would therefore recommend to raise twelve hundred dollars for deficiency and ordinary expenses.

Amount of personal property as estimated by the Overseers of Poor Farm at present time, including stock, hay, grain, and all eatables, is
                                       $514 35
Farming implements, tools, &c ,   75 00
                                      ——— $589 35

      Respectfully submitted.

               J. REYNOLDS,   } Overseers
               MOSES HOBSON,   }   of
               JAMES P. BROWN, } the Poor.
CONCORD, March 4, 1861.

Marriages, Births and Deaths in Concord, in 1860.

The following statement exhibits every material fact in regard to the Marriages, Births and Deaths which have occurred in the town, and have been registered during the year 1860.

MARRIAGES.—Whole number, 16. Of the parties, 22 were inhabitants of Concord, and 10 of other places ; 10 were born in Concord, 12 in other towns in Massachusetts, and 10 in other places. Of the males, 14 were first marriages, 1 a second and 1 a third marriage. Of the females, all were first marriages. As compared with the marriages in 1859, there were 3 less.

BIRTHS.—Whole number, 43, being 5 less than in 1859. Males, 28 ; females, 15. Of these only 14 were born of Irish parents, being less than one-third of the whole. Last year one-half were of Irish parents, so that America will have cause to be hopeful.

DEATHS.—Whole number, 38. Males, 18 ; females, 20. Of the males, 6 were married, 10 unmarried, and 2 were widowed. Of the females, 8 were married, 10 unmarried, and 2 were widows.

Of these persons, 23 were born in Concord, 7 in other towns in the State, and 8 in other places.

Of the males over 15 years of age, 4 were farmers, 3 laborers, 1 carpenter, and 1 gentleman.

Deaths between								males,		females,
Deaths between	90	and	100	years of age—males,				1—females,		0
"	"	80	"	90	"	"	"	1	"	2
"	"	70	"	80	"	"	"	2	"	1
"	"	60	"	70	"	"	"	3	"	1
"	"	50	"	60	"	"	"	2	"	2
"	"	40	"	50	"	"	"	1	"	0
"	"	30	"	40	"	"	"	0	"	3
"	"	20	"	30	"	"	"	0	"	1
"	"	10	"	20	"	"	"	0	"	1
"	"	5	"	10	"	"	"	0	"	1
"	"	1	"	5	"	"	"	1	"	3
"	under	1	year		"	"	"	8	"	4

Average length of life, 33 3-4 years.

Deaths by	Cholera Infantum,	7	Deaths by	Dropsy,		2
"	" Apoplexy,	8	"	" Lung Fever,		1
"	" Consumption,	4	"	" Scarlet Fever,		1
"	" Cancer,	2	"	" Measels,		1
"	" Infantile,	4	"	" Whooping Cough,		1
"	" Diarrhea,	2	"	" Typhoid Fever,		1
"	" Dysentery,	1	"	" Old Age,		1
"	" Softening of Brain,	1	"	" Suicide,		1

The names and ages of the persons who died in 1860, are as follows, viz. : —

George Atcheson, 1 y. 1 m. 8 d.
Nehemiah Ball, 69 y. 2 m. 11 d.
Martha Tilden Bartlett, 61 y.
Ruth J. Clark, 75 y.
Julia Collins, 1 y. 9 m. 16 d.
Mary Collins, 8 m. 16 d.
Ephraim Dakin, 86 y. 1 m. 24 d.
Mary B. Dakin, 55 y.
James W. Dean, 2 m. 6 d.
Margaret Fahan, 32 y.
Roxanna Flint, 55 y.
John Garrison, 91 y.
Mary Gleason, 9 m. 6 d.
Annie W. Goodnow, 4 y.
John M. Goodwin, 58 y.
Charles Gordon, 76 y. 9 m.
Milly Holden, 86 y.
Tilly Holden, 76 y.
Rufus Hosmer, 51 y.
Sarah L. Hutchinson, 18 y.

Edward Lamson Kent, 3 m.
David Murphy, 3 m. 8 d.
Catherine Murray, 2 y. 3 m.
Mary Newcomb, 81 y. 2 m.
Thomas Nolan, 1 d.
Theodore Parker Pratt, died in 1859, 16 y. 8 m. 18 d.
Jane T. Prichard, 69 y. 8 m. 27 d.
Lucia Simmons, 5 y. 5 m. 24 d.
Edward Hurd Skinner, 10 m. 2 d.
Martha W. Smith, 32 y.
Elizabeth A. Starkey, 35 y. 2 m.1d
(not named,) Starkey, 1 d.
Evangeline Surette, 3 m. 13 d.
(not named,) Waldron, 4 d.
Isaac Watts, 61 y.
Susan P. Weston, 27 y. 7 m.
Frank Wetherbee, 2 m.
Charles Wheeler, 49 y. 4 m. 15 d.

The deaths in 1860, were, according to the United States census for that year, as 1 to every 59 1-5.

GEO. HEYWOOD, Town Clerk.

Concord, Jan. 1, 1861.

OF THE

SCHOOL COMMITTEE,

AND

SUPERINTENDENT OF THE SCHOOLS,

OF THE

TOWN OF CONCORD, MASS.,

WITH

A NOTICE OF AN EXHIBITION OF THE SCHOOLS,

IN THE

TOWN HALL,

ON SATURDAY, MARCH 16, 1861.

CONCORD:

PRINTED BY BENJAMIN TOLMAN.

1861.

REPORT.

The School Committee for the current year, organized on Monday, April 2nd, by choosing the former Chairman and Secretary, and soon after elected the former Superintendent. They have proceeded to carry out the plans of last year, and take pleasure in reporting the condition of the schools, as, on the whole, better than at their last report, and such as to reflect great credit on the town. Some changes have occurred in the list of teachers, yet six out of the eleven are the same as last year. By a vote of the town the High School room has been divided, and is now used both by the High and Intermediate schools, — a change which has removed some, but not all of their inconveniences. A portion of the old Intermediate room not used for the library extension, has been devoted to the use of the High School for a recitation and apparatus room. As yet, however, there is but little apparatus, and the Committee desire to recommend the appropriation of not less than two hundred dollars for the purchase of suitable apparatus for the High School. In a few years we hope to obtain a permanent and useful collection.

During the year the Committee extended an invitation to the Massachusetts Teachers' Association, to hold their annual meeting here, which they did on the 26th and 27th of November. Our citizens freely opened their houses to our visitors, of whom some two hundred and fifty were thus entertained. The days spent here were mutually agreeable and profitable, and this convention has been one of the marked features of our school year.

It has been thought best to enlarge our annual report, and to include a list of all the pupils in the several schools, and an account of

143

the exhibition. This promises to become one of the pleasantest parts of our school system, and has so much to recommend it, that we are confident our successors will continue it. The Superintendent, in his detailed report, has touched upon this and nearly all the other points which we would present to the town. On some topics, however, we may enlarge.

I. THE HIGH SCHOOL. This school has changed its teacher during the year, and has also changed in other respects. Its numbers have increased, while its room has been diminished in size; yet the new accommodations have proved ample for the comfort of the pupils. The plan of teaching has been slightly modified, and there is a new interest in the studies taught. A greater proportion of the pupils are studying the languages and higher branches, and much progress has been made in elocution under the competent instruction of Mr. Shepard. The introduction of weekly lectures and conversations by the Superintendent and others, is a new feature which promises well, and is one of the many excellent innovations of Mr. Alcott. We see no reason why the men of learning and experience who adorn the town should not thus contribute regularly towards the better education of the children. Gymnastics, (by the system of Dr. Lewis,) have also been introduced by Mr. Shepard, and found of service, though not constantly practised. Perhaps few of the boys need them for the exercise, though many of the girls do ; but it helps both by the agility, precision and grace of movement which it gives, and its healthy stimulus.

II. EXAMINATIONS. The proper mode of examining schools has been much considered by the Committee, and the general opinion has been that stricter and more private examinations ought to take the place of the exhibition now given twice a year in each school. But so important is it to bring together the parents and friends of the pupils, which is done on these occasions, that we have not ventured to recommend giving them up. Still it should be remembered, that they are not *examinations,* strictly speaking, though of much value to the schools.

III. A WINTER SCHOOL. In our last report we hinted at the necessity of a separate school for a few troublesome boys who now do little but weary and annoy their teachers, and disturb the other pupils of the schools where they are. It has been suggested that these, to the number of a dozen or twenty, should be placed by themselves during the winter months, under a competent teacher ; and we offer this suggestion for the consideration of the town, well aware of the arguments against it, as well as in its favor.

It will be seen that the object of the Committee and the Superintendent for the last two years has been to modify and extend the school system of the State into one suited to the character of the town, and far more general and liberal than prevails commonly. Much has been done, but much still remains to do. We see no reason why the Concord schools should not be made to cover all and more than all that is done in the graded schools and colleges of the State. There is much illusion about our high schools and so called universities. The sciences and the arts taught there can usually be better learned elsewhere by the earnest student. They give golden opportunities, but throw a thousand obstacles in the way of using them. Worst of all, they seem to stifle that enthusiasm for learning and virtue, without which the highest culture is impossible. A Massachusetts township, with its central village, lying in partial seclusion, yet partly connected with the great world, is one of the best universities, or may be made so. In it, by a careful and well pursued method, we may train our children and youth to far better purpose than most colleges or cities can do. Nor let it be supposed that such a plan would require great expense, or a condition of things very different from the present. A permanent school committee representing all interests and all sections of the town, — permanent teachers who could see the fruit of their labors year after year,—a cordial interest of all the citizens in the liberal culture of the children, with a little change of method and a little lengthening of the time for which children shall be kept at school,—would gradually give us advantages greater than any public or private course of instruction in the State now offers. There is no lack of sound practical knowledge, nor of profound and elegant learning in the town ; we are free from the hurtful extremes of wealth and poverty, and enjoy a simple, democratic style of society ; there is great tolerance of diverse opinions, and an unusual degree of town pride and public spirit. What prevents us then from carrying out these plans, which to many may seem visionary ? We are convinced it lies within the power of the people of Concord to realize in a finer way the noble dream of Milton, in his Tractate on Education, — " that voluntary idea which hath long in silence presented itself to me, of a better education, in extent and comprehension far more large, and yet of time far shorter and of attainment far more certain, than hath yet been in practice, * * a complete and generous education which fits a man to perform justly, skilfully and magnanimously all the offices, both private and public, of peace and war."

We will not now offer the details of such a plan, farther than they are to be found in the report of the Superintendent, who has performed with extraordinary ability, enthusiasm and diligence the labors imposed by his office.

The usual tables will be found annexed to our report.

JOHN S. KEYES, Chairman, ⎫
F. B. SANBORN, Secretary, ⎬ District No. 1.
GRINDALL REYNOLDS, ⎭
EPHRAIM W. BULL,   No. 2.
FRANCIS A. WHEELER,   No. 3.
WILLIAM D. BROWN,   No. 4.
JACOB B. FARMER,   No. 5.
JOSEPH D. BROWN,   No. 6.
NATHAN BARRETT,   No. 7.

School Committee of Concord.

Concord, March 25th, 1861.

The Concord Districts are

No. 1, THE VILLAGE,

including the

NORTH PRIMARY SCHOOL,   EAST PRIMARY,

HIGH SCHOOL,

WEST PRIMARY,   INTERMEDIATE.

No. 2, - - -   THE EAST QUARTER.

No. 3, - - -   NINE ACRE CORNER.

No. 4, - - -   THE FACTORY VILLAGE.

No. 5, - - -   BARRETT'S MILL.

No. 6, - - -   BATEMAN'S POND.

No. 7, - - -   THE NORTH QUARTER.

SCHOOL REGULATIONS.

SECT. 1.—All the Schools in town shall commence at 9 o'clock, A. M., and 1 o'clock, P. M., and close at 12 M., and at 4. P. M., except the Centre Schools, which from April 1st to October 1st, shall commence in the afternoon at half-past 1, and close at half-past 4. The teachers are required to observe *punctually* the hours of closing as well as opening the schools, and to be present ten minutes before the opening of the school in the morning.

SECT. 2.—The government of the Schools is entrusted by law to the teachers, and they are expected to preserve strict order and discipline, and to pay constant attention to the language, the manners, and the conduct of the scholars in and about the schools.

SECT. 3.—The schools shall be opened in the morning by reading the Scriptures, and it is recommended that the Lord's Prayer, or a short written or extempore prayer, be offered.

SECT. 4.—No book shall be used in the schools without the sanction of the Committee.

SECT. 5.—If a scholar be absent from school, he or she shall bring a written excuse from the parent or guardian.

SECT. 6.—It shall be the duty of the teachers to see that no injury is done to the school houses or the premises belonging to them; and if there is, to give immediate notice to the Committee. Also, to see that their school rooms are properly swept, warmed and ventilated.

SECT. 7.—The schools shall keep five days in a week,—the High School giving Saturday for a holiday,—and the other schools adopting the same course or not, as the resident member of the Committee may decide. The following shall be holidays also: Fast and Thanksgiving, May Day, Fourth of July, Agricultural Fair, Christmas, New Years, and the 22d February.

SECT. 8.—Teachers will be allowed to visit each school in town once during the year, and for this purpose only, to devote one afternoon in a month, making in all cases the appointment therefor beforehand, and also will be allowed one afternoon in each month, if the Sub-committee do not object, for an excursion with the pupils, or a visit with them to other schools.

SECT. 9.—Candidates for the Intermediate School shall be able to read correctly in Hillard's Second Class Reader, and to spell and define common words. They shall pass a satisfactory examination in Colburn's Primary Arithmetic, in the four ground rules of Written Arithmetic, and in Cornell's Intermediate Geography as far as the 19th page ; and be able to point out and define the parts of speech and the marks of punctuation, and to write their names legibly.

SECT. 10.—Candidates for the High School shall be able to pass a satisfactory examination in Reading, Spelling, and Grammar, and be able to parse, analyse, and write correctly common sentences in prose. They must be familiar with the sounds of the letters, with accent and punctuation, and pass a good examination in Greenleaf's Common School Arithmetic as far as Proportion ; in Cornell's Geography and Maps, and in the History of the United States, and be able to write a fair hand.

SECT. 11.—Scholars may be admitted into these schools twice in the year, but in no case without the written permission of the Committee.

By order of the Committee.

F. B. SANBORN, Secretary.

June 4th, 1860.

SUPERINTENDENT'S REPORT

OF THE

CONCORD SCHOOLS

TO THE

SCHOOL COMMITTEE,

FOR THE YEAR 1860-61.

"Teachers shall exert their best endeavors to impress on the minds of children and youth committed to their care and instruction, the principles of piety, justice and a sacred regard to truth, love of their country, humanity and universal benevolence, sobriety, industry, frugality, chastity, moderation and temperance, and those other virtues which are the ornament of human society, and the basis upon which a republican constitution is founded. And to endeavor to lead their pupils as their ages and capacities will admit, into a clear understanding of the tendency of the above mentioned virtues, and, also, to point out to them the evil tendency of the opposite vices." —[*Law of the Commonwealth establishing Free Schools of Massachusetts.*]

FINANCIAL STATEMENT.

The amount placed at the disposal of the Committee by vote of town was —

Appropriation for Schools,	$3300 00	
Income of Cuming and Beaton Fund,	89 59	
Income of Massachusetts School Fund,	94 00	
Unexpended balance of last year,	72 15	
		$3555 74

Which has been expended as follows: —

Messrs. Allen and Shepard, teaching High School,	$647 60	
Proportion of fuel and care, charged by town,	99 42	
Books, chemicals and incidentals,	37 99	
Total cost of High School, 40 weeks,		$785 01
Miss Dillingham, teaching Intermediate School,	$246 00	
Proportion of fuel and care, charged by town,	66 28	
Books, chalk, brushes and incidentals,	24 41	
Total cost of Intermediate School, 41 weeks,		$336 69
Miss Hosmer, teaching North Primary School,	$60 00	
Miss Goodall, " " " "	133 50	
Fuel, care, books and incidentals,	44 30	
Total cost of North Primary School, 40 weeks,		$237 80
Miss Hosmer, teaching East Primary School,	$200 00	
Fuel, care, books and incidentals,	46 00	
Total cost of East Primary School, 40 weeks,		$246 00
Miss Richardson, teaching West Primary School,	$197 50	
Fuel, care, books and incidentals,	43 41	
Total cost of West Primary School, 40 weeks,		$240 91
Miss Hubbard, teaching East Quarter School,	$195 00	
Fuel, care, books and incidentals,	61 78	
Total cost of East Quarter School, 39 weeks,		$256 78
Miss Stearns, teaching Nine Acre Corner School,	$195 00	
Fuel, care, books and incidentals,	26 55	
Total cost of Nine Acre Corner School, 39 weeks,		$221 55
Miss Tinker and Miss Whitney, teaching Factory V. School,	$199 50	
Fuel, care, books and incidentals,	61 89	
Proportion paid Acton for scholars of this district,	35 86	
Total cost of Factory Village School, 38 weeks,		$297 25
Miss Prescott, teaching Barrett's Mill School,	$200 00	
Fuel, care, books and incidentals,	48 85	
Total cost of Barrett's Mill School, 40 weeks,		$248 85
Miss Bean, teaching Bateman's Pond School,	$200 00	
Fuel, care, books and incidentals,	40 96	
Total cost of Bateman's Pond School, 40 weeks,		$240 96
Miss Brown, teaching North Quarter School,	$185 25	
Fuel, care, books and incidentals,	36 86	
Total cost of North Quarter School, 40 weeks,		$222 11
Total cost of Schools, teaching,	$2659 35	
Fuel, care, books and incidentals,	674 56	
Total cost of Schools,	$3333 91	
Unexpended balance,	221 83	
	$3555 74	

SCHOOLS	TEACHERS	Whole No. Summer	Winter	Average Attend'ce Summer	Winter	No. over 15	No. under 5	Wages per month	Length in weeks	SUB-COMMITTEE
High School,	Charles A. Allen,	33	41	29 1-2	37	33	0	$800 pr.yr.	40	J. S. Keyes, G. Reynolds,
Intermediate,	Edw'd O. Shepard, Mary A. Dillingham,	51	60	36 11-125	50 8-75	10	0	$24	41	F. B. Sanborn. J. S. Keyes,
North Primary,	Susan Goodall,	54	43	41	33	0	0	20	40	Nathan Barrett. F. B. Sanborn,
East Primary,	Jane Hosmer,	78	59	54	52	0	0	20	40	E. W. Bull.
West Primary,	Sarah Richardson,	49	43	36	36	0	1	20	40	G. Reynolds, W. D. Brown.
East Quarter,	Abbie F. Hubbard,	27	30	22	23 47-74	3	0	20	39	E. W. Bull, G. Reynolds.
Nine Acre Corner,	Rachel M. Stearns, H. C. Tincker, C. F. Whitney,	19	21	15	17	0	0	20	39	F. A. Wheeler, W. D. Brown,
Factory Village,		41	42	31	33	1	0	22	38	W. D. Brown, F. A. Wheeler.
Barrett's Mill,	M. E. Prescott,	22	23	17 93-119	18 59-71	1	2	20	40	J. B. Farmer, J. D. Brown.
Bateman's Pond,	S. P. Bean,	18	23	15	18	4	0	20	40	J. D. Brown, J. B. Farmer,
North Quarter,	S. A. Brown,	13	12	9	9	2	0	20	40	Nathan Barrett, J. S. Keyes.

SUPERINTENDENT'S DUTIES.

I find my duties as Superintendent of the Schools defined as follows :

I. Visits.—The Superintendent shall make all the visits required by law, and such others as shall be necessary from time to time.

II. Reports.—He shall make a report to the committee at their regular monthly meetings of the condition and wants of the several schools, and shall attend said meetings for the purpose of affording the committee information ; and he shall also at the end of the school year make to them in writing a detailed report of the condition and operation of the several schools, with suggestions for their improvement.

III. Powers.—He shall have and exercise in concert with the sub-committee for each school all the powers and duties of the general committee over the admission, classification and discipline of the scholars in said schools.

IV. General Oversight.—The aim and object of the Superintendent shall be to elevate the standard of the schools, increase the average attendance and awaken the interest of the pupils, improve the methods of teaching, and promote a better understanding between the different teachers, and between the teachers and the parents of the pupils.

SUPERINTENDENT'S REPORT.

Gentlemen of the School Committee : —

It gives me pleasure to report our schools in good condition. The best of feeling exists in all of them between the teachers and pupils, and I believe between teachers and parents in the several districts. There have been few changes of teachers during the year ; with two or three exceptions the schools have been under the charge of one teacher, and the present teachers are disposed to continue them for the coming season. I know of nothing to prevent a still more successful year's prosperity.

SPIRIT AND METHODS. I have good encouragement also in finding the teachers devoted to their duties and successful. At my monthly visits I have sought to inspire them rather with confidence in their chosen ways than to interfere by counter suggestions of my own, be-lieving that here in this matter of teaching the following out each of her tendencies and views would best subserve the common interest. Teaching is a personal influence, for the most part, and operating as a spirit unsuspected at the moment. I have wished to divine the secret source of success attained by any, and do justice to this ; it seemed most becoming to regard any blemishes as of secondary ac-count in the light of the acknowledged deserts. We require of each what she has to give, no more ; not that this measure or method, this study or that, should be the one preferred by us. We watch results rather than processes.

Does the teacher awaken thought, strengthen the mind, kindle the affections, call the conscience, the common sense, into lively and con-trolling activity, so promoting the love of study, the practice of the

3

virtues ; habits that shall accompany the children outwards into life ? The memory is thus best cared for, the ends of study answered, the debt of teacher to parents, of parents to children, and so the State's bounty is best bestowed.

Nor shall we hold all amenable equally to the ideal standards. Let us judge each by her own, and hold her fast by its demands. Each is to be judged by temperament, training, opportunities, experiences ; the due allowance being made for all under the circumstances. The motive is the main-spring of the rest. A teacher entering her school for any reward other than the love of teaching, shall not claim the praises deservedly due to devotion and genius. Most of our teachers are young women, seeking, some of them perhaps with mixed motives, the earning of a livelihood, yet doing good individually as must every lover of children ; and sure of her recompense, since she who loves her work finds the best reward in the doing, and is thus twice paid. What comes from the heart finds the heart, and is approved by it for services readily rendered.

Teaching is an instinct of the heart ; and with young children particularly. It needs kindly sensibilities, simple feelings and sincere ; love abounding. Young women are better suited to the work, and more excellent than most men. This interest is essential in all, for admirable as one's qualities may be in other respects, and surpassing her gifts, the secret touch of sympathy is the sole spring of success. The heart is the leader and prompter. No amount of learning avails without it. The qualities of the dispositions blend with the truths to be inculcated, and become their conductors. A certain feminine essence mingles with the subtlest influences, and the most diffusive. Genius is of both sexes, and there is the genius of sentiment as of intellect, it has the best attributes of both—the tenderness and strength, tempered finely, and telling on the subject. So we see how swiftly and easily the vivacious teacher quickens the stupidest, and subdues the unruliest, by the pure power of her presence, the arts of her persuasiveness and command ; while yet another, more learned perhaps and accomplished according to the received judgments, shall painfully fail of getting the attentions, or winning the regards even of the best. Mind refuses to be driven by mechanism, it moves by magnetism. It hates routine, dislikes mere rote and repetition. Even the drill of lessons must have love and sense insinuated, to be relished by the child or long remembered.

The schools have been gainers largely in coming so generally under this music of persuasion, these kindly drawings of the heart. Any one loved by children and esteemed by parents is of necessity a good influence and the teacher we want. Speaking of the pleasures of study and of her school master, Lady Jane Grey says, charmingly : —

"Mr. Elmer teaches me so gently, so pleasantly; with such fair allurements to learning, that I think all the time nothing while I am with him," —

so absorbed is she in her subject, and all her sensibilities are so quickened by the magnetism of his touch. Now we may not be so fortunate as to put Elmer's, or genius like his, in our school-houses, yet we can have next best, namely : men or women there who love teaching and can instruct in the rudiments of good learning and the virtues. Moreover we can prove our regard for such by amply rewarding their services. If we would have good schools, we must pay the price for them ; nor can we overpay if we would.

Singing.   Singing is a favorite exercise in most of the schools, and practised daily.   Where the teacher does not lead, one or other of the scholars can.   There is a deficiency of suitable songs, adapted to the associations of American children.*   A book of school songs, set to music, the notes printed prettily a-top of the pages is wanted now. It should breathe the airs and poetry of New England life, and be set to the jubilant child-like heart.   Music is one of the magical arts, the oldest of any, the speech of heaven, and of memory ; a welcome influence, spiritualizing and refining the worst.   Pythagoras held : —

"That it contributed greatly to health, as well as to purifying the heart and the manners; and he called it a medicine, when he so used it, and a purification; and he conceived that each season had its particular melody. He placed in the middle a player on the lyre; and seated in a circle around him, were those who were able to sing. And when the person struck the lyre they sung certain peans, through which they were seen to be delighted, and to become elegant and orderly in consequence of the ecstacy; and he had melodies devised as remedies against the passions, as anger, despondency, complaint, inordinate desire; which afforded the greatest relief to those maladies. He likewise used dancing."

---

* Dr Mason's introduction of music into our schools from those of Pestalozzi abroad, has wrought out a good reform, and this has been done without detriment to study but a great gain,—to the heart a blessing so acceptable that scarce an objection or impediment has been interposed. Music and Arithmetic, the favorites now in the schools, are taught in the method of Pestalozzi, to whom modern education owes its chief improvements. Every teacher should make himself familiar with the principles and methods of that eminent school master and friend of mankind. His life and works are being published by President Barnard, of Wisconsin University, and Editor of the American Journal of Education.

A little gymnasticon, a system of gestures for the body, might be organized' skilfully, and become a part of the daily exercises in our schools. Graceful steps, pretty musical airs in accompaniment of songs, suiting the sentiment to the motions, the emotions, ideas of the child, would be conducive to health of body and mind alike. Any graceful drills are good at suitable intervals, as reliefs to studies—any steps and counter steps, with musical accompaniments which the genial teacher shall invent or adopt from others. Children have their favorites, and the games their seasons ; marble time, ball time, hoop time, skating time, &c. We shall adopt dancing presently as a natural training for the manners and morals of the young.

CONCORD SCHOOL STEP. Some thirty years since in our schools at Bristol and Cheshire, in Connecticut, we had something of the kind ; also at the " Salem street Infant School," and the " Temple School," in Boston. Among those practiced and a favorite with the children, was the " Hopity Skip," since called the " Concord School Step " by the children of our classic town. It has the merit of exceeding simplicity, as it can be extemporised at any pause of the school studies, and operates like a charm.

At a touch of the bell, a child rises and falls into the aisle ; the teacher beating time in measured strokes and bringing him round past his seat, the next child falling in and following round the circuit and so taking up the children one by one till the whole school is in motion on the floor ; weaving a sprightly musical trail of comely heads, flowing ringlets in serpentine figures or other caprices as the humor serves, through aisles and turns between ; feet a-step, blood a-brisk, faces a-glow ; the first up taking his seat first, the rest theirs successively one by one as they come round to their places, till all are down, all in place, and the studies proceed as before. It has the air and grace of a dancing march, and with the musical accompaniments becomes still more pleasing. This, with other pretty fancies, set a-foot by any lover of children, by the children themselves, would serve to exhilerate, give a zest to their studies, and relieve the tedium consequent on long confinement in doors.

At the risk of smuggling in the juvenile politics, I may allude to the patriotic style in which the boys played their *snow* game against secession South, dissolving that treason some weeks before the Illinois Splitter Elect set himself about removing the traitorous wedge from the cleft, to save the Union if he could for Young America. Perhaps Liberty cares as much for the boys and girls as for their seniors, and is proving their mettle meanwhile for the coming games.

RECITATIONS. I have witnessed a growing perception on the part of teachers and pupils of the true uses of books and of their place in the order of studies. The teachers have become interpreters in some sense of the text books, and the recitations are rendered more lively and profitable in consequence : information has been methodized in the mind, a greater accuracy ensured, a firmer grasp of subjects, and pleasure associated with study. The text has been taken as a thread for conversation, and a clue to the sense, the pupils being required to render this by translation or paraphrase. The method of conversation adopted by most, has put spirit and meaning into the exercises ; brought teacher and classes into livelier sympathy and correspondence with one another ; into intimacies more or less friendly according to the temperament and disposition of the partners. Perhaps this change is the hopefullest sign of improvement made in our schools. A child should be dealt with sympathetically and so helped to express himself gracefully and this help comes best by conversing.

CONVERSATION. Conversation is the mind's mouth-piece, its best spokesman ; the leader elect and prompter in teaching. Practiced daily it should be added to the list of school studies ; an art in itself, let it be used as such and ranked as an accomplishment second to none that nature or culture can give. Certainly the best we can do is to teach ourselves and children how to talk. Let conversation displace much that passes current under the name of recitation ; mostly sound and parrotry, a repeating by rote not by heart unmeaning sounds from the memory and no more. Good teaching makes the child an eye-witness, he seeing, then telling what is seen, what is known, or comprehended ; a dissolving of the text for the moment and a beholding in thought as through a glass. "Take my mind a moment," says the teacher, "and see how things look through that prism," and the pupil sees prospects never seen before or surmised by him in that lively perspective. So taught the masters : Plato, Plutarch, Pythagoras, Pestalozzi : so Christianity was first published from lovely lips ; so every one teaches deserving the name of teacher or interpreter. Illustration always and apt ; life calling forth life ; the giving of life and a partaking. Nothing should be interposed between the mind and its subject matter ; cold sense is impertinent ; learning is insufficient ; only life alone ; life like a torch lighting the head at the heart. Even so are the children made partakers of it; are asking for it every day over their books, in school-rooms and elsewhere, and getting some elsewhere in these times of activity ; all New England and the West being an open college, admitting the populations old and young during half the year to the school master's lectures and lessons ; while the newspapers and magazines are fast superseding in prospect, primers, text books and professors in part ; graduating bright boys and girls at every hearing, every issue, every shop and fireside, everywhere.

Still we are wont to associate college acquirements, books, erudition, with the office of teaching, and to consider learning as the teacher's chief qualification. It is a sad mistake, and the schools have been the sufferers for it. Books were thoughts first, their contents the results of thinking, they should be baits for thought and study. We need minds whose thoughts are the substance and soul of books ; persons of good gifts, having thoughts and feelings, and can impart these in lovely ways ; can dissolve the book and show its contents outside of its covers ; meeting their classes, first, to hear all they can recite out of their books, and then to pour from a glowing mind a flood of light over the page, and create the subject anew before their eyes, inspiring them with the soul of creation. We want living minds to quicken and inform living minds. A boy's life, a maiden's time, is too precious to be wasted in committing words to the memory from books they never learn the use of.

USE OF BOOKS. Next to thinking for themselves, the best service any teacher can render his scholars is to show them how to use books. There are better or worse ways of studying, and a child should be helped to possess himself of the contents of a book in manners most consonant to his tastes and aptitudes. No two persons read after the same fashion, nor can books be studied alike by different persons; the author's method may be good in itself, but not ours, and each finds by instinct what is his. The wise teacher is the key for opening the mind to the books he places before it. If he has not the key to open each he shall help none to open the books to profit. He must read the temperament and disposition of his pupils, and assist each to make the most of his gifts, correcting what is deficient or amiss chiefly through the student's choices. He is there to form good habits of studying and of using books to help himself with afterwards.

"The genial school master, that hath a hand
To institute the flower of all a land,
Gives longest lessons unto those whom Heaven
The ablest wits, and aptest wills hath given."

Doubtless we remember the pleasure we felt in our childhood on first opening some interesting book that chanced to fall in our way ; perhaps making an era in our youthful experience. Good books are only second in their influence to that of persons ; oftentimes on such as chance to come seldom under the power of cultivated persons, a book is an education. It is to be regretted that our family and school libraries are not better furnished, and that the love of reading choicely is so little cultivated in our families and schools. A taste for books, and good habits of reading, is an omen of good things to come for the reader. Our town library is doing something to serve the wants of old and young, and is perhaps the most beneficient influence the town has inaugurated, not second to the lyceum itself, that liberator of the mind of New England. Who shall tell what this has done for our rural population ?

" For here for the last twenty years have come our towns-people from season to season to the peaceful games of our Lyceum, from which a new era will be dated to New England, as from the games of Greece. For if Heroditus carried his history to Olympia to read, after the cestus and the race, have we not heard such histories recited here, which since our countrymen have read, as made Greece sometimes forgotten ? "

A kindly consideration of the wants of the young for which the town has cared and provided so generously in its flourishing library, will I doubt not, open for them still ampler opportunities and privileges in a well selected assortment of books for their special benefit. I believe the very valuable Quarterly Journal of Education, edited by Dr. Barnard, has not yet been added to the collection.

SCHOOL BOOKS.

The following is the list of Books sanctioned by the Committee :

For the Teachers' Use.

Picture Testament.
Pilgrim's Progress.
Krummacher's Parables.
Constitution of the United States.
Declaration of Independence.
Constitution of Massachusetts.

Primary, Intermediate and other Schools.

Philbrick's Tablets.
Mrs. Barbauld's Lessons and Hymns.
Miss Edgeworth's Easy Lessons.
Tower's Gradual Primer.
"   Introduction to Gradual Reader.
"   Gradual Reader.
Hillard's Second Class Reader.
Town's Progressive Speller.
Emerson's Primary Arithmetic.
Colburn's First Lessons.
Greenleaf's Common School Arithmetic.
Tower's Algebra.
Parley's History.
Weld's Grammar.
Fowler's Manual of Conversation.
Fowler's Book of Synonyms.
Payson and Dunton's Writing Books.

High School.

CLASSICAL AND FRENCH BOOKS.

Andrews' Latin Series.
Arnold's Latin and Greek Series.

Moore's Virgil.
Johnson's Cicero.
Sophocles' Greek Grammar.
Xenophon's Anabasis.
Homer's Iliad.
Fasquelle's French Grammar.
Fasquelle's Reader.
Chouquet's French Lessons.
Nouvelles Genevoises.

ENGLISH BOOKS.

Shakspeare, Milton and Thompson.
Gleanings from the Poets.
Plutarch's Lives.
Sargent's Fifth Reader.
Green's Grammar.
Greenleaf's National Arithmetic.
Day's or Sherwin's Algebra.
Davies' Legendre's Geometry.
Hill's First Lessons in Geometry.
Olmstead's Astronomy.
Tate's Natural Philosophy.
Stöckhardt's Chemistry.
Cornell's Geographies.
Fitch's Physical Geography.
Tenney's Geology.
Jarvis' Physiology.
Gray's Elementary Botany.
Hanaford and Payson's Book-keeping.
Worcester's Comprehensive Dictionary.
Quackenboss' U. S. History.
Miss Peabody's Universal History.

I should like to add to this list, Webster's Dictionary, and The Book of Agriculture which is being prepared by the State. Also Rei Rusticæ, recommended by Milton, and Evelyn's Gardener and Acetaria.

The Books authorised in the High School may be used in the other schools of the town.

Pursuant to law a sufficient supply of the above books has been procured, and the same can be obtained at A. Stacy's Bookstore, at cost.

4

NEW BOOKS. The new books placed at the teachers' desks as books of reference, have been found very useful, and the class books have served to give a tone of sprightliness and fluency to the readings very agreeable to witness. The books have been read more or less, and given out as rewards for good scholarship or good behavior at intervals of study. No objections, save in one district where the skill of the teacher in making the most of her materials made the want less felt by the children, have come to my knowledge.

The classes who have used Miss Edgeworth's admirable Lessons as a reading book, have made very great improvement in reading ; that pleasing art ; owing in good measure to the suitableness of the matter and style to their understanding and taste.

The Book of Synonyms has been used to profit also. It has been used as a book for spelling and defining, and for exercises in paraphrasing, and as a dictionary in general. Next to Miss Edgeworth's Lessons, it seems to be the most popular of any in the class list. I believe it has been used in nearly all of the schools.

The book entitled How to Talk has been less tried. It was introduced rather as relief lessons for the grammar students, than as a regular class book ; though it is very well suited for the study of beginners, containing many useful hints for teacher as well as scholar. A better book is much wanted.

Plutarch's Lives has been studied by some of the advanced classes. As a book of reference it is of inestimable point and value ; a taste for it is a certificate of genius for the student of its pages. The Committee have shown their regard for the rising talent in the schools by admitting it into the company of this mellow sage and master biographer of antiquity.

Krummacher's Parables is the best book of the sort in our language. It stands next to Pilgrim's Progress in the estimation of its many readers, and is coming into general favor as a family book wherever it is known. We were fortunate in securing a good edition from the press of Bohn, of London ; an elegant book at a reasonable price.

Miss Elizabeth Peabody has added some valuable books to our list : her fresh version of the Legend of Saint George, from Spenser ; her book on The Crimes of the House of Austria, and Hawthorne's Liberty Tree. The last has been read with delight by the younger children ; his Wonder Book and Tanglewood Tales should be in every childs' hands. Miss Peabody's Universal History stands also on our list of school books for any classes that shall be formed in that study.

I am sure the Committee have offered a good suggestion to other towns in putting into our schools copies of the Constitution of the United States and of the Declaration of Independence.

The Picture Testament being a Harmony of the Gospels and the Acts of the Apostles, beautifully illustrated, the several topics discriminated and printed in sections, with a full table of contents, and making an attractive volume of this Scriptural classic, we have been unable as yet to obtain. I believe this edition is out of print; it should be in the hands of every parent, in every family and school. Mrs. Barbauld's Lessons and Hymns, designed as an attractive reading book for the primary classes, it has been difficult to find in a suitable shape for a school book.

PILGRIM'S PROGRESS. The Pilgrim's Progress stands next to the parables of the New Testament in the value of its insinuating moralities. It should be on the desk of every teacher, and in every home library throughout Christendom. It never tires; it cannot be read too frequently; it is never finished, and the thousandth perusal is as new and as charming as the first. It has been accepted wherever it has been circulated, and this is only second in extent to the Christian Scriptures. It cannot be too early given to the fancy and heart of the young, that its homely sense so Saxon and so strong its lively images may dwell with them as long as they live.

My indebtedness to it is great. It was the first classic next the New Testament, that opened upon my eyes, and took captive all that was best in me; I read it again and again through all my childhood and youth; and have read it to thousands of children during the last thirty years, in schools private and public, in Sunday schools and families, where I have chanced to be. And during the last year I have repeated this pleasure, having read part first in all the districts, in paraphrase, omitting impertinent passages, and following the thread of the allegory, giving free interplay of episode and conversation to carry the moral more surely to the heart of the listeners. The children in all the schools have been well pleased with this part, and are waiting for the rest. I consider this about the best service it has been in my power to render to them and their parents.

STORIES. Stories are the idyls of childhood. They cast about it the romance it loves and lives in, rendering the commonest circumstances and things inviting and beautiful. Nor do I know any means equally acceptable and so immediately conducive to the ends of teaching; insinuating so softly and persuasively the purest morals for the fancy and the heart. I never visit a school without coveting a life for its opportunities for enjoying the pastime of telling tales, every faculty and affection finding free scope in this play of all delights. The old memories waken and youth returns again : —

> " Yea, a deeper import
> Lurks in the legend told our infant years,
> Than lies upon that truth, we live to learn :
> For fable is Love's world, his home, his birth place;
> Delightedly dwells he 'mong fays and talismans
> And spirits, and delightedly believes
> Divinities, being himself divine."

POETRY AND FICTION. Fancy liberates us from the senses, and is ever a pleasant companion. Parables, poems, histories, anecdotes, are prime aids in teaching; the readiest means of influence and inspiration; the liveliest substitutes for flagging spirits, fatigued wits. The great teachers from Pythagoras down,—the sacred teachers of all time, have sanctioned the use of them ; and the human race still testify to the delight it receives from these masterpieces of genius : the smallest child according to his capacity of enjoyment, as the maturest mind. Plutarch is delightful for his anecdotes ; Shakspeare is the joy of all wherever his name and books have penetrated, — Spenser too, Chaucer and Milton. Scott is a general favorite : then of the earlier and later minor poets ; — Herbert, Crashaw, Vaughan, Cowper, Thompson, Gray, Burns, Tennyson, Wordsworth ; at home, Bryant, Whittier, Longfellow. Channing has written some delightful verses that should be better known to be enjoyed by all lovers of pure poetry. Of the Sacred poets, Cattermoles is the best collection I know ; and Dana's contains nearly all the best pieces in our language. A choice selection including poetry and prose from English literature is still wanted for family and school reading; it should contain only the very best. The young should have access to the wisdom and worth of the fruits of genius.

It is proposed to compile from the writings of our townsmen and women a Concord Book. Such a collection would embrace suitable pieces from Buckley, its founder, Wood, Ripley, Hoar, Shattuck, Frost, Jarvis, Mann, Peabody, Bradford, Hawthorne, Channing, Thoreau, Emerson ; and if well prepared would be a work of great historical and literary interest. There seems no reason why a volume of this attractive character should not be published at once.

PRIMERS AND CLASS BOOKS. It were well if there were at hand in our schools a little library of suitable books for reference and recreation ; for the smallest children, portfolios and pictures. Whatever can be addressed to the eye is a gain, and next to the ear.

A Child's Picture Primer and Mother's Aid is wanted. It should be some suitable story founded on American life, disposed as exercises in thought, behavior, talking, reading, conversation, and marking ; it should be illuminated in the tastiest style of art ; its moral insinuated, not obtruded. Children are the best judges of books for their own reading. Only what interests and to which they turn again and again, is good. By a happy instinct, as lovers of the good and true, they find what is for them, and leave the rest. A proper supervision is supposed to be given to the books they open, as to the company they keep ; since a bad book may corrupt in manners that an improper companion cannot. In this respect we might take wise counsel from past times.

Plato comprehended education under the two heads of gymnastics for the body and music for the mind, beginning with fables and musical arguments ; fancy fashioning facts to please and harmonize the mind, and graceful exercises the body ; by which means he sought to draw the young to the practice of health and virtue, to genius and good behavior unconsciously. In his Laws he enjoins upon the State the duty of exercising control over the poets, to the end that mothers and nurses shall fashion the young and tender more by chaste and well chosen fables than their bodies by their hands. He thought the selection of leaders in the gymnastic contests was by far the greatest of the chief offices in the State. For he said : —

" As the first budding of every plant when it runs in a beautiful manner to the excellence of its nature, is the most powerful to take on a suitable finish, so of animals tame or wild and of man, who, when favored by nature and instruction becomes an animal most divine and tame, but when he is not sufficiently or not properly brought up, is the most savage of all animals the world produces: so the legislator ought not to suffer the bringing up of children to be a secondary thing, or as a by-work."

The Reading books should be simple and addressed to the ages and comprehension of the classes. Children cannot read with spirit and grace what is not theirs by fancy, by sense ;—nothing that lies out of their affections. Good reading is a gift, an inspiration, a matter of the heart. Not a little of the bad reading in the schools arises from the difficulty of finding meanings where none are meant for them in the text, and so they mouth and mar their utterances. Voice and sense should suit. Give sense : a text charged with meaning and suitable to a child's years and he shall express himself elegantly and well. A boy carries a good deal in his head, but it is not ponderous enough usually for Webster's speeches to enter and flow freely off his tongue, or Everett's periods mellifluously. The training of the voice proceeds on the affections, as melodized by their flow : eloquence being fluent thought, dissolving views passing before the eyes and melodies to the ear. Nor should we call on gentle boys and girls to read pieces they dislike or did not cordially select. They may not understand the sense always, but should be attracted to the sound by the subtle significance of its fitness ; their tastes and elocution being so cultivated best. It is a pity the flowers of rhetoric, the strong Saxon phrase should be plucked so freshly in the sports and conversations of the young, yet spoiled, or marred so badly in parlors and schools,—places one would think specially designed for cultivating the art of discourse.

PHILBRICK'S TABLETS. Philbrick's Tablets introduced into the primary and district schools, have more than satisfied the expectations of the Superintendent and teachers, as ingenious devices for interesting young children in the elements of learning through the eye and hand, those leaders along with the ear of culture in every department. They have been used to good profit, and to the pleasure of teachers and classes. Next to Colburn's books, and Dr. Mason's music books, I consider them the best thing that has been done for the schools since the revival of education amongst us. Some improvements may be suggested to suit the growing demands of the mind ; perhaps colored types for the vowel sounds, illustrated fables, calisthenic postures, mythology, costumes, cards of songs, maps ; and giving the new art of photography to the service of education. Pictures have wrought wonders during the last thirty years for human culture, and the youngest children in families and the schools are beginning to get their share in the new improvements.*

---

* A word on the Tablets. They are something new and but lately introduced to notice by the Boston Superintendent. They consist of ten cards, 21 x 27 inches, and each card containing two tablets, one each side, and complete in itself. The subjects illustrated are the alphabet, penmanship, punctuation, figures, numerals, sounds of the letters, drawing, and words and sentences for spelling and reading. They are designed for using in the primary, district, and intermediate schools, serving the purpose in a measure of books for the younger classes. Every primary and district school should have them. If any parent questions it, an hour spent in school will bring him round to take the part of his child's comfort and progress. The set of twenty costs $5; a single tablet, .40. They would serve a school for years.

SLATES AND PENCILS. I find the slate and pencil have come into general favor. Every child is expected to bring these with his primer on entering for induction into the mysteries of learning and the mind. The least can print their spelling and reading lessons from the pages of their primers, and some not over five or six years of age mark elegantly or print as they call it, in a clerkly style; all taking pleasure in the privilege. The slates are found a ready means of insuring order and diligence; and afford agreeable pastimes during intervals that would be tedious otherwise: besides sparing them the pains of sitting idle with folded hands, or from the penalties of mischief in self defence. Given out as rewards, the slates give interest to their exercises, and under proper restrictions can be used for picture sketchings, or any caprice they please to indulge in.

They tell a story of a boy cut off from schools and books who took to his fingers; saving his coppers for buying chalk, and in the want of black-board and foolscap, cut his flourishes on the snow or the uncarpeted floors, and so learned to write. These snow tablets are always available in winter, and games at flourish might be drawn at noontime if the scholars chose.

DRAWING. This pleasing and really useful art has been hitherto much neglected in the schools. It is practised in some of them and should be included in the list of studies. It is but a form of writing, and connects intimately with geometry, and with the manual and ideal arts.

FORMS AND IDEAS. A little Atlas of the Body mythologically shown from the artist's points of view, the plates displaying the person to the eye in a set of draped figures, is a book much wanted for first lines in drawing. The figures should be colored and gracefully executed by a master. Add a Greek Pantheon as a gallery of forms for illustrating the first metaphysics in an attractive style to the senses. A child's piety is seen in its regards for its body, and the concern it shows in its carriage and keeping. Of all forms, the human form is most marvellous and the modest reverence for its shadings intimates the proper

---

[NOTE.] FOR DRAWING AND IDEAS. Use Pinnock's Iconology. For Studies in Mythology, in Nature, and in Human Forms, Hermes' Drawing Books, comprising easy lessons in drawing, in five parts; landscapes, do., in forty-seven do.; flowers and fruits, do., eighteen do.; arabesques, do., twenty do.; studies from still life, do., eight do.; animals, do., twenty-two do.; the human form, do., twenty-nine do.; geometrical drawing, do., eight do., and the picture book containing sixty-four colored pictures of objects.

mode of studying it rightly and religiously as a pantheon of powers. The prime training best opens here as an idealism, the soul fashioning her image in the form she animates, and so scrutinizing piously without plucking the forbidden fruits. As far as the mind can be symbolized in forms, it should be, and so shown to the eye in colors to heighten the effect. Studies in anatomy are best deferred : they are not taught at any time without some hazard and best as mythology. The ends of science are sometimes served at the cost of innocence and of humanity ; the scientific mind finds its opportunities in museums and the dissections.

There is a want of suitable aids to the studies of these mysteries. The best books I know are poor enough. In the want of a better, we name for the study of matter in its connection with the mind, including the proper considerations regarding health and temperance, Graham's Laws of Life, a rather dull but earnest book ; and for smaller classes and beginners, Dr. Alcott's House I Live In. Miss Catherine Beecher's book for studies in Physiology and Calisthenics, is a practical treatise, and should be in all the schools. Sir John Sinclair's Code of Health, contains a re-publication of the Wisdom of the Ancients, on these subjects, and is a book for all persons and times. Some of the best things said about health, temperance, and holiness of culture outside the Gospels, are found in the sayings of Pythagoras, from whom a word further here. Of food he held : —

"That whatsoever obstructs divination, or is prejudicial to the purity and sanctity of the mind, to temperance, chastity, and habitual virtue, should be shunned; also that which is contrary to purity and defiles the imagination at any time. That the juvinile age should make trial of temperance — this being alone of all the virtues, alike adapted to youths and maidens and women, to all of advanced life; and that it comprehended the goods both of body and soul, and also the desire of the most excellent studies. He thought boys were especially dear to divinity, and exhorted women to use words of good omen through the whole of life, and to endeavor that others may predict good things of them." Again one of his disciples has said,—" Our first duties go abreast, comprehending the care of the mind along with the body. Parents are protectors of families and States; they stand for comfort, for nobility; for earth-husbandries, and man-culture, not as Cattle Gods and Pantry Providences only; but for State and family interests largely considered and beautifully combined; for temperance, for thrift, humanity and the future."

He paid great attention to the health of body and mind, using unction and the bath often, wrestling also and leaping with leaden weights in the hands, and used pantomimes with a view to strengthening the body, studiously selecting for this purpose opposite exercise.

It is sufficient to say, in praise of the excellency of the Pythagorean school, that in it were formed the noblest persons of antiquity, Socra-

tes, Plato, Plutarch, Pericles; and if any question the matter of reg-
imen for the body, we need but add to the list the name of Milo, the
wrestler, and the strongest man of antiquity.

TACTS. We should consider the inestimable value of self-help in
early training, and take pains to give schooling to hand and eye along
with the head, using every occasion for educating these by natural
means, that their skills may not come too late to help at the instant.
The child takes to them by instinct and mother wit at the beginning.
And the best education comes from actual dealings with things and
persons, this being the most direct, and efficient for the chief ends of
life : a tact applied at once to things and events as they rise : not waiting for the training that books can give or the drills of the schools.   In
such wise are men self-made and successful.

GYMNASTICS. We come late to disciplines of this noble nature;
yet physical training has received some attention here lately, and is
practiced in some of the schools.   But I need not enlarge upon its
benefits to you, Gentlemen of the Committee, several of your members having taken strenuous parts in the class gathered in this Hall,
under the leadership of Dr. Lewis,—invited here by your Secretary,—
who has kindled an enthusiasm that has spread throughout the town,
and still brings its classes of gymnasts of all ages, professions, callings;
from school boys and young ladies, to grave seniors — including many
of the teachers, along with the farmers, the merchants, the Hon.
Chairman, the tall Secretary, and the Rev. Minister.   Teaching,
preaching, pleading, trading, farming, house-keeping; hearth-sides,
studies, the neighborhood, the landscape, are all of them the sweeter
and the lovelier for these; and as recreative to the seniors as to the
young people, and taken as a natural religion by instinct.   Body
and mind are yokefellows and love to draw together in these life
tasks and pleasures of ours.   All need meat and drink, fresh air, the
influence of sunshine, exercise out of doors, and a chosen task; if
imposed, the more is the need of those incitements, as reliefs and relays
for us in disguise.   Play is wholesome.   A sound mind proves itself
best by keeping its body sound and swift to serve its turns; its senses
keen, its limbs strong and agile for the moment.   Nature is the broad
church of All-Souls for cheer and satisfaction, strange as the houses
may seem and the doings in-doors.

5

The homely Nurse doth all she can
To make her foster child, her inmate man,
Revive the glories he hath known,
In Paradise from whence he's flown.

AMUSEMENTS. Young people find ways enough of amusing themselves, and we best leave them much to their choice in such matters;
yet some slight superintendence seems becoming—some interest shown
by us in their pleasures—since these exert a commanding influence
in forming their tastes and characters, and cannot be safely neglected
by their guardians. They are a school for the fancy and the heart;
they may play the part of the school of virtue or of scandal, as well
or ill chosen. The streets are the gymnasia of the young, the
world they live in largely, the widest, the freest range they know
and are permitted to enjoy. Herein are they fairly launched into
life, and left free to follow their inclinations—masters of themselves for the time, and servants of their senses and devotees. "Let
us play" is the privileged version of their creed, and they enter with
the unction of enthusiasm into the sweet sports they love. Then they
show what they are; casting all reserve aside their souls leap sun-
ward glossy gay in their abandonment to fancy and fun. And now
is the teacher's golden opportunity for learning the temper, and
tendencies of these enthusiasts at their pastimes outside. Nor
need his presence mar their sports. Any indifference to these matters shows some defect of sensibility and an unfitness for his task.
A teacher should have much good company in him and tact at making
himself as agreeable out of doors as inside. Sound health, flowing
spirits, sprightly wits, sympathy, sane sense, a genial temperament,

---

[NOTE] KINDER GARTEN. For little children, a ray of sunshine has fallen on
their path from the kind soul of Fræbel, in his carefully devised system of Recrea-
tions and Gifts for them. 'Tis the school master in the nursery and garden; the
genius of sensibility set fairly to work for their edification and delight. "It developes
the faculties in a pleasing manner, gives perception of form, beauty, and color, manual dexterity, and lays the foundation for intellectual and moral culture."

FRŒBEL'S BOOK. The book from which the needful information may be drawn,
is published by Hodson & Son, 22 Portugal street, Lincoln's Inn, London. It is an exposition of Fræbel's system of Early Training, and prepared by John & Bertha Ronge.
The title is as follows:— A Partial Guide to the English Kinder Garten, (Children's
Garden,) for the use of Mothers, Nursery Governesses, and Infant Teachers, being an
exposition of Fræbel's System of Infant Training, accompanied by a great variety of
instructive and amusing games, and industrial and gymnastic exercises, also numerous songs set to music and arranged to the exercises. I believe some good friends of
children are about bringing his system before the minds of parents, by opening a little school and publishing his books and gifts.

tell best; a harmony of tenderness and grace that draw love and confidence at once. Everywhere the laws of influence are the same and operate alike. Dullness is intolerable, and dreaded by all—by children particularly. The teacher must touch the sensibilities and strike the fancy, or they will not listen long ; his the fault, theirs the misfortune. He does not play well on his instrument, the human heart, if he lack fancy, enthusiasm, health, humor ;—"if he pipe ever so hard, they dance not ; if he sorrow they don't weep" as he would have them, and the game is wearisome to all ; all parties have enough of it. For whoever speaks not to the love and wonder of mankind says little deserving of lasting interest.

Conceive the quicksilver a child is, and wonder by what surprising skill he is held civil and fast to his books, by what grace preventing he has borne with the impiety that has made him the scape-grace and by-word of literature, from Chaucer old down to the Committee man of to-day ;—

> The whining schoolboy with his satchel
> And shining morning face, creeping like snail
> Unwillingly to school.

So Shakspeare sang, and his snail still creeps of right toward all houses destitute of love and humanity inside. For if children are not first magnetized and charged with life by the teacher's vivacity, getting something as genial as they give, inspiration answering to animal spirits, they have the best of it, and lead as they list, he following frowning in self-defence and seeming command as he may. What wonder, then, if getting little or nothing touching him quickly, the boy drops his enjoyments with his cap in the entry as he comes in, and pushes his way outside as soon as his profitless task is over. 'Tis a defeat ; the victory is his, and with spirit won ; the shame his master's, else the mind hates knowledge, defies good manners, and distrusts virtue as unprofitable and false. Young America is generous, if met justly and generously ; as it loves rule, so it loves to be ruled in honest Saxon mood. "Any boy can teach a man, but it takes a man to teach a boy anything," said the old countryman Fuller with his usual good sense and sagacity. Hear further what he says of the schoolkeeping and teachers of his times :

"THE GOOD SCHOOLMASTER. There is scarce any profession in the Commonwealth more necessary, which is so slightly performed. The reasons whereof I conceive to be these: First, young scholars make this calling their refuge, yea, perchance before they have taken any degree in the University, commence schoolmasters in the country, as if nothing else were required to set up in this profession but only a rod and a ferule.

Secondly, others, who are able, use it only as a passage to better preferment, to patch the rents in their present fortune, till they can provide a new one, and betake themselves to some more gainful calling. Thirdly, they are disheartened from doing their best with the miserable reward which in some places they receive, being masters to the children and slaves to their parents. Fourthly, being grown rich, they grow negligent, and scorn to touch the school but by the proxy of an usher. But see how well our schoolmaster behaves himself.

His genius inclines him with delight to his profession. He studieth his scholars' natures as carefully as they their books, and ranks their dispositions into several forms. And though it may seem difficult for him in a great school to descend to all particulars, yet experienced schoolmasters may quickly make a grammar of boys' natures, and reduce them all, saving some few exceptions, to these general rules.

1. Those that are ingenious and industrious. The conjunction of two such planets in a youth presage much good unto him. To such a lad a frown may be a whipping, and a whipping a death; yea, where their master whips them once, shame whips them all the week after. Such natures he useth with all gentleness.

2. Those that are ingenious and idle. These think, with the hare in the fable, that running with snails (so they count the rest of their schoolfellows) they shall come soon enough to the post, though sleeping a good while before their starting. Oh, a good rod would finely take them napping.

3. Those that are dull and diligent. Wines, the stronger they be, the more lees they have when they are new. Many boys are muddy-headed till they be clarified with age, and such afterward prove the best. That schoolmaster deserves to be beaten himself who beats nature in a boy for a fault. And I question whether all the whipping in the world can make their parts, which are naturally sluggish, rise one minute before the hour nature hath appointed.

4. Those that are invincibly dull and negligent also. Correction may reform the latter, not amend the former. All the whetting in the world can never set a razor's edge on that which hath no steel in it. Such boys he consigneth over to other professions.

He is able, diligent, and methodical in his teaching; not leading them rather in a circle than forward. He minces his precepts for children to swallow, hanging clogs on the nimbleness of his own soul, that his scholars may go along with him. If he hath a stubborn youth, correction-proof, he debaseth not his authority by contesting with him, but fairly, if he can, puts him away before his obstinacy hath infected others.

He is moderate in inflicting deserved correction. Many a schoolmaster better answereth the name of a teacher of wrestling or gymnastics, than one who teaches or trains boys."

Perhaps we are correcting the old affection for flogging at some risk of spoiling the boys of this generation,—girls have always known how to cover with shame any insult of that sort,—but the power of persuasion comes slow as a promptitude to supersede its necessity. Who deals with a child deals with a piece of divinity obeying laws as innate as those he transgresses, and which we must treat tenderly lest he put spiritual interests in jeopardy. Punishment must be just, else it cannot be accepted as good ; and least of all by the wicked and weak. Even animals are amenable to sentiments superior to their instincts, and the man in man may be debased to the brute.

The accomplished teacher combines in himself the arts of teaching and of ruling: power over the intellect and the will, inspiration and persuasiveness, — qualifications not always found united in one person and constituting genius properly. And this implies a double consciousness in its possessor that carries forward the teaching and ruling together, noting what transpires in motive as in act : the gift that in seeing controls. It is the sway of presence and of mien ; a conversion of the will to his wishes, without which other gifts are of little avail. Nature is strong, yet manageable by her master genius, the mind, whose way is one and the method of all ages ; namely, humor, dealing with the mind tenderly, descisively. The simpler it is and the swifter, the more salient the sally, and the sooner its coming round. The method is one of speed, dropping no faculty on the route, mind passing entire as a conductor. Talent cries halves and is lost in the labyrinth of things, while genius is torch, guide and clue-head on shoulders of things below. Drill there might be, it is indispensable, so is the pleasure in study. Let them alternate in the shape of task and pastime keeping the mind and memory sweet and study a pleasure. The dullest child likes learning when he is so fortunate as to get a taste of it ; is the more eager as he is dull, because his hunger is less satisfying, the emptiness so deep. We should give him the bread he asks for in his heart though his tongue ask amiss ; not the poor stones insultingly. The deepest impiety I know, the boldest blasphemy, is that brutality of soul which would club down the springing faiths of the little victims it tyrannizes over, by its cold contempts ; — the blighted tree forever accursed from whose twigs no lovely sensibilities shall ever bud !

ARITHMETIC. To name Euclid, Pestalozzi and Colburn, is but naming the most and best we know concerning Geometry, Algebra and Arithmetic, and the proper methods of teaching these sciences, which are the alphabet and prime symbols of natural things. Perhaps these branches of learning are better taught than any others ; and this is owing to the almost utter impossibility of teaching at all unless it be done rightly and accurately. Colburn's books have wrought a revolution in this respect, by bringing numbers and their relations within the grasp of the senses and the intellect of the youngest child ; assisting him simply to use the counters nature has pointed out in the fingers and toes as the units and tens of all rotation, and thus conducting his mind from his body into nature for nominating and numbering the objects of his senses. Pestalozzi gave practical examples of the natural method of teaching by the fingers and natural objects, and his disciple, Colburn, applied this prime doctrine to the mind. President Hill, in his little treatise on Geometry has done something to make the mind of Euclid tell on the schools of our day. Dr. Bowring has given a most charming account of the history of written numbers, in his *Decimal System*, a book that should be at the desk of every teacher for reference, and to interest pupils in that science.

ATLAS OF CONCORD. In my last year's report I ventured some suggestions on a simple mode of studying nature as it lies about us here in our own town, and add a word further here.

I find it difficult to propose to our teachers any improvement in our methods of studying Geography without giving them the advantage of a fair beginning. Geography is studied in all the schools, and by very young children; and while they answer questions on the maps and recite from their text books, it is not quite kind to put questions about things outside, or to expect them to find the places in the town named and delineated in the little map of Concord hanging on the wall. They probably know the little or big house they live in and come out of and return to; where they feed and sleep, and their pleasure grounds very well, but never too much of the districts remote from them, far less of the great world they live in and study about. The natural method begins at home. And happily we have a sort of resident Surveyor-General of the town's farms, farmers, animals, and everything else it contains, — who makes more of it than most persons with a continent at their call. Will he just set his ten senses at work upon an illustrated Atlas for the citizens, giving such account of the world they inhabit, with such hints concerning the one he lives in, as he pleases? Such a book would suit us all, and become a model text book for studies out of doors, and a gift to our children for which they could not be too grateful.—The town should find ways of using its best men. This every town owes to itself and to its children especially since they are its fairest productions. It cannot afford to deny to the humblest of them the services if they can be obtained of its favored citizens. Much less can it do so if it be enriched with any gifted with more senses and a stronger wit, with genius and adaptabilities surpassing most men; any who might educate them in ways so agreeable in its geography, its natural history, its antiquities, or the poetry of literature, the history of their minds, their natures and callings. Still better if led by these wise eyes along our fields, wood-paths, river-lands, brook-sides, and the plain landscape they know, these children were helped to seize at once and at first hand their mys-

teries and uses; so stealing the secrets of things, of animals, and the
human intelligence it hoards in its humble homes and environs.

GEOGRAPHY AND NATURAL HISTORY.   We must be near to nature
and of simple heart, to study and learn what she can teach us.   A
child must view the landscape he is studying, or he gets very slight
knowledge of it from the second sight his maps afford or the dry statement of his text books.   An actual view of the objects studied as far
as may be, is essential.   Walking presents the best method, — that of
observation, — which globes information to the senses in the living
way.   " Seeing is knowing," " seeing is believing," — these proverbs
affirm the secret doctrine of education; the eye being the professor
elect of the faculties of the mind, giving shape and substance to the
rest, while each member and power follows its leader in turn and shares
in the elucidation.   The eyes are travellers and fancy their draughts-
man sketching things seen on the journey.   So fancy's pictures help
the mind afoot, but cannot take it far from the school room, the town
in which the student resides bodily.   He must take to his legs, carrying
his maps in his pocket if he please, but seeing with very eyes the
objects described therein, thus impressing the originals on the globe of
his brain, through ideas, the mind's eyesight.

A globe serves him next best.   And if some skilfull worker in plas-
ter would construct the hemispheres in bas relief, giving the globe to
the eyes as it rolls in nature or appears fixed to the senses, he would
help the ends of primary instruction in a kindly way.   Let these hemispheres project boldly from the sides of the school room presenting the
surface to the eye without illusion ; and to strike the fancy all the more
they should be colored as natural objects are.   Children, the devotees
of sense and sympathy, and ready to translate objects into ideas, find
their fancy embarrassed by the effort of dealing with the lines and
dots they see pictured on the plane maps, and get by consequence
little beyond the names and signs of them as represented on the maps.
They study these and not the world they traverse outside.   This
dot is all they see of the city named London or Constantinople ;
that line is all they take in of the Missouri or Amazon; that
hump is veritable Apennine or Andes.   The names, even, are empty
of sense, at best but sounding words, suggesting vague somethings,
having nothing in common with things known and seen from the school
windows ; not good grounds for climbing, ball playing, honest currents
for boating, solid for skating, as are the Common, Lee's Hill and

Concord River; all dreamland, dreary droil, as barren of interest as of whortleberries or pickerel, an impertinent paper hanging on the wall, a roll call of hard names, not the reveille for play they are waiting for.

Then put the map of Middlesex County into the schools, with such illustrations as may be drawn from town histories, Thoreau's books, the Historical and Agricultural Transactions, monthly walks with Atlas and the teacher, and something of life and reality might be given to the studies Geography, History and Biography, with the elements of the natural sciences generally, and Geology and Botany particularly. Then at night there is the firmament for the study of its spangles and poets to read the children Mythology to their delight. I can conceive of the surveyor employing some of the understrappers for studying under his eye by carrying his chain for him, each young Agassiz and Kane taking his turn as it came.

TALKING AND WRITING. The child begins the study of words properly from the lips, conversing about their sense and meaning as they are dropped in lively discourse. As soon as he is able to use it, put a little Thesaurus or word-book into his hands to assist him in forming his vocabulary. Put one at his desk at school to be used for spelling and defining. Let him write his words on his slate before he spells them from the book, and so learn to write with his pencil, beginning with imitating the Roman letter, sliding by degrees into the italic character, and thence into the current script as he advances. Beginning thus and being taught by the natural sense of his eye and by daily practice at hazard to follow out his taste in the formation of a characteristic hand of his own, he learns rapidly. I have never known an instance in which practice in this simple way did not give a power over the hand and eye at less pains of time and effort than by the ordinary methods.*

---

*Children are always ready for almost any exercise of their limbs, their sense of sight, the voice or the ear. A pleasing use is made of this love of activity in giving the classes lessons in elocution, or the proper training of the voice and ear for reading and speaking. Mr. Philbrick has prepared a tablet of the gamut of sounds as given by Prof. Russell, who is esteemed authority in such matters. His scale runs thus:—

One.	Two.
1. Ah.	1. All.
2. Am.	2. Orb.
3. I.	3. On.
4. Air.	4. Old.
5. End.	5. Ooze.
6. In.	
7. Eve.	
8. Up.	

VOCABULARY. Spelling should go hand in hand with defining, to the end of getting a good vocabulary of our tongue for daily use in conversation and composition. It would be a curious exercise, yet perhaps the best a teacher could put his classes about, for each member to hunt through the dictionary in alphabetical order for the words most significant and used in his conversation ; each writing his list and submitting it to be discussed at length under the guidance of the teacher with the aid of the authorities and as a test of acquirement in language. I think any experiment of this kind would reveal the exceeding poverty of our culture, and show the need of taking at once in hand the study of our Saxon tongue historically, and as a classic. Some of the worst samples of language are to be found in the writings of distinguished educators, — not Saxon, but Latinized to an extent horrible to read.

The statistics of these things are curious. Marsh in his lectures says : —

"Shakspeare's vocabulary was the largest of our English writers, and next comes Milton; the former used about fifteen thousand words in all his works, and the latter not above eight thousand. Not more than ten thousand are used by the best of our writers at the present time; and the number in ordinary writing and speaking is not above three or four thousand. The number of words not obsolete but found in good authors, or in approved usage by good speakers, does not fall far short of one hundred thousand."

GRAMMAR AND COMPOSITION. We should remember that the study of language does not of necessity include the study of its grammar as a beginning ; but more properly the tracing of its elements to their genealogies and roots in nature and the mind. These are the proper text books, — nature being the mind's phrase book and dictionary, of which speech is the illustrated alphabet. Language should be studied in its simplest renderings to the senses by means of words written or spoken, and less from the books than from a sense of the things themselves. Whatever is written out or copied from books should be written back again, and set and seen in its roots and grounds by the hand of logic and the eye of thought. This is translation properly, and composing also. Good writing involves both, — a sight into the originals of things and a clothing of these in their proper foliage and forms. It implies a sensibility and a sympathy, a perception of the fitness of things ; taste and the rhetoric that a sound criticism dictates, — every object, every action, quality and relation taking its name felicitously, every thought and thing standing truly in its place. Conversations on words, paraphrases, transposition of sentences, to dislodge the sense and seize better the connexion, re-composition, trans-

6

lations, are the natural methods for pursuing this study. Books of synonyms are of service here. Dean Trench's Monographs upon the Study of Words and Proverbs, and his Glossary of English words; Swinton's Rambles Among Words, White's Edition of Shakspeare, and Richardson's Dictionary, will be found good helps. To the list should be added Rogers's Thesaurus, Bailey's Universal Etymological Dictionary, Russell's Exercises on Words, Cardell's Grammar, Holloway's Originals, and Marsh's Lectures on the English Language, just published. The works of the Philological Society are invaluable studies for the teacher, and, as a neat vocabulary for the use of the classes along with the dictionary, Worcester's Spelling Book.

PHONETICS. The new system of phonetic writing and reading claims the notice of parents and committees from the ease and speed of its method in overcoming the difficulties of learning the elements of language. I once witnessed a trial of skill in reading and spelling between classes taught by the common method and this. The phonetic classes swept the stakes, taking the prizes from the brightest and best instructed children in the old system;—neophytes of six months' training, surpassing those of their ages and older who had been students for years. It was a triumph of the new art not for once and a generation but for all time to come. Certainly parents equally with children should rejoice in the prospect of learning to read and spell so easily and so soon, by this simple device of giving to each distinctive sound in the language its unvarying character and name; thus removing by a simple stroke of genius, impediments over which children have stumbled here at the threshold of letters for centuries;—a method so simple and natural that any child with six months' training shall outstrip others taught in the usual way, and hold fast besides the keys to every future acquisition in language. This reform in education, anticipated by the Edgeworths theoretically, is now reduced to• practice in an art founded on philosophical principles and operating beneficent improvements in teaching. The change is so easy and the basis assured to the beginner.

LETTERS AND DIARIES. Every child feels early the desire for communicating his emotions and thoughts, first by conversation and next by writing. Letters and diaries are his first confidants: the records of life and the stuff of its living literature. With the writing of these let composition begin. A child commits his experiences naturally and with a little assistance to his diary; and soon learns to write epistles to his mates, and loves to do it, as his effort gives him the sense of power and converts his learning early to practical uses. Teach him tasteful ways of folding his letters and of superscribing them correctly. The post-office is his by birthright, let us encourage him to find uses for it early as a foretaste of his little stake in affairs of State. And schools might correspond in a similar manner, delivering these little mails on stated days as exercises in spelling and composition. The keeping of a diary is an education in itself.

ANALYSIS. If a child have any thoughts and feelings, we should help him to get right names for them, for this is instructing him in the originals of language and the essence of things physical as well as metaphysical, which all names express and signify, and the knowledge of which is grammar and humanity. If he have none of these, it is the province of education and the teacher's first duty to give him some, and so rescue himself along with his pupil from nonsense and idiocy. There is no other basis for any teaching outside the mind and its powers. Every object, quality and relation is expressed by some name,— every thought and thing. To classify these under their appropriate heads, assorting thus our thoughts and things by essence and substance, properly opens the study of language and its grammar.

Thus for a beginning and with the smallest children, take the words from the lip or from the primers, and set the things seen or suggested under the following heads, in a scale written upon their slate or the black-board, naming them as the pupils observe and conclude, each for himself.

There are four classes of thoughts and things, these, namely ; —

I.	Objects.	III.	Qualities.
II.	Actions.	IV.	Relations.

Let them classify the lessons accordingly, and place the results under their proper heads in the columns.

Or the Parts of Speech may be grouped for analysis, thus : —

I. Verbs,	naming,	Flowing Being, its motions and transitions.
II. Nouns.	"	Fixed Being, at rest, or
III. Adjectives,	"	Qualities and States of the above.
IV. Particles,	"	Relations between these, connecting or disjoining.

A little practice on words serves to draw out distinctions and discriminations of differences, and is a delightful exercise in thinking and analysis for a class. If any one doubts, let him try it and see what life and reality it puts into the study.

A School Newspaper. We all admit that a boy comes into the world to learn something about it; first of the world nearest and of to-day, next and afterwards of past times and things remote. Let him have his information instant and at first hand if possible. Everybody takes a newspaper now-a-days, a paper of some sort for his family reading, but the schools await theirs. A good one would take wonderfully, and as wonderfully improve the pupil's reading by interesting him in the contents. They need boys and girls alike, new class books adapted to their comprehension and celebrating their ordinary life, their extraordinary, their impulses, aspirations and inferences; their modes of thinking and feeling. We have none suitable. Nothing better nor surer to stimulate and feed an interest in their studies of the world than the introduction into their school of a class reading sheet. Call it The Globe, if you like,—The Atlantic News,—and give the classes the pleasure of opening it of a morning as it comes fresh from the world outside wet with intelligence, as we have ours—thanks to the post office and telegraph in whose generosities the schools should largely share also. Let it be a magazine of biography, of sports, amusements, games, costumes, customs, accounts of museums, of libraries, of nature and art, of the sciences, of country life; let it contain anecdotes, and reports of the shows, the philanthropies, enterprises, discoveries, the lectures; the bright side and the right side and all sides of matters, of men and of the times;—something of politics also, of administrations; the life of the moment, well assorted and sifted to the ends of virtue and intelligence and suited to his reading and pursuits. Certainly the boys and girls are deserving of something good enough to be spared from being used as wrapping paper for their luncheons and shoppings. Such a gazette would serve the Young America running about so greedily after the village gossip, at picture shops and news rooms—every novelty it can lay ears eyes and hands upon; and prove a school master it would rather like.

Teachers' Interchanges. The half-days allowed the teachers for visiting each other monthly and taking their scholars with them, have given pleasure to all, both teachers and pupils, furnishing occasions for observing the methods pursued by each, and the benefit of any suggestions such opportunities may afford. I believe all have availed of the permission and found pleasure in it. It has brought them together professionally and proved instructive. Next to teaching is the instruction derived from seeing how others teach ; and next to seeing good examples of the best, is witnessing bad ones. Very good too and proper this following the Superintendent, that they may judge the better of his judgments concerning their gifts. Besides, they have too few chances for varying the school routine, wearisome oftentimes, from the excessive draughts made upon their spirits as well as upon the childrens' tempers from week to week.

The permitted walks to the woods and through the fields monthly, and sometimes the sleigh rides, have found favor ; and the arrangements, so far as I have learned, have been acceptable to all parties. The children have enjoyed them of course. They have less of novelty than they love, at the best, and lose their freshness too soon in consequence. Perhaps the best part of their schooling comes the cheapest,—not paid for by the State or town tax,—but taken thus unconsciously and at hazard out of doors, unsuspected and providentially, through the tuition of person and things, operating on their susceptible hearts.

SUNDAY EVENING MEETINGS. Following out our plan of interesting parents in their home duties and their relations to the school, I have held Sunday evening meetings at the school houses in the several districts. They have been well attended generally and by the children largely. So far as I have learned they have been profitable to all. The sub-committees have sometimes been present and addressed the company. I can conceive of no better disposition of an evening than the meeting together of parents and children to converse or hear discussions on the family relations, the duties of neighborhood, the spirit of childhood, the laws of life and of the virtues. On looking over my notes I find the subjects actually considered to be intimated as follows : —

Relation of Parents to Schools.   True and False Idea of Education.
Family Life.   Moral Culture.
School Books.   Methods of Teaching.
Religion in Education.   Experiences in School Keeping.
The State's Duties to Children.   The Good School Master.

Perhaps no greater service could be rendered to this generation by the leading men in our towns, villages and districts, than by assembling occasionally during the winter months to consider the great questions that interest them as men, as parents and as neighbors, in a calm and conversational way, at the school houses. Such meetings would presently become second only to the lyceum in interest and profit, while the place and company would offer opportunities for discussing some of the most cordial themes now brought before them at the churches, in a manner quite unobjectionable, and more likely than any other to promote charity and a genial piety.

The Rev. Mr. Reynolds, and the Secretary, as well as the resident Committee-man, have sometimes accompanied me and spoken at these meetings. Our meeting in the Centre at the vestry, was addressed by Hon. Simon Brown, Professor Russell, of Lancaster, (to whose services as editor of the first American Journal of Education, and as promoter of reforms since carried forward, the State and the country, are so largely indebted,) and also by the Secretary. It was then proposed to have a series of meetings at the Town Hall, but the numerous engagements of our people have thus far rendered this impracticable.

COMMITTEE AND TEACHERS' MEETINGS. Our meetings for conversation have been fewer than the teachers desired. They have been well attended and accepted I believe both by teachers and Committee as among the most important and useful of our several novelties for promoting the interests of the schools. We have discussed the following among other topics : — " Ought pupils to be carried along in Arithmetic farther than they can understand ? "

" The method of governing a school by calling on the pupils for reports."

Modes of Examination.	Modes of Correction.
Recitations.	Text Books.
School Checks.	Conversation.

Most of the teachers usually took part in these discussions.

MONTHLY ROUNDS. No one, however favored by long residence and the advantages of birth, can hope to enjoy an intimate acquaintance with the separate families of his townsfolk, much less a fabulous Superintendent of short standing and slight opportunities for forming an acquaintance so general and confiding. He must be content to draw on his fancy as he walks his monthly rounds through the districts and by the dwellings of the people, for the human influences that are moulding the inmates, save as he learns these from the little groups the neighborhoods send to their school houses, which he is by their kindness permitted to enter. It is a privilege he values and would not abuse ; a pleasurable variety of his year's gardening,—the tillage of soils without and of souls within.

HOME INFLUENCES. The school is an index to the family, the key to home influences ; it is the readiest reading of the town's population. As the family, such is the school, such is the neighborhood, the institutions, the man. Is is the world in little. Socrates comprised all objects of his search in

> " What e'er of good or ill can man befall
> In his own house,—his homestead, sole, "

rightly conceiving this to be the seminary of the virtues, and the foundation of States.—There it stands the ornament of the landscape, and for the handsomest hospitalities. We cannot make it too attractive. Let it be the home of the affections ; a parlor for conversation, a pantry of comforts, yet not reminding us too broadly of the brute satisfactions. Let its chambers open eastward admitting sunshine and the sanctities, for our and still more for the children's sakes. They covet the clear sky ; delighting in the blue they left so lately ; nay, cannot leave in coming into nature, whereof they are ever asking the news of it. The gay enthusiasts must run eagerly and never have enough of it. How soon the clouds clear away from their faces, how sufficient they are to the day and the joy it brings for them. Their poise and plentitude rebuke us. So the poet sings sadly yet truly for some of us : —

> " Happy those early days when I
> Shined in my angel infancy ;
> Before I taught my soul to wound
> My conscience with a single sound,
> Or taught my soul to fancy aught
> But a white celestial thought,
> Or had the black art to dispense
> A several sin to every sense :
> But felt through all this fleshly dress
> Bright shoots of everlastingness. "

If any one thinks him romancing about children, let him turn to Matthew, chap. XVIII, verses 1 to 7, and read what the best authority has said concerning them. It is sad to consider how long a time is necessarily consumed in wiping away the stains which have been insinuated into our breasts, during these earlier years and up to coming manhood, to what we call the maturity of our powers. Life is too much for us; it survives only in our doubts: yet cannot perish clean out of us. So much of age, so little company in so many of us; living in the moment and so dating us with the memory of its burden. We think we once were not, and fear the like fate may overtake us again, as if time were ancient and older than our minds. We always were, and so cannot trace our beginnings to the atheism of no-being, or our resolution to nothings. Children save us; rather we are saved by being children, as Christ said. We all know too well where lie the chief difficulties, and the paternity we have in them. Reform begins at the beginning, with parents personally, and at home. Every family is a little seminary and world of its own; has its climate, characteristics, its manners and morals; each the reflex and image of its heads. How different the effects, atmospheres, and modes of life in each, — one might take the moral census of the population by looking inside of our houses. But that were uncivil, and looking too curiously; we must be content with the advantages the schools open in this respect.

PARENTS' VISITS. The school stands nearest the family of all our institutions,—is indeed an extension and image of it, and claims its fostering interest and sympathy. It should enlist the parents' affection, and get some of their freshest hours. Its teachers deserve to be taken into their hearts as friends, the friends of their children, and their assistants in the work of training them in the ways of learning and virtue. Sympathy is the least they can afford to give for so much bestowed, and the best part of the teacher's success. I fear it goes ill in those families, whose heads are seldom seen inside the school houses, to learn for themselves how their children are managed, and to encourage the teacher by their presence and considerate judgments concerning her school. I know no plea that can be pronounced without shame for any negligence of this kind. The schools are no longer the dismal places some of the old people remember; if they were, who would think of sending his children there, or, sending them, would take his part of the infliction by entering them occasionally. Certainly the place where a child passes so large a part of the most impressible period of his life, should be the resort of his parents sometimes, and be made as charming as possible. Perhaps something of the old prejudice against them as places for mischief and dulness, still lingers amongst us to their detriment. I can vouch for the vivacity and pleasant manners of some of them, to say the least, and confess to the good it has done me to enter them rather often. I may safely recommend a trial to everybody, and advise any who shall fail of being interested from a visit, not to own it, lest they make thereby an unexpected confession. A visit cannot fail to benefit all and parents most if they enter as parents should. Free thoughts and a fresh heart shall find freedom and freshness inside. Dull visitors carry dulness of course, and bring away the dulness they carry. The kindly spirit finds scenes of life and of activity; handsome heads, pleasant faces, mischief sometimes, idleness most likely, but more of diligence and satisfaction reigning. Where these are, the school is cared for if frequently visited; nor are our ends fairly gained till our towns people are awakened to the beauty of the school interest and the schools become attractive places of resort; our best minds contributing their best things to the children and parents. And what more convincing proof can we exhibit, in a country town like ours, of the duty of all good citizens to complete our republican theory of general education for all, by all, in the Commonwealth?

TOWN INFLUENCES. We have great advantages of place and population. Our people still follow the callings and profession of Paradise, whose occupant was a farmer. Next to man culture, agriculture is the eldest of pursuits, and these united are the best means of living. Planters of ourselves and farmers, we cultivate the nobler animal, being members most of us of the Middlesex Society of husbandmen and house-keepers; but we esteem the family crop the fairest we can gather, and see that for its growth and tillage the farms were stocked. Then Concord has retained the primitive manners, and for a village so near the metropolis has still much of the air of the olden time, the population being largely agricultural as from the first, and the descendants of the original settlers remaining to keep their names fresh in our memories. The social refinements and simple habits of our people are highly friendly to the promotion of learning and sobriety. In these advantages the scholars of course largely partake. These social out door influences seem favorably blended for moulding the manners and morals of the people. Boating, riding, field sports and games,—the schools owe much to these also, and in important senses are indebted to them for what our drawing rooms, graced as they may be with the gifts of culture and of virtue, have not to give. So difficult is it to match nature with the corresponding wholesomeness of mind and serve the human needs to the full.

7

Company, conversation, exercise, amusements are foremost studies in the lively university whence our children graduate, getting here the best part of their discipline ;—which is liable of course like all free things to be perverted to uses the worst. Society,—the power of persons and spells of company, the giving and taking of conversation, the fine commerce of personal qualities and gifts,—in fine, an exhalation of life itself ; this is to youth a surprise,—an ecstacy of surprises, and charming from its novelty. Especially are these the more potent in swaying the roving fancy, just coming out of its childhood, and entering the intermediate state, half way between the child and man or woman. To youth the opportunities and humors of village life offer allurements to pleasures which hold a place, to be sure, in their culture, but should be guarded with all the more care and solicitude, as exerting an influence unsuspected at the time on all the coming years of their life.

The town is properly the house the citizens live in, its social hospitalities being the apartments and offices opening out all around. The village comes in for the central share, and is the largest partner in the responsibility. Now were it as wholesome as nature is, then were it an out-of-doors pleasure ground, wherein the children might range unrestrained by check or oversight of their elders, who should seek by all careful measures to make and keep it such, as the guardians of honor and virtue for all. Perhaps our village hospitalities are spread abroad on a scale of wider and more mixed enjoyments than the young can innocently partake of, thus exposing them to some temptations not so easily withstood.

The State's Duties. Every one knows it is more difficult to manage the same number of children in a village than in districts less exposed to the social temptations; there is the greater conceit, and the moral pressure is so much the lighter, while the opportunities are so much the greater for concert and complicity in evil doing. Perhaps little can be done to reach the sources of evils of this kind. Though the State can do little against the wishes of its citizens, it still has duties to perform for them, for it is the parent of parents and their guardian. The best government is what domestic economy is to the household, providing carefully for the breeding and educating into virtue and intelligence of every member of the Commonwealth. Nor can a State resist safely the conviction which facts are fast confirming, of the enormous cost of ignorance, with its consequent crime, impiety and danger. The strong government is best and most popular in the end with all parties. And when power takes the side of the weak against the wicked we cannot have too much of it. The trouble is that legislation comes too late ; its yoke frets the citizen's neck whose passions are unused to the restraints of sobriety and self-rule. A parent may enforce what a State cannot. The virtues may be cherished in the family rightly and legitimately, but when the State sets about dealing with the appetites and passions of its citizens, its right to interfere in these matters shall be questioned gravely, and may be set at nought. They plead indulgence in any evil as their prerogative and personal right, and legislation comes too late. We must begin at the beginning, or any good beginning becomes difficult, if not impossible. The vice of intemperance, for instance, is older by some generations than any set of drunkards or tipplers, or any individual of the set oftentimes, or the generation he lives in ; having been fostered and confirmed by the social customs of his time, his neighborhood, his family, very likely, and only vicarious in him ; and it may need as many influences conspiring to effect its cure. Every transgressor is the State's accuser. Prudence dictates the wisdom, the safety of educating the people to habits of self-restraint, to sentiments of reverence, before committing them to themselves entirely; and this becomes all the more necessary in a government possessing the advantages a republican rule affords. Philo, the ancient republican, said well, " that the State's best policy was to teach the citizens how to govern themselves."

It is difficult, as I have said, to reach the sources of ignorance and consequent crime in a community like ours, calling itself free, and boasting of its right to do what it will. But freedom is a social, not less than an individual concern, and the end of the State is to protect it. The first object of a free people is the preservation of their liberty. It becomes, then, their first duty to assume the training of all the children in the principles of right, knowledge and virtue, as the only safeguard of their liberties. We cannot afford to wait at such hazards. The simplest humanities are also the least costly and the nearest home. We should begin there. The State is stabbed at the hearth-side, and here liberty and honor are first sold. It is injured by family neglect, and should protect itself in securing its children's virtue against their parents' vices ; for by so doing can it alone redeem its pledges to humanity and its citizens' liberties. A virtuous education is the greatest alms it can bestow on any of its children.

> " Some great estates provide, but do not breed
> The mastering mind, so both are lost thereby;
> Or else they breed them tender, make them need
> All that they leave. This is flat poverty;
> For he that needs ten thousand pounds to live
> Is full as poor as he that needs but five."

Says holy George Herbert.

States have ever been too busy with their laws to care for the children primarily and immediately. Even ours, with the best of rulers, is still open to the satire of the philosopher who said he chose rather to play with the children than to be much encumbered with the insufficient management of the Commonwealth; since here, he said, he could play justice and humanity to advantage, and rule a republic wishing to be governed by them, at least.

HORACE MANN. This eminent educator had right notions of the State's and the statesman's duties. He began at the beginning, or if not quite there, with the common school, the nursery of States and the family offshoot whereunto the citizen is born, and sent thence qualified better or worse to serve States and the world at large. His first Report on Education advocated reforms which have been largely adopted and carried into practice to regenerate our morals and manners, and confer stability and honor on the people. Here are a body of arguments for education, showing the cost of ignorance, crime, poverty and disease which States assess and uphold; and suggestions bringing heavily home to us those higher obligations to educate children for citizens and responsible agents in the world. It is pleasing to find what he attempted and perfected as far as the time permitted, at last adopted in good part, and carried far in the direction of his aims, under conditions favorable to final success.

Good purposes never perish nor come to nought; as seeds sown on the snows of mid-winter, they find the earth and take root in the coming spring-time, to bear their autumnal fruits for the future generations.

It is proposed to place Mr. Mann's portrait in all the school rooms of the Commonwealth, and four of our schools have already done this. The money thus contributed goes in part to pay for the bronze statue to be erected in honor of Horace Mann in Boston.

NATURE AND CULTURE. The noblest productions of a people are its best men. They are its praise and prosperity. Every one takes pride in them and in some sort partakes of their gifts. And proud as we are of our privileges, perhaps this healthy sentiment of New England best shows itself in having made every town a schoolmaster, and so opened opportunities for every child's becoming one of its best persons if he will. Yet the best opportunities prove profitless to any but those who can use them. Mother wit graduates all who take the honors and pay for them afterwards. For though culture is this graded affair, we take our schooling as we can get it, often in unsuspected ways, and are least indebted where we think ourselves the most.

Persons first, we are wont to consider, and books next in the order of influence. But both disappoint and deceive more or less ; nature taking the larger share in our culture. Books aid us as we have the skill to use them to advantage ; persons best by indirect means as if they served us not. Nature converts us to ourselves and against our knowledge or consent. For it is still a questionable matter how far our best arts are subordinated to her intents or thwart them ; the art of education being as yet a business of so much difficulty and so complicated and incalculable, that, with all the experiences of past times to aid us, the most striking persons have oftenest been of those who, having escaped the trammels of the schools, were formed by the direct influences of things operating under the pressure of necessity, and what we call accident.

Nature is the armory of genius. Cities serve it slightly, books and colleges chiefly as they celebrate nature. The mind craves the view of mountain, ocean, forest, lake and plain, the open horizon, the firmament — an actual contact with the elements ;—familiarity with the seasons as they rise and roll ; thus getting the grasp the scope and poise which cities fail to confer. Nature is the first school of eloquence ; her images bait the senses to pluck free and fair the befitting rhetoric. A good writer is a pensioner of sun and stars, of fields, woodlands, water, skies, the spectacle of things ;— agencies these, more than libraries or universities— competing successfully for the prizes of inspiration. Take them from the student's landscape and his studies are of small account. Nature contrives to blend her substance with the mind's essence, thus tincturing with life and color the phrases of discourse as neither books nor professions can. Literature shows pale and poor from inside chambers and halls ; and whoever would strike effective strokes for truth and ideas, for the times, must be afoot often and early to import the stuff of things into his thoughts ; the sprightliness and point that tell tenderly and deeply upon the soul of mankind. "Afield all summer and the winter spent in studies in-doors" is the good Anglo-Saxon rule, and as good for the Anglo-American of to-day. We must take the seasons into us, drinking off their cup daily, if we will live in earnest and take life with the zest that life is and the health it gives. For never is the mind weaned from nature or ideas; pasturing at these meadows she plucks their fruits unrestrained loving to be abroad musing and amused.

CORRECTION. Recreation is the sacrament of the mind, the second creation by renewing the exhausted spirits. Country children are less likely to lose from want of out-door exercise than from too close confinement at school. Perhaps both mind and morals would be gainers if the fresh morning hours were set apart for study, the rest of the day being given to exercise. Health is the basis of sanity, the flowering of genius;—eyes, and every sense serving the body and the mind in beauty and bloom. We should feed a boy finely and all the more chastely as he gives himself to study and takes to the liberal learning we wish him to call his: the sound sense, right sentiments, the classic speech, the flowing manners, which an elegant temperance promotes. Mind and body dine together: his meal sharpens his wits or dims them; is a spur to study or mischief as it goes round its circuits. Learning is sweet in itself, let him taste it at the fountains; with keen coy appetites both of body and of mind, let him whet them on relishes for sense or sobriety, enthusiast as he is and greedy of delights. Give him his allowance of satisfactions tempered finely and tinctured with out-door sports, nor separating solemnly his pleasures from his duties: naming these play, those studies, this work; he defines for himself and refines according to his likes, his dislikes. He knows what he likes or dislikes; let us see to their springs in him. Perhaps he is careless about observing the ten commandments he finds written for him, the spoken twenty, being the more curious about how they are kept by his betters in the religion of examples. Words! he has heard rather too many to mind them much: precepts unamiably pronounced to set lovingly by them and take them cordially as he would. Very likely his heart needs changing: well—there is grace abounding and about him correcting its waywardness, if we give as much for the good mediation; he takes all we have for him when thus warmed into life and poured mild and molten into his affections. Be sure the liveliest dispensations, the holiest are his, his as cordially as ours, and sought for as kindly;—we must meet him where he is. Best to follow his bent if bent beautifully; else bending him gently not fractiously lest we snap or stiffen a stubborness too stiff already. Gentleness now; the fair eye the conquering glances straight and sure ; the strong hand if you must till he fall penitent at the feet of Persuasion ;—the stroke of grace before the smiting of the birch : for only so is the conquest complete, and the victory the Lord's.

> " 'Tis vain to flee; till gentle mercy show
> Her better eye the farther off we go
> The swing of justice deals the mightier blow.
> The ingenuous child corrected doth not fly
> His angry mother's hand, but clings more nigh
> And quenches with his tears her flaming eye."

If she is good enough she may strike strong and frequent till thanks come for it; but who is she, much less he, that dares do it more than once, nor repents in sorrow and shame for the strokes given ? Only the " shining ones " may do it for good.

> " Then I saw that he commanded them to lie down, which when they did, he chastised them sore to teach them the good way wherein they should walk; and they thanked him for all his kindness, and went softly along the right way toward the Celestial City."

They say the household pieties are fading fast from our hearthsides and disappearing. How could they remain after the general closing up of the fire-places and the consequent irruption of these Dragons into our drawing rooms backing out the friendly flame, — the old hospitalities all deferred for the Comforter who never comes. Company enough gathered inside with no company in them—and without an altar piece. He said significantly, there were " many mansions in his Father's house," did he forget the children's apartment ?

BEHAVIOR. The graces of behavior spring from a sense of beauty planted in all minds even the meanest, and its prevalence is the symptom of a genial culture distinguishing man or child from the brute he were otherwise. There is a fine religion or the seed and scion of sanctity seen in that blushing diffidence by which the loveliest souls are characterized and shown unconsciously to themselves by implication. A bashful child is still in Paradise, the flush of innocency mantling the cheeks and the maid is apparent there. I consider the case hopeless where reverence is gone and the blush that is its ornament. Any blight is better than shamelessnesss ; no bloom like innocence and simplicity. It is useless, I should say impious to clothe for show merely ; as useless to teach manners as to give innocence : we must guard and keep the last, that the graces of good behavior may maintain the gloss of their own and be fine manners indeed,—an emanation of the soul, and the gesture of the mind ; self-respect and sensibility being their ground work and showing. While the child is pure, the person innocent, there is the fine behavior of necessity and the natural piety that graces its owner as counterfeit piety cannot. Good hearts are always graceful and take captive against any blemishes of nature.

ANCIENT CULTURE. The wise teacher has a tact at discriminating the character of his pupils as portrayed in their physiognomy of countenance and complexion. The Greeks called boys of fair complexions the children of the sun, and those of brown skins they esteemed for their courage. Certainly in these matters of aspect and discipline they had some advantage practically which we have lost. They studied the mind as the subject matter of education, to which they gave the best talent and the whole of life. They were masters and makers of men in senses common and uncommon : for they read the laws of culture from the book of things, and could predict and secure results in the character of their pupils.

Let us see how the Great Master, Pythagoras, went to work.

"He prepared his disciples for learning by many trials. For he did not immediately receive into the number of his associates all who came to him, till he had subjected them to various examinations. In the first place, he inquired after what manner they associated with their parents and relations generally; next, he surveyed their unseasonable laughter, their silence, their speaking when it was not proper; and farther still, what were their desires, their intimacies with their companions; their conversation; how they employed their leisure time, and what were the subjects of their joy and grief. He likewise surveyed their form, their gait, gestures, and whole motion of their body; their voice, complexion, and physiognomy; considering all these natural indications to be the manifest signs of the unapparent manners of the soul. Having thus subjected them to this scrutiny, he next suffered those whom he thought eligible to pass a good while seemingly unobserved by him, that he might the better judge of each one how he was disposed towards stability and a love of learning, and whether he was sufficiently fortified against the flatteries of popularity and false honor and glory. After this he advised such to observe a long silence, that he might observe how far they were — experimentally — continent in speech; and that most difficult of all victories,— the victory over the tongue.

Thus practically he made trial of their aptitudes to be educated, for he was more anxious that they should be modest and discreet than that they should speak unadvisedly. He likewise directed his attention to every other particular; such as whether they were astonished at the outbreaks of immoderate passion and desire. Nor did he superficially consider how they were affected by these; or whether they were contentious or ambitious; or how they were disposed as to friendship and strife. And if, on his surveying all these particulars accurately, they appeared to him endued with worthy manners, he next directed his attention to their facility in learning and memory; first considering, indeed, whether they were able to follow what was said with rapidity and perspecuity; and in the next place, whether a certain love and temperance attracted them towards the disciples by which they were taught, and whether they loved to learn, and to be governed; and how they were disposed as to gentleness, which he called elegance of manners; considering all ferocity of temper as hostile to his mode of education. For impudence, shamelessness, intemperance, slothfulness, slowness of learning, unrestrained licentiousness, disgrace and the like, are attendants of savage manners; but the contrary of these are gentleness and mildness."

I know of no book better deserving the study of teachers and parents than this Life of Pythagoras, from which my extracts are taken. The book is not easily obtained. Mine is a translation by Thomas Taylor of Jamblichus's admiring biography of his master, and contains attractive selections from the Ancients. Everything of his comes commended to us of to-day by its elegancy and humanity, giving us the sense of the worth and wisdom of this founder of the Greek School of Philosophy.

> " In all he did
> Some figure of the Golden time was hid."

In saying this much in his praise I am not blind to some of his defects. But I wish rather to look at his surpassing merits as an educator and thinker for all times. We must remember that we are still using his eyes, so far as most of us have eyes in use, in almost every department of thought and activity into which pure humanity and ideas can enter ; in art, science, literature and religion itself.

"The aim of Pythagoras was at once a philosophical school, a religious brotherhood, and a political association; and all these characters appear to have been inseparably united in the founder's mind. It must be considered as a proof of upright intentions in Pythagoras, which ought to rescue him from all suspicions of selfish motives, that he chose for his school persons whom he deemed capable of grasping the highest truths which he could communicate; and that he was not only willing to teach them all he knew, but regarded the utmost cultivation of the intellectual faculties as a necessary preparation to the work to which he destined them. He instituted a society, an order as we may now call it, composed of young persons, three hundred in number, carefully selected from the noblest families, not only of Crotona, but of the other Italiot cities."

STUDIES IN THE MIND. In common with every interest of a social or spiritual nature, education has shared the misfortunes arising from the extreme absorption of mind in affairs, and the consequent impoverishment of ideas that thoughtful and devout persons complain of so generally. For when the pure mind is forgotten, or dropped aside from men's regards, institutions, men themselves, are already unsound at the core ; the culture and fashioning of men becoming of secondary account.

The mind with its faculties and powers are the tools we use in this work of living. By these invisible implements we deal with things and affairs. Our bodies are handles for them. And the prime office of education is to put us fairly in possession and instruct us in the sleights of their uses; their bearing directly and skilfully upon life and its opportunities. Yet singularly enough we have nearly omitted the Mind from our list of studies, and children grow up instructed better in everything else than in the knowledge and use of themselves. We have no available metaphysics and speak at hazard concerning the springs of thought and sensibility, as if definite perceptions of our powers and implements were superfluous, and self-knowledge might be dispensed with by us without detriment or loss. We teach or affect to teach the encyclopedia of things, but make the merest mention of ideas which give rank to all we know or conceive of knowables; and our youth are growing up, as ourselves have grown, better instructed in all matters else, than in the mystery of the mind. Of physics and affairs all gain some knowledge since these are components of our parts visible and animal, we dealing sensibly with them and daily. But the powers thus engaged are not theirs: they are above and beyond them; metaphysical in essence, and spiritual;—the mind itself, personal and transcendent. Now it may not be easy to present this essence distinctly to our eyesight, distributing its parts as seeming territories of the globe outside of us. Still the teacher and student should enjoy an alphabet and image of its faculties, its modes of operation, its aspects, its traits, as a standard of reference and a scale for his thinking. Let us deal with it tenderly since the mind is the subject of our operations in teaching. And we should endeavor in every lesson to address some sense distinctively as the prompter of the rest, thus aiming at calling forth the mind entire, thus bringing its full forces to bear directly and intensely upon the object of thought or sensibility which our argument requires—sensibility in the teacher touching the sensibility and so quickening thought in his classes. This is inspiration and teaching in the natural method, invoking moreover the supernatural agencies and graces of the spirit.

Life is a suggestion of the Spirit through the mind and giving us news of Him in guise of queries for beginners in the study of it. I print with diffidence a vague anagram or alphabet of the Spiritual Powers in a scale for the black-boards and as means of aiding the classes in their studies. Let them try their wits upon it and help me to revise it from time to time by their illuminations. If it cannot stand this test fairly it is useless and an imposition on their faith and simplicity.

THE QUERESTS AND FACULTIES;

THEIR OBJECTS AND FUNCTIONS.

SPIRIT.

Being.   **God.**

```
WHO?........SOUL.................PERSONS
WHENCE?...INSTINCT............LAWS
WHAT?......CONSCIENCE........RIGHTS
HOW?........IMAGINATION......IDEAS
WHY?........REASON............TRUTHS
WHICH?.....FANCY..............FORMS
WHERE?....UNDERSTANDING..FACTS
WHEN?......MEMORY............EVENTS
```

Body.   **Substance.**

MATTER.

SACRED READINGS.—

> Nor nibble longer there
> Since nothing fresh ye find
> Upon those rocks;
> Lo! meadows green and fair,
> Come pasture here your mind
> Ye bleating flocks.

Our teachers open their schools with readings from the New Testament. And this reading is in some of the schools (and would but for a diffident piety be) followed in all by devotions and the singing of some suitable morning hymn. The spoken prayers and praises are not enjoined by our rules; and we think we show therein that tender courtesy to the faiths of the heart that true piety loves and cannot overstep. An earnest and sweet disposition is the spring from which children love to taste; and best always if insinuated softly in mild persuasions and so leading to the practice of the loves and graces that soften and save. Gentle hearts are not persistent in pronouncing the peace they know preferring rather its sunny smiles and silent syllables, as if suspecting that he

"Who speaks his virtues name or place has none."

A course of readings from the Picture Testament might favor the best ends of spiritual culture. A child should be approached with reverence as a recipient of the Spirit from above. The best of books claims the best of persons and the gracious moments to make its meanings clear, else the reading and listening are but a sounding pretence and of no account. The spirit within must invite and prepare the heart instantly—inspiration answer inspiration and so answering, informing and renewing ;—a Pentacost and an awakening from on high. I have wished these books were opened with the awe belonging to the eminent Personalities portrayed therein, thinking them best read when the glow of sentiment kindles the meaning into life in the morning hour ; the teacher opening her school by opening their leaves. Read otherwise these oracles but touch the ear and fail of their good effects, since, " if they tend not to cleanse the heart, it cumbers the head and cloys the appetite, and men shall do with them as children do with birds, either they crush them or let them fly away."

ANTIQUITIES. It would give an increased interest to our Annual Reports if we had a reduced map of the town, with the several districts and subdivisions indicated and the families in the quarters and neighborhoods. Such a picture would not only be valuable as an historical document for the antiquarian and our towns-people, but a means of interesting the schools in the studies of geography, topography, and localities, besides subserving in many ways the agricultural interests. I have ascertained the cost of a work of that sort, and am told the artist's labors on it would come under a hundred dollars, which includes the best part of the expense that would be incurred in the undertaking. It seems as if this sum might easily be raised by private subscription, as every family would like to have one, the house-holders and land-owners generally. Our town history is one of more than ordinary significance, and though it has been compiled ably by one of our townsmen, the book is out of print, and the Committee have been unable to put copies into the schools as books of reference for teachers and pupils, as they designed. Besides the local traditions are fading out and will soon be obliterated in good part if not rescued soon. The elder people are fast leaving us and taking much with them that their descendants should not suffer to be forgotten. It is good to foster that pride of place which has borne the fruits of good and brave deeds, and so keeps its honors fresh and green in the descendants of the first settlers, especially, when in all our towns though less in ours than most, local causes are fast obliterating the old lines, regardless of spots and boundaries : a dense overgrowth of new concerns fast blotting out the traces of our early history in the several districts. We care for them and every vestige and relic of the olden time : the primitive boundaries, bridle-roads, wood-paths, homesteads: the customs, manners, dialect, dress, their creeds even have a venerable significance yet: the anecdotes that still linger on the lips of our oldest inhabitants ; a well sorted and sifted edition of which would be a relic of information to the young and a valuable contribution to our personal history. Then we are rich enough in having an Herodotus and Plutarch to compile these for us.

Every one knows what sensations attend our surprise at reading familiar names and spots for the first time in print, how literature transfigures the commonest objects and events and makes them new again, makes us children and partakers of the common gifts of our nature. Our landscape wears a plain russet aspect and charm us so, and while some of its pleasing features have been celebrated in prose and song, there remains much of beauty and comfort for the scholars' and poets' pen : and these we have also to say and sing them too. Our town records are still to be read only in their originals.

It might sound a little strange to the ears of even descendants of the first settlers and planters of these grounds, this " Grant of the General Court of the act of Incorporation, dated at Newtown, September 2, 1635."

" It is ordered that there shall be a plantation att Musketaquid, and that there be 6 myles of land square to belong to it: And that the inhabitants thereof shall have three years immunities from all public charges, except training."

All know very well about the training charges and how they were paid : the children recite the story often and visit the spots

" Where walked our fathers when the English braves,
Who deemed they owned the land our fathers' tilled,
Flush with red jackets marched along the banks
Of our slow River creeping to the sea."

Our river winds through the meadows still : and Fair Haven, Nawshawtuc, Walden Pond, Conantum, the Easterbrook Farm, Ponkawtassett, Poland, the Virginia Road, Annursnuck, Winthrop's Place Brother's, Spenser's and Mill-Brook, (Dunge Hole, Hogpen Walk, the Forge, are names now obsolete to us,) are parts and parcel of us daily, all passing into literature for our children if not for us. I take my share of credit for holding fast by the old names of the districts against the scandalous numerals they were threatening to own, and intend they shall resist to the death. Centre shall be centre, not No. 1, and acknowledge its mill-dam, common and square, its meeting house, Buckley's house, Wright's tavern, (Jethro's tree is gone

without recovery) ; then there were the Garrison house and the pound—
outside are the battle ground, the monument, old north bridge, and the
graves. The quarter's East and North, (South quarter has lapsed,)
Bateman's Pond, Barrett's Mill, are fresh as ever, while Factory
Village, Derby's Bridge, Nine Acre Corner, sung to us but yes-
terday. The old school houses are gone, but the spots show new
ones ; and " Grassy-Ground river " with its Concord of Assabet and
Sudbury streams, still runs winding through our farm-lands, still tilled
by farmers, still as ever—

> " The patient earth sets platters for their food,
> Corn, milk, and apples and the best of good."

SCHOOL HOUSES. I think we may take some pride in ours, new as
they are and comfortable, convenient, and for the most part well placed ;
only one or two of them standing apart inhospitably on spots whose
surroundings add nothing to the pleasure the buildings would otherwise give us. Road-forks seem the most inviting places for these little
hives of industry and mischief, taking on so gracefully the ornaments
of shrubbery and of flower-gardens to complete the picture and add
beauty and finish to the landscape. Ours need shade-trees. The
yards of one or two have been platted prettily and set with rose
bushes, to grace alleys and approaches and afford pleasure to the children in caring for and cultivating them. I wish the example may be
imitated in the other districts. Mrs. Emerson has generously repeated
her offer to supply the yards with roses and flower seeds; and if the
sub-committees will second her generosity by planting rows of trees
on the grounds these bleak and lone spots will be charming in a few
years. Play-grounds are matters not beneath the notice of the lovers
of children; they have their share — and an important one it is —
in the culture of body and mind. They should be ample, attractive ;
and were every one as eloquent in their praises as our neighbor in
praise of his flowers, they would presently be made the delight of all
eyes.

[NOTE.] Good Maps are essential in any studies of nature or the heavens. The
Ptolamaic Charts printed in the Coast Surveys, Coale's Essay on Maps and Charts in
the Smithsonian Reports, and Blodget's Chronological Charts are highly commended
by Mr. Thoreau as the best he knows. And Globes are as necessary as Charts. The
High School has one, but the Committee have not been able as yet to furnish them for
the other schools.

SCHOOL PORTRAITS.

The teacher is the frontispiece to the school. He is the central figure of the group; the neighborhood appearing in the back-ground in perspective, its colors all reflected warmly in his countenance from the faces of the children. Any portraitures of the schools must be taken from originals thus living and large to be of any value, and what the schools deserve at the artist's hands. Yet how delicate the task, and venturesome, as difficult as delicate, and short comings at best. One might try his hand at the teacher without so much distrust of his skill: but there is something in a child, in a school of children, in the youthful group not caught at once nor easily, so passing is it, so elusive : like a dove's neck so changeable, like a dream. And one should not wonder if the schools were entered less for their pleasing pictures of our humanity as it seems, but as intimations of those traits of it our eyes wait to see. Pleasing task too and a tempting one might we lift veils from comely faces and yet sink the names.

HIGH SCHOOL.—Mr. E. O. Shepard, Teacher.

Pupils.	Ages.	Pupils.	Ages.	Pupils.	Ages.
Addie E. Adams,	16	Emma C. Hunt,	17	Charles E. Bowers,	17
Martha A. Adams,	19	Carrie Marble,	16	Henry T. Brown,	17
Jennie M. Adams,	17	Mary H. Moore,	14	Hersey Brown,	15
Hattie A. Adkins,	16	Ellen J. Nealy,	16	Charles J. Dakin,	17
M. Augusta Bowers,	15	Ella Pierce,	15	M. Joseph Gleason,	16
Hattie L. Eaton,	15	Eliza P. Potter,	17	Edward Gleason,	17
Anna E. Gregory,	15	Anna W. Stewart,	16	Ephraim M. Hatch,	15
Alice A. Hall,	16	Mary D. Wheeler,	18	J. Galen Hoar,	17
Lizzie Hatch,	19	Mary C. Wheeler,	15	Nathan H. Hosmer,	17
Hattie A. Hoar,	15	Ida A. Wilson,	15	Samuel H. Rhoades,	15
Annie E. Hosmer,	19			Reuben Rice, Jr.,	17
Ella S. Hosmer,	16	Frank A. Adams,	14	Henry Walcott,	15
Susan D. Hosmer,	16	Charles H. Bartlett,	17	Caleb H. Wheeler,	18
Hannah R. Hudson,	14	Cyrus W. Benjamin,	16	Wallace Wilson,	16

We may consider ourselves fortunate in having secured the services of a teacher so spirited and strong as we find Mr. Shepard to be. He has taken the school forward since it came under his charge in a manner most satisfactory to parents and committee. All the scholars are, I believe, his fast friends. He brought good testimonials for his scholarship and ability, and has made these abundantly good in practice. He certainly has the essentials of a schoolmaster for our times; energy, decision, and manliness. I regard him as a good sample of the kind best suited to take charge of our free young people, and suspect he owes his popularity with them to his allowing all the freedom which they ought reasonably to take within the limits of self-respect; and which, if not given, is apt to be taken as due, notwithstanding. All this he allows, reserving a jurisdiction which he makes felt rather than seen in the show of authority; spurring forward by looks and a secret free-masonry which the school understands and instinctively regards. He comprehends the advantages of waiting for the work he wants, as of getting it done seasonably. Then he has the advantage of a good voice, which is no slight merit in a school.

I have occasionally conversed with his scholars on Friday afternoons, at a set hour, and have invited other persons to give the school a conversation or a lecture, though fewer than I could wish have done so.

LECTURES. Mr. Emerson has given the school a conversation on persons and books, telling lively anecdotes of both, interesting the school and offering useful hints about reading and study. He gave them some criticisms on their reading and speaking, read himself from Shakspeare, and recommended some favorite authors for their perusal, namely:

Plutarch,	Shakspeare,
Gibbon's Biography,	Chronicle of the bid,
Franklin's Biography,	Herbert's Temple,
Tom Brown at Rugby,	Scott,
Tom Brown at Oxford,	Life of Socrates.

To which I would add

Emerson's Essays and Addresses,	Holmes,
Channing's Near Home, and other poems,	Cowley's Essays,
	Evelyn's Diary,
Thoreau,	Town and General Histories of N.
Hawthorne,	England and the U. S.,
Whittier,	Biographical Dictionary,
Bryant,	Lippincott's Pronouncing Gazetteer,
Irving's Washington and Columbus,	Worcester's Dictionary.

Mr. Pratt has read an exceedingly interesting paper on Flowers and Flower Culture, giving a catalogue of the principal favorites, and the best mode of raising them in our houses and gardens. Mr. Sanborn has also read a paper on the History of Numbers, full of curious information, and of great interest. Mr. Bull's engagements have prevented his giving some account of the discovery and culture of the Concord grape, as he had partly promised the school. It has lost, besides, I regret to say, something promised by Mr. Thoreau on his favorite theme of Nature as the friend and preceptor of man.

RECITATION. A recitation should be a creative hour, a meeting of master and disciples in genial communion, a dealing with the subject matters face to face, in the free and felt ways of discourse. A rough manner puts the best things out of the head, and makes sages seem simpletons under the stroke. Persons of strong temperament become overbearing often, and against their wishes; they would gladly hold themselves in reserve, but cannot. The consequences are paralyzing, and operate as a panic. Children feel the least incongruity of disposition and recoil from it. Painful to find it standing at the head as driver, never by possibility at the heart of the group as its leader. Touches of tenderness and humor are the natural foils of power in its displays, and particularly in all dealings with children. The good shade kindly and shelter infirmity of any sort; they help the child to find his thoughts, and out of his confessions.

STUDY OF THE MIND. With such views to guide me, I have wished to interest the more advanced classes in the several schools in the study of the mind, for which a place has not been assigned in the order of exercises, owing to the want of a suitable text-book. Believing that something might be done, meanwhile, I have ventured some conversations in some of them, taking our scale of the faculties as a thread for discussion, using the black-board for rendering our analysis the more obvious as we proceeded. It needs more time than we have at command to take soundings in these depths of the life-powers, and deliver them to the light and to the senses. But these attempts, imperfect and unsatisfactory at best, have proved beyond question how easy it is to interest the young in those studies. A sensible teacher shall get ready responses from the Sphynxes, since nothing is so charming to mind as the mind itself when interrogated aptly and to the point. Indeed, this study, conducted ably, would

9

open the Academy for our children and Plato's dialogues be reborn in our school rooms.

THE LANGUAGES. It is a common mistake to suppose that the study of Latin is useless, because it is no longer a spoken tongue, and has even ceased in great measure to be the vehicle of science and learning. Nor is it chiefly for its literature that we should study either the Latin or the Greek, unequalled as the latter is for the wealth of its literature. The mental discipline is what the pupil needs, and what the study of another language than his own best affords him, especially a language regular and fixed, and incapable, because unspoken, of further change in its grammatical forms. The effect of translating from another speech is the best stimulus to thought and a knowledge of our vernacular. Of course the study of Latin can be carried too far; we would not have our children waste their time in writing bad hexameters, or reading useless authors; but there is little danger of excess in that direction. I could wish that all the pupils in the High School learned at least the rudiments of Latin, and that half of them should go through the common text-books. Beyond this few will go, and yet there are fair fields beyond to which the studious few ought to have access. Let me suggest a few books in Latin and Greek which I would gladly see a select class reading during their years in the High School. Cæsar, Virgil, and the select orations of Cicero, are good, but by no means the best Latin. Let the more advanced try Sallust, Cicero against Verres, or his philosophical books, portions of Livy, and most of all in prose, Tacitus. In verse they might glance at Ovid, but read Horace, half of Catullus, and all Lucretius. Juvenal and Persius, Lucan and Martial, and the rest, might be read if there were time. But let no student think he has got the kernel of Roman literature till he knows Lucretius, the fragments of Ennius, Catullus and Tacitus. In Milton's catalogue the Rei Rusticæ Auctores appear very early; of these Cato and Varro are the best, though Columella and Palladius are good. But these we have elsewhere recommended. Pliny's Letters and portions of Seneca might be added.

In Greek we use Xenophon and Homer; but we should add the Memorabilia and the Odyssey to the Iliad and Anabasis. Herodotus by all means should be read, and parts of Plutarch, in spite of his Roman Greek. Æschylus is difficult, but worth the labor. Next among tragedians is Sophocles, though Milton's favorite was Euripides.

Hesiod and Pindar, and the spurious Orphics, may be reached; but
not until the student has tasted a little of Aristophanes in comedy,
and Plato in graceful philosophy. Thucydides and Aristotle are for
the veterans and the thinkers; when one can read them in Greek with
ease and enjoyment, he need not blush to be called a scholar. Professor Goodwin's "Greek Moods and Tenses" will aid the student
greatly, especially in his readings from Demosthenes, whom I must not
forget to name among the foremost in the list. The Euchiridion of
Epictetus and the Meditations of Marcus Aurelius should be read by
all who would know the sweetness of the Stoic philosophy.

EXAMINATIONS.   An examination is one thing and an exhibition
another. The first should be a private matter, and conducted by the
committee and teacher; it should be searching and thorough, dealing
more with principles than the text, more with the motives that prompt
than any special attainments, and taking always the teacher's compe-
tency into the account. A certain tenderness is becoming, seeing but
not declaring too much. We must not put the victims under the com-
pound blow-pipe of a consuming scrutiny, and search amid their ashes
for any merits that may remain there to declare. We see blemishes
soon enough. 'Tis well while seeing to oversee such in the larger cir-
cumspection which detects that striven for, though it may not have
been reached by pupil or candidate. Culture is characterized by
a tender consideration of infirmities; softly reproaching, so far as
reproach is implied in proffering its own eyes, and so leading to the
prospect desired; endowed with a sense of justice also, too just to
impeach any or wound by words even.

Perhaps no examination answered these conditions so well as that
of the High School. There was less to exhibit and more to be examined than usual. The classes were mainly large, and they were
questioned indifferently by teacher and Committee; showing by their
answers that they had studied the subject, as well as the book. Of
the forty pupils, thirty-seven were present, and of these twenty-five
study Latin and nine French. Mr. Shepard seems to have given his
pupils short lessons and shown them how to learn them. A little
more attention to the grammar of the languages studied, would not
be amiss, and we would like to see exercises written in them. In
Mathematics the Committee found much improvment, and recommend
the study of Geometry to be carried farther.

There was very little of the timidity once so embarrassing on exami-

56

nation day apparent at this time. Certainly the school has come far out of its reserve and speaks for itself. Messrs. Sanborn, Farmer, Barrett, Reynolds, and Brown were present, and the school acquitted itself greatly to their satisfaction. There was an air of ease and cheer prevailing, a good understanding between teacher and school, as a consequence of the freedom he allows. I consider this one of the most marked features of improvement under Mr. Shepard's instruction. He strives to be thorough and to ground the mind in principles. Consequently he shares largely in the general dissatisfaction with the current modes of teaching English Grammar, and is hoping to adopt better methods hereafter, by availing himself of suggestions offered in our pages. His studies have lain in this direction, and we hope to see the fruits in his proposed attempts in teaching.

INTERMEDIATE SCHOOL.—Miss M. A. Dillingham, Teacher.

Pupils.	Ages.	Pupils.	Ages.	Pupils.	Ages.
Jennie Barrett,	10	Mary Neagle,	15	Frank Holden,	12
Sarah Benjamin,	13	Anne Reynolds,	13	Charles Holbrook,	12
Alice Brigham,	13	Elizabeth Rhoades,	13	Albertus Hosmer,	13
Kate I. Bowers,	12	Emily Rhoades,	13	Alfred Hosmer,	10
Margaret Byron,	12	Abbie Staples,	10	John Lynch,	18
Julia Carey,	15	Emma Todd,	11	Francis Lynch,	16
Mary Carey,	14	Mary Todd,	13	Norman Meek,	12
Emma Collier,	12	Elizabeth Warren,	10	Charles Monroe,	13
Edith D. Davidson,	8	Mattie Wheeler,	12	John McDonough,	17
Mary Eaton,	11	Amelia White,	14	Patrick Madden,	19
Susan Farwell,	13			Frank Pierce,	11
Mary Foss,	17	Joseph Barrett,	10	Edward G. Reynolds,	11
Mary Garrity,	14	Richard Barrett,	12	Michael Ryan,	14
Minnie Goodnow,	11	Charles Brown,	10	William Shannon,	14
Adelia Hobson,	11	William H. Brown,	12	Frederic Skinner,	11
Fanny Hosmer,	10	Thomas Bulger,	16	Charles Watts,	12
Susan Hubbard,	12	Asa Collier,	13	Charles H. Wetherbee,	15
Mary Kelly,	12	Orlando W. Fay,	13	Frank Wilson,	13
Mary Lynch,	13	Edward Garrity,	16	Charles Walcott,	12
Ellen McManus,	15	Confucius Hayden,	16		
Laura P. Meek,	14	Willard Hobson,	13		

I believe I speak for parents and children in commending this pleasant school so worthy of their confidence. The children have been uniformly studious and respectful during my visits. They are kept close to their studies and to the rules. Miss Dillingham has great skill in getting work done and of ensuring diligence, good behavior and the love of study. I consider her an example of strength, tempered with kindness and good will, cheerfulness and decision. I should like to multiply copies of such winning authority for other school houses in the land.

I have given the school an hour on Fridays during the last term, hearing lessons and conversing with the children. These interviews have been agreeable to me ; the scholars conversing with readiness and sprightliness. I have read frequently from Krummacher's Parables—

a favorite book in all the schools—the Cave of Mammon from Spenser's Fairy Queen, besides the first part of the Immortal Dream. The children testify to the pleasure these readings have given them and have often asked me to come and read again ; a pleasure I shall gladly repeat.

I consider these interviews as the most profitable to the schools of any I am permitted to enjoy in them ; offering us the best opportunities for cultivating the neglected gifts of conversation, the graces of style, and a taste for elegant literature. There has been a culpable oversight in this matter to the disparagement of our language, as a slight observation of the current conversation-of our cultivated people will show. For still, and against the boasts of the schools, the stalk and flower of mother tongue are plucked less by orators and poets than by the innocent and ingenuous young people—the best poets left us. Shakspeare and Ben. Jonson ought not to be bad company off the stage, nor the dictionary expurgated too coyly, nor the fancy dismembered, to spare the modesty of conversation and authorship, on the plea of giving us " English pure and undefiled." Nor should a flood of spirits be sinful ; nor tropes of rhetoric magdalens disgracefully admitted into the sentence. What is thus gained in decorum is lost in strength of expression, in sprightliness, in breadth ; in proof of which, witness the effect following the utterance of a spoken thought, the swell of an emotion, the outbreak of any passion ; and see how the fancy overpasses conventional barriers, leaping, like a boy into the ring, intent on making itself felt and victor forthwith, to the delight and relief of all. Our language is rich, racy, significant ; good for all things and occasions : genius having anticipated for us and made the word, the phrase we wanted, the very one and best ; none so pertinent so consonant ; the current world of to-day accepting the sign and its necessity in the using it. So the human body is the orator's liveliest phrasebook for plucking his plumes from, proffering its figures, blood-warm and flesh-colored to his fancy ; and he who culls gracefully and boldly for speech or page, carries all mankind, the fancy and the heart, at once ;—for the fig leaves are poor shields for hiding illicit fancies however primly disposed or decorously draped, still they blazon the more openly their owner's immodesties—pruriances that shall soil an angel's wardrobe even and pollute the snows.

Proper guards should be set against any abuses of the tongue, of course, and discreet persons, parents, teachers and public men, best know the value of bridles for the fancy as for the tongue : and especially in the ranges of our villages and affairs.

Of the Committee, Messrs. Keyes, Farmer and Sanborn were present at the examination. The classes showed the effects of the teacher's faithful methods in the quickness and general correctness of their recitations. Forty-one were present. The new room set off their pleasing faces, and gave the school a new charm. It was noticed that the Arithmetic classes were a little puzzled by problems requiring thought, and seemed to have been trained too exclusively in the problem of the book,— but we were all delighted with their familiarity with those. The new books have taken well with the reading classes, and both reading and speaking were better than usual. Miss Dillingham is disposed to make trial of Dr. Nutting's new Grammar with one of her higher classes. I think the book an effort in the right direction.

EAST PRIMARY SCHOOL.—Miss Jane Hosmer, Teacher.

Pupils.	Ages.	Pupils.	Ages.	Pupils.	Ages.
Jessie Barrett,	5	Martha Pierce,	9	Robert Downing,	9
Jane Bartlett,	6	Mary Ryan.	7	Harrison Fay,	8
Josephine Bartlett,	9	Catharine Shannon,	8	James Ferguson,	6
Margaret Battles,	6	Annie Skinner,	6	Morton Gannon,	7
Gertrude Bowers,	8	Martha Walcott,	9	James Garrity,	11
Catharine Bulger,	9	Alice Watts,	6	John Garrity,	9
Fanny Burke,	7	Mary Watts,	12	Nathan Haynes,	8
Caroline Dean,	8			Edmund King,	6
Harriet Dean,	12	George Bartlett,	8	Edward Howard,	6
Mary Dowd,	11	James Battles,	10	Francis Lacy,	5
Lillah Downing,	6	John Battles,	7	James McManus,	7
Sarah Downing,	12	James Bulger,		Michael McManus,	12
Ora Foss,	11	Charles Bulger,	7	Charles Mullet,	6
Catharine Gannon,	10	John Bulger,	6	James Nolan,	7
Catharine Garrity,	6	Edward Burke,	8	John Nolan,	6
Elizabeth Howells,	8	James Burke,	6	Martin Nolan,	11
Anny King,	8	Michael Craig,	6	John O'Brien,	6
Margaret Lacy,	11	Joseph Dean,	7	Thomas O'Brien,	8
Ellen McManus,	10	Frank Derby,	6	Everett Reynolds,	10
Mary Murphy,		John Dowd,	8	Patsie Pindus,	6
Catharine McManus,	9	John Dowd,	6	John Shannon,	10
Elizabeth O'Brien,		Frank Dowd,	7	George Walcott,	7
Julia O'Brien,	7	Batty Downing,	8	Horace Walcott,	9
Ida Pierce,	6	John Downing,	12	Willis Watts,	9

Miss Hosmer still gives her best endeavors to this little company of children. Her school is one of the liveliest and busiest of the central primary groups, and shows under every varying aspect and movement the tact and adaptabilities of its mistress, who seems to know just what is in every little head, how the land lies in and out of them, and to serve them one by one as they need. It is a stirring little bevy ; the quick-witted Green-Islanders setting off to advantage the common sense of our children, acting as counterspurs and checks to one another, and working off contrasts agreeable to witness. It must take at least a generation or more at this rate to blend the two peoples into one, and get off a nationality that America can fairly claim as hers. Twenty-two were present.

Young America is fast passing ahead of the New England, as she has outstripped the Old country by a century or so, as if intent on proving the limits of freedom and authority for herself and the generations in advance. Forty-eight were present at the examination. They came neatly dressed, and made a pretty appearance. A class gave the points of the compass, told the streets of the village, the names of the neighboring towns, as an introduction to answering questions on the maps. They have a variety of little songs which they sing at intervals, and some geometrical and other manual exercises. The reading of the Orange Man, from Early Lessons just introduced into the school, showed the courage and confidence accompanying the reading of a text when understood by the reader. Messrs. Sanborn and Farmer were present. The room was tastefully dressed with evergreens, and the performances left a pleasing impression of this school.

NORTH PRIMARY SCHOOL.—MISS SUSAN GOODALL, Teacher.

Pupils.	Ages.	Pupils.	Ages.	Pupils.	Ages.
Elizabeth Flagg,	10	Agnes Edna Tolman,	9	Daniel Hosmer,	11
Abby Garfield,	6	Elizabeth Wood,	11	Herbert Hosmer,	6
Hattie Garfield,	8	Catharine Wood,	10	Edward Keating,	5
Emma Goodnow,	9			Daniel King,	6
Frances Hall,	9	Edward Adkins,	11	Bryan McDonough,	14
Annie Hosmer,	5	William Adkins,	12	Charles Meek,	8
Mary Hosmer,	8	William Bisbee,	8	George Meek,	10
Catharine Keating,	7	Philip Carson,	7	Michael Moore,	8
Lilla Keyes,	6	Nicholas Coclin,	5	Benjamin Nealey,	11
Ellen Murray,	6	John Dowd,	8	Charles Newton,	10
Sarah Murray,	11	Ward Davidson,	5	William Sexton,	5
Alice Prescott,	7	George Flagg,	12	Edward Simmons,	8
Caroline Rhoades,	8	Thomas Foley,	8	Daniel Surette,	5
Ellen Sexton,	7	John Garrity,	9	Louis Surette,	7
Ella Todd,	7	Charles Hosmer,	8	Charles Willis,	12

Here we have a cunning little company, quite young most of them, in a pink of a house, and under charge of a pains-taking, precise, school mistress, assiduously doing her best to maintain the fair repute the school acquired under the excellent management of her predecessor. So much earnestness and intensity should ensure the best success. And the examination proved that her exertions had borne good fruits. The children made a pleasing show, spoke their pieces prettily, and read with fluency and grace. Their skill in marking was noticed, and their singing sweet. Twenty-two were present. Messrs. Keyes, Reynolds and Sanborn examined them kindly. They have been charming listeners to my Pilgrim, stirring and lively — a prompt little Allegory themselves, whose precise meaning, by Bunyan or Spenser, has not clearly transpired.

WEST PRIMARY SCHOOL.—Miss Sarah E. Richardson, Teacher.

Pupils.	Ages.	Pupils.	Ages.	Pupils.	Ages.
Jennie S. Barrett,	8	Agnes Lynch,	7	John Flannery,	12
Elizabeth Bean,	7	Mary McManus,	6	Patrick Flannery,	8
Ella Bigelow,	10	Lucy Reynolds,	9	Willy Garty,	7
Mary Jane Byron,	7	Ida Smith,	7	Horace George,	10
Catharine Byron,	9	Minnie Hall,	14	George Haggerty,	10
Anne Barney,	7	Anne Wetherbee,	10	James Haggerty,	7
Joanna Carey,	10			John Haggerty,	13
Elizabeth Carey,	9	Le Baron Austin,	10	Thomas Haggerty,	5
Mabel Dennis,	8	Frank W. Barrett,	6	Frederic Harlow,	11
Sarah Farrar,	8	Frank Bigelow,	10	Charles Hobson,	8
Ella Gorman,	7	Henry Damon,	8	Cyrus Hubbard,	11
Julia Haggerty,	7	Edward Dempsey,	6	George Hubbard,	10
Ellen Haggerty,	8	James Dempsey,	9	Daniel Lynch,	10
Fanny Hayden,	7	John Dempsey,	13	Stephen Lynch,	13
Elizabeth Hoar,	6	Michael Dempsey,	8	Philip McManus,	7
Ida Hobson,	9	Frederic Dennie,	9	George Tulis,	8
Fannie Hubbard,	7	John Dennie,	8	John Tulis,	7
Mary Lynch,	14	William Fararr,	11	Patsy Tulis,	5

Miss Richardson's good sense and self-possession have taken this mixed school forward far during the year, and done well by it. She is to be commended again for her discretion and moderation; for taking the necessary time, and for her persistency and kindly courage in carrying reserved ends to their issues. Then she has the motherly virtue of not playing "I spies," seeing too much that may be going forward and so extemporizing a culprit at convenience. I think this a grace specially commendable, and wish it may spread as a religion proper for the school-keeping and house-keeping both. Here, at least, it has worked admirably for the spirits and studies as the examination showed. The speaking was spirited; the reading was specially noticed, and the blackboard exercise in marking. We heard some cheerful singing besides. In examining them, the sub-committee of a minister gave an example that should be imitated for its liveliness and speed of questioning, or for kind consideration of their age and capacity. Forty were present, and of the Committee, Messrs. Reynolds and Brown.

They contrived, also, to cast a net over the Superintendent, and did actually catch him in the meshes of their threaded allegory, and got a shiftless speech out of him before they let him out.

EAST QUARTER SCHOOL.—Miss A. F. Hubbard, Teacher.

Pupils.	Ages.	Pupils.	Ages.	Pupils.	Ages.
Susan E. Adams,	15	Mary J. Tibbets,	14	Georgie A. Everett,	10
Lucy Balcom,	5	Sarah J. Tibbets,	13	Harley Gowing,	
Mary E. Bull,	14	Ida M. Tibbets,	10	S. Douglas Mason,	12
Katie Burke,	14	Alice A. Wheeler,	12	John Moore,	7
Virginia E. Cleveland,	15	Lizzie M. Wright,	18	Samuel Nye,	7
Julia Dempsey,	10	Ella Wright,	11	Arthur Paine,	6
Annie Hall,	14			Henry N. Wheeler,	11
Etta F. Hall,	7	Ephraim W. Bull,	11	James Wright,	17
Emma M. Hatch,	8	Johnny C. Bull,	9	George Wright,	14
Amelia Russell,	15	George Clinton,		Eddie Wright,	9
Georgianna Russell,	15	William Connor,	14		
Elmira Russell,	8	Eddie Connor,	11		

This school brightens with time and the accomplishments of its excellent mistress, who brings learning and fine dispositions to her task. She wastes no time on the many impertinences inseparable from the genius of children, but goes forward without perplexity or hurry, as a genial and persistent influence. These graces of learning and of heart have won the confidence of the school and left her free to instruct them agreeably. The order has been uniformly good, a certain republican strength and plain power is intimated in some of the best heads ; we had a recitation on the Constitution in proof of it ; some sound thinking on Grammar and Algebra, with a declamation of the union sentiments in Washington's Farewell Address, and the famous piece "You'd scarce expect one of my age," was in true Boston. A little class recited together the names of the towns in Middlesex County and of the counties in the Bay State. Here too little Frank is a favorite reading book. There were present Messrs. Bull, Sanborn and Reynolds.

The Committee bestowed their unqualified praises, and gifts of pictures were awarded by Mr. Bull to the more meritorious scholars, according to a record of behaviour and scholarship kept by the mistress. They have practiced gymnastics under the lead of an accomplished member of Dr. Lewis' class, as also under the guidance of the teacher. To this gentleman the school is indebted for the gift of a set of apparatus for the games. The sub-committee has taken an active interest in every movement for the good of the school.

NORTH QUARTER SCHOOL.—Miss Sarah A. Brown, Teacher.

Pupils.	Ages.	Pupils.	Ages.	Pupils.	Ages.
Carrie R. Buttrick,	16	Abbot Lawrence,	7	Francis H. Tarbell,	14
M. Lizzie Dakin,	12	Alvin Taylor,	6	Edward P. Litchfield,	13
Ellen F. Green,	9	Rockwood Flint,	15		
Fannie Holden,	7	George H. Hunt,	12		
Emeline A. Stacy,	12	Charlie Green.	8		

Though we have a dozen names in the printed list of pupils for this school, that number was seldom seen on any day seated in the desks ; and several classes consisted of one member only. Several lived at a distance and had bleak paths to traverse, and yet, as if to publish the irregular attendance of some, a resolute boy living at the greatest distance never missed a day during the term, and was earliest at the school every morning besides. Our chairman has made honorable mention of his name, with others, as examples for general imitation. We could wish that parents would feel more generally the importance of steady attendance, and contrive to serve the mind as punctually as the body. The evenings of our winters so friendly to cultivation,

need not be wasted in frivolous or idle ways. While all families have
access to the newspaper and the library, it would seem as if the best
part of education were within the reach of all, and that home life
would of necessity stimulate the mind to greater exertions at school.

Miss Brown has been teaching under many difficulties. She has
done a great deal of honest work here with an earnest heart and a
capable mind, which if not answered by a corresponding sympathy, is
yet helping forward the children in solid learning, and is the best
preparation for her calling elsewhere. Parents will remember the
demonstration of a problem in Cube Root at the exhibition as proof of
her teaching. Six scholars appeared at the examination, and Messrs.
Barrett, Keyes and Reynolds, of the Committee. The black-board
exercises in spelling were very good. The older scholars have had
exercises in tracing synonyms and found the book useful. We saw
some graceful hand writing also.

BATEMAN'S POND SCHOOL.—Miss S. P. BEAN, Teacher.

Pupils.	Ages.	Pupils.	Ages.	Pupils.	Ages.
Ella Adams,	9	Lucy J. Melvin,	11	John Heald,	
Charlotte Adams,	6	Louise Melvin,	8	James Jones,	6
Nellie Brown,	16	Charlotte Stowe,	9	Dennis Keefe,	22
Abbie Brown,	15			Charles Melvin,	15
Lizzie Brown,	12	Benjamin W. Brown,	14	James Melvin,	13
Amelia Brown,	11	Joseph D. Brown,	11	James C. Melvin,	13
Charlotte Brown,	8	Richard Collins,	24	Francis W. Wadleigh,	12
Mary Brown,	7	Micah Collins,	13	Henry Wetherbee,	8

If all schools conducted themselves after the manner of this, we
should have little use for any but the superlatives in speaking of them.
Miss Bean has the credit of being its teacher; but I have never been
able to satisfy myself on that point fully. It is my private opinion
that there are as many teachers as there are pupils, including herself
as one of the last, making just twenty-two of them, and that by some
concert of secret sympathy they conduct the school reciprocally and
admirably together. I will assume this to be so and say that Mrs. Sympathy is certainly one of our best school mistresses, and gives universal
satisfaction to every one—to children, teacher, district, and committee;
as one of the most motherly and mild matrons they have had the pleasure of meeting at the several examinations, and whom they unite in
commending to the admiration of the districts as a perfect model in
her pleasant ways, and so have written her certificate for all time to
come as their preferred candidate for all the schools in town and
elsewhere; for good, better, very best, and as admirable for the
worst. Miss Bean, I believe, agrees with us, and defers her special
claims modestly to her kind comforter who has done so much for her;

and has promised, I understand, to adopt her as her successor when the infirmities incident to persons of her years shall make it necessary for her to decline further service, which we trust will not be during our superintendency of the Concord schools, as we mean to maintain our growing reputation for the superlative, with accessions of admiration for the coming periods forever.

The twenty-two were all present at the examination, and behaved in their best manner, and to the acceptance of the Committee ; Rev. Mr. Reynolds doing his part for the praise and pleasure of all ; Messrs. Brown and Farmer also being present. A little class read charmingly from Frank, then printed their lesson on the blackboard and read from the tablets prettily. The next class of nine read from Rosamond, spelled from dictation, writing the words on the blackboard, and told the story one by one after the reading ; also recited the tables of measures, months, &c., and wrote the figures from dictation ; they worked out sums in the simple rules accurately, and recited some verses, and finished their doings by reciting the story of Pilgrim's Progress without prompting from their teacher, who conducted the exercises of the morning without book.

We heard some graceful reading by the young ladies, who showed a good knowledge of Algebra and American History ; and they gave a Latin translation. There was an analysis given of a sentence by the scale, and by Greene's method. Some maps of Concord drawn on a large scale were exhibited, and our foreign gentlemen read " Longfellow's Launch of the Ship," in classic brogue, analyzed " The quality of mercy is not strained," from Shakspeare, showing a familiarity with the sense and structure. They had a paradigm also on the black-board. We were shown some fine specimens of penmanship; and the letters and diaries of the class of little girls were very curious. The parents as usual were many of them present, and the Admiration Committee rained their roses at the close. This school owes much to the unity of feeling in the district, and the interest and energy of the sub-committee.

BARRETT'S MILL SCHOOL.—Miss M. E. Prescott, Teacher.

Pupils.	Ages.	Pupils.	Ages.	Pupils.	Ages.
Elizabeth Brooks,	9	Mary G. Shaw,	14	John Carter,	5
Eliza A. Carter,	8	Ann A. Winn,	16	Alfred B. Dakin,	12
Ellen A. Carter,	11	Laura A. Winn,	9	Lewis George,	16
Eliza A. Dakin,	11	Sarah A. Winn,	12	George F. Leet,	12
Mary R. Dakin,	9			Andrew Rhoades,	10
Caroline E. Hildreth,	11	George Barrett,	9	Nathan B. Smith,	10
Adaline Robbins,	7	Herbert Barrett,	13	Clevin Winn,	6
Alice Robbins,	6	Stephen G. Brooks,	10	Horace E. Winn,	14
Ella A. Shaw,	8	Herbert Brooks,	7		

Great improvements have taken place in this school and district, owing to the good sense and discretion of the teacher, assisted by the advice and good councils of the sub-committee. Every one is pleased with the change; the school is prosperous, and its acquirements were shown at the examination. Miss Prescott has great practical ability and breadth of action in her teaching. She aims at thoroughness and does what she attempts without too large an expenditure of means. There is a good deal of activity and animation in this school and lively sports without. Miss Prescott has interested herself in Calisthenics and has some manual exercises for varying the studies. She has that best of all graces, the winning manners which children cannot resist. Great accuracy was observable in their attainments at the examination, and a wider range of studies than usual. They were familiar with the arithmetical tables, gave the names of the towns in Middlesex County, names of the counties in the State, and there was some rapid Addition on the black-board. The class in "Frank" had made good improvement in reading. Twenty-three pupils were present, and the Rev. Mr. Reynolds examined them in his best manner. At the close the Mutual Admiration Committee, consisting of Messrs. Reynolds, Keyes, Farmer and the Superintendent, sowed their compliments broadcast, and the Rev. Mr. Ballard, of Carlisle, gracefully addressed the school.

FACTORY VILLAGE SCHOOL.—Miss C. F. Whitney, Teacher.

Pupils.	Ages.	Pupils.	Ages.	Pupils.	Ages.
Lizzie Auty,	9	Emma Puffer,	13	Frank Puffer,	16
Hannah Auty,	6	Abbie Puffer,	11	John Puffer,	10
Ellen Cash,	9	Bridget Ryan,	9	Charles Puffer,	5
Maria Cass,	10	Eliza Ryan,	13	William Priest,	
Ella Casley.		Ella Sampson,	13	Henri Priest,	10
Mary A. Dorothy,	8	Angie Tarbell,		William Ryan,	12
Nancie Hayward,	18			John Ryan,	11
Lillian Hayward,	12	Jonas Auty,	7	Franklin Stone,	
Laura Hayward,	12	George Carr,	15	Nelson Wood,	14
Emma Hayward,	6	John Cass,	13	Michael Wale,	14
E. Hosmer,	12	Melvin Church.		Gilman Willis,	12
Clara Hoar,	10	Edgar Church.		Charles Woodbury,	12
Martha Leonard,	9	Frank Munroe,	8	Howard Willis,	10
Alfarata Noyes,	12	Clarence Moor,	10		
Janiata Noyes,	12	Edward Nolan,	11		

I am sorry this school has lost its excellent teacher. Miss Tincker was called home a few weeks before the close of the last term, and her place was taken by Miss Whitney. It is hoped she may remain for the coming year. The school enjoyed uncommon advantages under its former mistress. She has energy, tact, practical sense, decision, and dealt well with her mingled materials; the school being mainly composed of children from the village, and needing just the gifts of command which she possessed and used so efficiently in their management. There is a deal of mischief in young heads, and all the more cunning as they are bright and sure to break out unless they are kept busily about something interesting for the time and absorbing. This is the largest of the schools in the outer districts and of late has had the reputation of being the least manageable of any. But Miss Tincker found ways of engaging hers agreeably ; she sent them out to play when they were tired, refreshed her exercises by a variety, putting a class under the tuition of an advanced scholar, wasting no time in needless supervision which should be given to teaching. It was a working school under her guidance ; a business matter, alive, and delivering results with surprising rapidity and freshness. She taught them the use of books and the necessity of thinking and reasoning, insisting on clearness and precision of statement and utterance in everything undertaken ; more especially in arithmetic, spelling and reading, in all which her scholars are superior. They excel in penmanship, in singing, in which she led with spirit and melody. We had an example at our exhibition that all remember. I think for perfection of drill and power of spurring forward she has no superior.

I regret that on the occasion of her leaving the school and at the late examination, the weather prevented my being present. I have understood that the children parted with her sorrowfully, and the district would have gladly kept her with them. Considering the difficulties attending the management of this school, arising from its mixed elements, and the unfortunate situation of the school-house, it might be advisable to offer better inducements to the teacher, so that any temptation to leave might not arise by advantages offered in other places.

NINE ACRE CORNER SCHOOL.—Miss R. M. Stearns, Teacher.

Pupils.	Ages.	Pupils.	Ages.	Pupils.	Ages.
Lizzie M. Garfield,	10	Frank Edson.		Edwin Wheeler,	15
Sarah F. Lee,	11	Joseph Fitz Patrick,	10	Harvie Wheeler,	13
Henrietta Miles,	13	Herbert Haynes.		Elbert Wheeler,	11
Mary Lizzie Wheeler,	10	Thomas Heyhoe,	19	Alvah Wheeler,	12
		George Heywood.		Cyrus Wheeler,	8
Daniel Callagan.		Granville Miles,	15	Willie Wheeler,	9
Alfred Dakin,	12	Edward S. Wheeler,	17	David Williams.	
James Edson.					

Our quiet and capable school mistress goes through her daily round of duties with measured promptitude and success. Taking the school from one of our gifted teachers, she has had the more difficult task of maintaining its reputation for solid strength and smartness. I believe she has acquitted herself to the acceptance of the district. The scholars retain their former enthusiasm for study and they have the art of getting at what the books contain. This appetite for information seems a little peculiar to our Nine Acre Corner Republic and looks as if these sober young citizens had no thoughts of being cornered but stood ready to conquer any thoughts invading their territory. This school still wears its business air and plain manners. It is full of sense and intelligence, goes straight to the work, knows as well how to do it, as when it is done, and can give the proof and reasoning if asked for. The scholars use the black board for almost all their exercises and daily practice has made many of them very handy at figures and the pen and pencil. Geography is a favorite study, they speak patriotic pieces and sing a variety of songs of which the " Echo" is the liveliest. The late·snow storm on the day set apart for Examination prevented the attendance of the Committee.

In framing our sketches I have not been unmindful of the delicacy of my task. I have aimed at drawing what I have seen in the schools and to portray their spirit as reflected in teacher and taught. 'Tis useless to blazon blemishes—and wicked beside. Art, literature and religion deal with life ; with what is, and not with what is not. It is the living images that grace our firesides and schools in which the children see themselves, whose likeness they carry in their hearts, that concern us.

Gentlemen, I am sure you are feeling with me,—what in the absence of our Secretary you will wish me to say,—that any report of our Schools were incomplete if his services as a teacher and a man were passed in silence. In adopting him so affectionately to its heart the town is harvesting some first fruits of that liberal spirit, learning and practical ability, which have made our village the resort of so many young persons to grace our drawing rooms and make classic our streets by their lively airs and accomplishments.

In closing, allow me to thank you for that courtesy and confidence which has given me the opportunity of spreading these suggestions before you. I wish they may be promotive of good. Accustomed as we are to speak in terms of commendation of our school system, it behooves us to make the most of its extraordinary privileges. You, Mr. Chairman, must feel gratified in having revived this earnest of our first planters as a town experiment : I believe you have the sympathy and support of our citizens, that all are glad to avail themselves of the ancient wisdom and foresight. I am sure they will spare neither pains nor possessions to make these tell directly on the generation committed to our keeping and who are fast rising into heads of families and members of the Commonwealth. We cannot be reminded too often of their principles, nor quote the admirable summary they give of these on the title page of this my Annual Report,—now

Respectfully submitted.

A. BRONSON ALCOTT.

CONCORD, April 1, 1861.

THE SCHOOL EXHIBITION.

Saturday, March 16th, the day first appointed for this annual festival, opened with a severe snow storm, in consequence of which the Committee of Arrangements postponed the exhibition to the following Monday. At the appointed hour — 1.30 P. M. — the Town Hall was nearly filled with the happy faces of the children and the expectant parents and friends, who had come in sleighs or on foot from all parts of the town. At precisely two o'clock the Chairman called to order, and the performances went on according to the following

ORDER OF EXERCISES.

Remarks by the Chairman.

Prayer by Rev. Mr. Reynolds.

Remarks by the Superintendent.

SONG.

Air, — "All the Blue Bonnets are over the Border."

I.

March, march, mothers and grand-mammas!
Come from each home that stands in our border!
March, march, fathers and grand-papas!
Now young America waits in good order!
        Here is a flower show,
        Grown under winter snow,
Ready for spring with her sunshine and showers;
        Here every blossom grows
        Shamrock, thistle and rose,
And fresh from our hillsides the Pilgrim's May flowers.

217

II.

Here is the New World that yet shall be founded;
Here are our Websters, our Sumners and Hales,
And here, with ambition by boat-racing bounded,
Perhaps there may be a new Splitter of rails.
        Here are our future men,
        Here are John Browns again;
Here are young Phillipses eyeing our blunders;
        Yet may the river see
        Hunt, Hosmer, Flint and Lee
Stand to make Concord hills echo their thunders.

III.

Here are the women who make no complaining,
Dumb-bells and clubs chasing vapors away,
Queens of good health and good humor all reigning,
Fairer and freer than we of to-day;
        Fullers with gifted eyes,
        Friendly Eliza Frys,
Nightingales born to give war a new glory;
        Britomarts brave to ride
        Thro' the world far and wide,
Righting all wrongs, as in Spenser's sweet story.

IV.

Come now from Barrett's mill, Bateman's blue water,
Nine Acre Corner, the Centre and all;
Come from the Factory, the North and East Quarter,
For here is a Union that never need fall;
        Lads in your blithest moods,
        Maids in your pretty snoods,
Come from all homes that stand in our border;
        Concord shall many a day
        Tell of the fair array
When young America met in good order.

INTERMEDIATE SCHOOL. — Miss M. A. Dillingham.

Song. — "This is our yearly jubilee."
Recitation. — "Then and Now."
Recitation. — "There is a reaper whose name is Death."
Song. — "Do Good."
Recitation. — "Shamus O'Brien."
Song. — "Little bird, little bird, come to me."
Concert Reading. — "Autumn," from Hawthorne.
Recitation. — "Watchwords."
Song. — "There is no home like my own."

EAST CENTRE PRIMARY SCHOOL. — Miss Jane Hosmer.

Song. — "We are little flower buds."
"The Little Classmates."

NORTH CENTRE PRIMARY. — Miss Susan Goodall.

Song. — "Come and join us, dear companions."
Recitation. — "Contented Life."
Recitation. — "Marian's Dream."
Concert Recitation. — "The Rainbow."
Recitation. — "We are Seven."
Song. — "Cleanliness."
Recitation. — "Willie and the Apple Tree."
Recitation. — "The Ants."
Recitation. — "Jesus, tender shepherd, hear me."

WEST CENTRE PRIMARY. — Miss S. E. Richardson.

Song. — "Vacation Days."
Dialogue. — "Boston Boys and Gen. Howe."
Song. — "Gentle Annie."
"Pilgrim's Progress."
Recitation. — "Minutes."
Recitation. — "The Union."
Exercise Song.

Remarks by the Secretary.

RECESS.

EAST QUARTER SCHOOL. — Miss Abbie F. Hubbard.

Declamation. — Extract from "Washington's Farewell Address."
Children's Geographical Exercises.
Reading. — "In Rome."
Recitation. — From "Evangeline."
Gymnastics.
Song. — "Bonny Eloise."

NORTH QUARTER SCHOOL. — Miss S. A. Brown.

Recitation.
Song. — "The Chrystal Hunters."
Explanation of Cube Root.
Declamation.

BATEMAN'S POND SCHOOL. — Miss S. P. Bean.

Scenes from "Pilgrim's Progress."
Printing.
Reading in Concert.
Dialogue. — "The Mathematician."
Reading.
Declamation. — "I love little Pussie."

BARRETT'S MILL SCHOOL. — Miss M. E. Prescott.

Song.
Dialogue. — "What is most beautiful."
Geographical Chant.
Dialogue. — "Metaphysics."
Manual Exercises.
Song. — "Johnnie Sands."

FACTORY VILLAGE SCHOOL. — Miss C. F. Whitney.

Song. — "Light Canoe."
Declamation.
Dialogue.
Song. — "Happy Land."

NINE ACRE CORNER SCHOOL. — Miss R. M. Stearns.

Declamation.

Song. — "The Seasons."

Spelling.

Dialogue. — "The Four Wishes."

Song. — "The Echo."

Dialogue. — "The Letter."

___

HIGH SCHOOL. — Mr. E. O. Shepard.

Speech by Charles E. Bowers.

Remarks by Mr. Shepard.

Song. — "Farewell, ye kind friends."

___

Remarks by Mr. Emerson.

___

Song. — "Auld Lang Syne."

Mr. Keyes spoke briefly, and in this gave an example which all the speakers followed. He said that this was the children's day, and that the Committee had no wish to engross the time. He would give over to the Schools, their Teachers, and the Superintendent, the whole of the afternoon's exercises, hoping that all present would remember that the praise of what they would see was their own praise, as parents and citizens, and the failure, if there should be any, was also theirs; and that the Committee could justly receive neither credit nor blame.

The Rev. Mr. Reynolds then offered prayer, after which the Superintendent, Mr. Alcott, addressed the company as follows:

"Parents, Friends, and Townspeople:

This is our day of jubilation, the anniversary of the mind for our schools, assembled now for their offerings to their parents and friends. Auspicious is the occasion, with its sunshine and snow, the suitable rhetoric for innocence. We think you have come with love and hope; we will try not to disappoint expectation.

"But we have no speeches to make; the day is the children's—the young people's. We, the Committee, can only do our best to show them to advantage as they bring forward the fruits of their season, and spread them before you. We think you will like them right well. It has fallen to the Superintendent of the grounds to show them as they present their gifts from the separate plots and parks of our school domain. He knows how impertinent any delay would be. You are all waiting, not for words from him, but for things done and spoken to your senses. Let him stand behind the screens and advertise the comers as they rise. And first a strain from the bards of our *arboretum* shall open our exercises."

Mr. Emerson then read Miss Alcott's lively song, which was charmingly sung by Misses Wilson, Hosmer and Adams.

The Superintendent then introduced the Intermediate School — fifty in number — "fresh varieties from our conservatory," he said ; " good stocks, and music hopping about from twig to twig." This school is the largest in town, and appeared excellently, both in its songs and recitations. To be sure, it had the advantage of coming first, which in a long afternoon is no small thing.

The East Primary School sent to the platform but twenty-five of the sixty pupils present, but these represented all the families in the District, and did the work of sixty. Mr. Alcott named them " samples not grown under glass, foreign and native flowers together, lively exotics, but they sing, too, and speak." They fully justified this description by their active and melodious exercises. Their pretty dresses, too, and the flower baskets which they bestowed so gracefully on the Committee, might well prejudice us in their favor. Certainly this school and the town owe much to Miss Hosmer.

The North Primary School was represented by twenty-one pupils only, sickness having much diminished its numbers. They were described as "too tender, some of them, for transplanting, but musical also." Their songs and recitations were much applauded, and the innocent boldness with which the little things spoke and sung. We shall hardly venture to call any names where all did so well — except the faithful teacher's.

The West Primary School sent forty-three pupils. " Varieties again," said the Superintendent, " domestic and imported, but all patriotic and revolutionary, Unionists, too, and can drill. Yet they dream, and can tell their dreams." One of their most characteristic performances was their recitation of the story of Pilgrim's Progress, in a manner entirely their own. This showed at once their way of receiving the Superintendent's instructions, given from this immortal book, and was gratifying to him and to all. The patriotic and Union-loving pieces were much applauded. All did great credit to Miss Richardson.

The Secretary's speech was of the briefest kind, expressing the hope that this festival would be perpetual, and the entire satisfaction

of the Committee with it.   After this a recess of ten minutes gave all
the children a mouthful of fresh air.

Mr. Thoreau being kept at home by sickness, his place was filled by
Master Freddy Harlow, who surprised the Superintendent by presenting him, in the name of the school children of the town, with a fine
copy of George Herbert and of Pilgrim's Progress.   Master Harlow
said :

" Mr. Alcott :

The children of the schools of Concord ask you to accept these
books, thanking you for your mild and wise counsels, and the interest
you have taken in us at your monthly visits."

Mr. Alcott replied :

" Children :

You have given me the very books I wanted most to put into my
library ; and both mine now by your choice and gift.   The Pilgrim's
Progress I value more than any book, perhaps, in the world.   It was
the first book that interested me deeply when a boy scarcely older than
the youngest of you ; and I borrowed it again and again from a cousin
of mine who had a beautiful copy of it, though not so beautifully illustrated as this costly book which you have given me.   I did almost
covet it as it lay at Mr. Stacy's bookstore, borrowed it to look at,
and kept it three weeks, I believe, before I could return it ; for I felt I
was not rich enough to buy it.   But you have now enriched me by
making it mine.   I thank you heartily for it, and the sweet book of
poems, its mate ; I shall thank you every time I look into either.
The Pilgrim's Progress is a sacred classic, and so is this.   Now, to
show you how glad you have made me, I will promise to come and
read them to all of you in all the schools in my very best manner.
Thank you, thank you."

Miss Hubbard's East Quarter School was introduced as " The Concord Grapery, whose clusters you are now to taste."   None of the
schools exhibited more individual character than this, or had a greater
variety of exercises.   Their declamations and dialogues were spirited
and amusing, their badges set the children off prettily, their Geography was well conned, and their dumb-bell gymnastics were lively and
rhythmical.   They numbered twenty, and bore faithful witness to good
training at school and at home ; and we thought we could see, too,
evidences of the good works of the resident committee man.

The North Quarter School is the smallest in town.   Its proportion present was as good as that of some other schools, yet it sent but six. Their performance was good, especially the demonstration of the problem in Cube Root. It was a hard nut to crack, but it was done, as Mr. Alcott assured us it would be, when he named the North Quarter "the Nut Grove." Miss Brown has shown admirable qualities in the management of her small flock — which ought to be increased.

The Bateman's Pond " Posy Bed," as Mr. Alcott said, came next, numbering eighteen pupils. The first recitation from Pilgrim's Progress, different from Miss Richardson's class performance, showed, like that, into how good ground the seed of allegory had fallen. By this time the children were growing tired and restless, and it was not so easy for Miss Bean to do her school justice as for some of those before her. One needs to visit the school itself to see how effective her work is.

Miss Prescott's "Beehive," from Barrett's Mill, swarmed next, eighteen in all. They buzzed about Geography in a very audible style, and the spirit of their songs and speeches overcame the fatigue of the children, and showed the activity of their teacher.

Miss Whitney next set the spindles of the Factory Village running merrily, to the number of twenty-five. The children did well, and their part was well closed by the melodious voice of one of the older pupils, whose gift at song attracted universal notice, both this year and last.

From the Nine Acre Corner, Miss Stearns brought sixteen pupils. This was the Conantum Park and Orchard District, we were told, and called to note the flavor of Baldwins and Russets. Coming so late as they did, these exercises were less lively than some, but showed diligence and faithful teaching.

The High School marshalled thirty-five pupils for the platform, and presented Master Bowers as their spokesman, who said :

" One year ago the School Committee conceived the plan of bringing all the schools of the town together, for the purpose of introducing the teachers and scholars to each other ; and also to afford the parents and friends an opportunity to witness the progress that had been made, and enjoy an innocent and pleasant entertainment.

" To us it was a season of unalloyed enjoyment, and I would take this occasion to thank the Superintendent and Committee for their kind interest in our behalf. The favorable manner in which our friends welcomed us, and the generous plaudits that greeted our humble performances, induced the Committee to promise a similar entertainment at the close of the next school year.

" I said that last year all the schools participated in the exercises. To-day one takes no part. In behalf of that one,—the Concord High School,—I wish to assure you that it is from no spirit of alienation or rebellion that we do not appear to-day. We have not seceded; ' secession ' is a word we have erased from our vocabulary. Our union is fraternal and indissoluble. It is cemented in pleasant friendships and in generous purposes to qualify ourselves to act well our parts in the great drama of life. To this union we hope to be forever loyal. But the time being limited, and the number of schools to be exhibited so large, we have deferred our exhibition until Saturday evening next, at 7 1-2 o'clock, when with the assistance of our accomplished teacher, we will do our best to give you a pleasant evening's enjoyment.

" Before closing, I wish to thank you for the interest you take in our welfare ; for the opportunities you afford us for the highest culture. We hope none of us will disappoint your expectations. Young as we are we are not unmindful of passing events. The extremity in which we find our country at the present crisis will inspire us with a love of justice and freedom. Its history presents no period so interesting or sublime as the one in which we are called to be actors. Thank God, the past is not the present. For its opportunities and duties we are not responsible. It is for us to discharge the high duties that devolve on us, and carry our race onward.

> ' New occasions teach new duties, time makes ancient good uncouth;
> They must upward still and onward who would keep abreast of truth.
> Lo! before us gleam her camp-fires; we ourselves must pilgrims be,
> Launch *our* Mayflower and steer boldly through the desperate winter sea,
> Nor attempt the future's portal with the past's blood rusted key.'

" Dark as the present hour is we will not despair ; fearful as is the present crisis we have faith that righteousness and justice will triumph.

> ' Gray Plymouth rock hath yet a tongue, and Concord is not dumb;
> And voices from our fathers' graves, and from the future come;
> They call on us to stand our ground, they charge us still to be
> Not only free from chains ourselves, but foremost to make free.' "

Mr. Shepard, teacher of the High School, then spoke in the name of the teachers. He said :

" I had promised to say something upon this occasion, but I had not purposed, nor do I now intend to do anything half so formal as the announcement upon the programme might lead you to expect of me. At this late hour, and after the bright examples of the ' soul of wit,' set me by my elders, it would ill become me to detain you with formal remarks.

"I am glad of this opportunity in behalf of the teachers to tell so many citizens of Concord what our brief residence among you has taught us to think of you, and to thank you for the generous treatment which we have always received at your hands.

"We have all been delighted,—I think that is not too strong a word, —with what we have seen and heard this afternoon from the different members of this promising family of schools. I need say nothing of this. But back of this singing and speaking and acting, I see what is to me the pleasantest feature of it all—the spirit among the citizens that prompts this union of the schools and carries it out so harmoniously. Nowhere but in New England, and nowhere in New England but in Concord, would such a plan have been thought of, or if thought of in the minds of a few, it would have gone no further.

"I speak of this, because to me it is only another expression of the truly catholic spirit which pervades your whole community,—and which raises it above all sectional jealousy and personal prejudice. We, the teachers, see it in the policy of your school committee—in the liberal scope they give to us in our work—in the provisions they make for the wider culture of the scholars by placing within their reach books outside of the ordinary routine of school studies, such as Plutarch's Lives, Pilgrim's Progress, and selections from the poets. If at any time the committee have seemed to depart from this liberal policy so far as to recommend a plan which had simply the 'virtue of economy,' I am sure they did so because looking upon it as a *temporary* arrangement it seemed the best that could then be made.

"It shines out in the life of your Superintendent, whose genial smile and pleasant words brighten our school rooms from week to week—to whom we owe what we have enjoyed to-day and to whom, for his quiet but culturing influence upon your children you owe more than you can ever repay.

"This liberal spirit is seen also in the eight beautiful homes for those schools, which adorn your town. I trust we 'shall soon see it manifested still further in the erection of a handsome building for the High School, which I can assure you from my actual experience in the little room below, is absolutely demanded of you, and that without delay.

"In conclusion, let me say if there is any one thing outside of my school and its associations to which I can attribute the love and admiration which has grown up in me for Concord, it is the same whole

2*

souled principle of thought and action manifested in the every day life
of all classes of her citizens.	It appears in the salutation by the way-
side — at the firesides of your homes — in the social gathering — ev-
erywhere.	Whether this is owing to your glorious history or to the
influence of the private life of your distinguished men and women of
to-day, or to both of these, it matters not.	Enough that it is here —
and while Concord may well be proud of that history and these famous
men and women, she may take a juster pride in keeping active this
principle of liberality that distinguished herself.

"I cannot better express my thoughts of you than in the words of
your own poet, Channing, who sings the praises of New England by
describing the daily life and homes of his own townsmen :

> But all about me live New England men,
> Their humble houses meet my daily gaze—
> The children of this land where Life again
> Flows like a great stream in sunshiny ways;
> It is a joy to know them, and my days
> Are filled with love to meditate on them,
> These native gentlemen on Nature's hem.

> Who sings the praise of women in our clime—
> I do not boast her beauty or her grace,
> Some humble duties render her sublime,
> She the sweet nurse of the New England race,
> The flower upon the country's sterile face,
> The mother of New England's sons, the pride
> Of every house where these good sons abide."

The Intermediate School now took the platform again and sang a
parting song.	Amid some confusion of the little folks Mr. Emerson
said a few words to the children and their parents.	He had served
his campaigns in the public schools years ago, but such a day as this
revived old recollections.	He spoke of the style of declamation as
needing some attention and quoted a story from Alexander Carlyle to
the purpose.	He also alluded with much feeling to the death of young
Faulkner, so well known here for his scholarship and his virtues.	In
conclusion he declared the highest interest of the state to be the training of its children.

While the company sang Auld Lang Syne the children were served
to the cake and fruit which had been provided in an ante-room.	Bas-
kets and plates were quickly emptied by the hungry ones, and with a
pleased and satisfied manner the assembly broke up,— not however
before the Chairman had read the names of those pupils who during
the year had been neither absent nor tardy.

The whole number of pupils in the schools during the year has been 405. There were present at the exhibition at least 300, and probably 325, or 50 more than last year. The exercises were a little protracted ; with this exception everything went to the satisfaction of all, and as children and grown people went home in the dusk of evening we are sure they wished for many returns of such a day.

HIGH SCHOOL EXHIBITION.—In consequence of the severe storm of March 21st, blocking up the highways, the High School Exhibition announced for the evening of the 23rd has been postponed to April. We regret that this will prevent our giving an account of it.

REPORTS

OF THE

SCHOOL COMMITTEE,

AND

SUPERINTENDENT OF THE SCHOOLS,

OF THE

TOWN OF CONCORD, MASS.,

WITH

A NOTICE OF AN EXHIBITION OF THE SCHOOLS

IN THE

TOWN HALL,

ON SATURDAY, MARCH 15TH, 1862.

CONCORD:
PRINTED BY BENJAMIN TOLMAN.
1862.

REPORT.

The School Committee organized on the 1st of April, 1861, by choosing the former Chairman and Secretary, and on the 6th of April re-elected the former Superintendent. Their mode of action, though less laborious, has been substantially the same as for the two former years. Leaving the Superintendent, as heretofore, to give a general view of the schools, we would present some special considerations.

I. POWERS OF THE COMMITTEE. We fear it is not generally known how extensive are the powers, granted by law and sustained by judicial decisions, now lodged in the school committee. These officers, though chosen by the towns, are in reality filling a State office ; they continue in power for three years, they have practically an absolute control of the school money raised by the town and appropriated by the State, they have the selection and dismissal of teachers, the admission and rejection of pupils in all the public schools, and the power of compelling the attendance of all children between the ages of eight and fourteen, unless disqualified by some mental or bodily malady, at some school for at least twelve weeks in the year. These and many subordinate and included powers are placed in their hands by the State, and cannot be annulled by the parent or the town. Of course they are subjected to a legal responsibility, but whenever they are accused of maladministration the law presumes they have acted properly till the contrary is clearly proved. It may be doubted if there is in the Commonwealth another office to which, within its proper field, so much authority is allowed,—or any in which it is so little liable to abuse. The committee are supposed to be chosen for some natural or acquired fitness, they can scarcely find opportunities for serving their own interests, and since they deal with a public interest common to each family, they are made socially responsible to all their neighbors of both sexes. These considerations ought to be kept in mind by all interested in the public schools ; and it should be remembered, farther, that no school can be useful to the public which is not well classified as well as well taught,—that graded schools, especially, require a careful system of admission and exclusion to make them of any advantage, and that the chances are always in favor of making this system too lax, rather than too rigid. Nor can any of our citizens complain that the laws of the State or the regulations of the committee are obscure or difficult of access, since the former are arranged as a manual in the last report of Gov. Boutwell to the Board of Education, of which every school district in town has a copy, while the committees' rules are printed in our last report for every tax-payer of the town, and have been besides distributed to every family and posted in every school house.

II. The High School.   What has just been said is of importance in connection with the present condition of the High School, and we would call the attention of the town to it.   This school is established for the benefit of the more advanced scholars of the whole town ; it is supported at an expense much greater than that of the other schools, and therefore should be made as effective as possible.   To do so, it should admit only those qualified to carry on profitably the proper studies required by law or custom to be taught therein.   If others are allowed to become members of the school, they only clog the classes and waste the time of the teacher.   Furthermore, the size of the present rooms of the High School sets a limit to the admission of pupils.   A room which can only seat forty, of course should not be used for fifty or any larger number.

At the end of the last school year the number of pupils in the High School was forty-one, — the average attendance thirty-seven. The number on the register this winter has been fifty-six,—the average attendance forty-eight.   In the opinion of the committee these numbers are too large and should be reduced.   To what is the increase owing, and how can the evil be remedied ?

We answer, it is owing solely to the unreasonable desire of children or their parents to be admitted to a school which they think it more reputable to belong to, or which has greater advantages than others, and to the good nature of the committee, who have allowed such pupils to enter and to remain in the school, though they were unable or unwilling to keep up with their classes. The evil may be removed by giving the High School teacher the charge of a preparatory department, to be taught by the present assistant,* in the Intermediate School room, and admitting into it the upper class in the Intermediate School; while the lower classes in that school should be removed to another school house, and put under a separate teacher. In this way the High School might have forty pupils in each department, and the Intermediate School would seldom rise above that number; while the time of the High School teacher could be devoted mainly to the teaching of the higher branches such as properly fall to his share.

The committee unite in recommending this change in the present organization of the High School, since it does not increase the expense or the labor of the teachers, and they further recommend that a new room be obtained for the Intermediate School.

III. School Discipline. In nearly all our schools there are serious obstacles to a regular and thorough course of discipline. Some of these are the irregular attendance of pupils,—their absence in the latter part of the day in consequence of " getting dismissed,"—their unwillingness to obey the rules made by the teacher, and the want of hearty support of the teacher by the parent. The evils mentioned have become so common as to require notice here :

1st. *Irregular Attendance.* By a reference to our Table, it will be seen that while the whole number of pupils in the schools last summer and fall was 449, the average attendance was but 343 1-2, or little more than three-fourths. During the past winter the whole number was 406, the average attendance 327 1-3, or about thirteen-sixteenths of the whole. What has made this average so low? The frequent and chronic absence of about a hundred pupils for whose instruction the town pays. Of course some of these absences were unavoidable, but if parents would seriously consider that a day's absence every week takes away half the benefit of the school unless the child

---

* It will be seen by referring to the Superintendent's report that we have employed an assistant in the High School, who has also taught classes from the Intermediate School. Miss Hunt filled this place for a few weeks and was succeeded by Miss A. P. Hosmer, who has done much to improve the efficiency of both schools.

is very studious, and that frequent absences give the teacher much additional labor and vexation, we feel sure that the absences could be diminished at least half.

Quite as important, though less noticed in the school registers, is the loss of time by early dismissing pupils at their own or their parents' request. There are thirty school hours in a week,—if a child daily gets excused for an hour and a half, which is not uncommon, it amounts to seven and a half hours in the week, or a fourth part of the whole. It might be well to make a rule allowing each scholar only so many excused hours,—say one a week,—and that only on the written request of the parent. The improvement in the child's progress would soon show the advantage of such a rule.

2nd. *Insubordination.* There will always be pupils who find it inconvenient or disagreeable to obey the rules of the teacher, and when this unwillingness to submit is encouraged at home, as is sometimes the case, the pupil is apt to become a constant source of trouble in the school. The authority of the teacher has been of late years so much limited by public opinion that there is little danger of its becoming excessive; indeed one fault of all the children now growing up is that they are too little subjected to reasonable authority, at school and at home. Would it not be well then to allow the teacher all the means of discipline remaining in her power, and ought not the parents to have sufficient confidence in the mild and conscientious young lady who teaches their children, not to lessen her already scanty authority? A common way of testifying dislike of a teacher is by taking the child from school; this may sometimes be advisable, but such cases are very rare. An incompetent teacher is usually better than none, and to indulge a child's whim against a teacher is one of the surest ways to make that child's education impossible.

In connection with this subject should be mentioned the bad consequences of school children frequenting the shops and places of amusement in the village. Setting aside the chances of their meeting unfit companions, and being too early introduced into the amusements of men, the waste of time alone is a sufficient reason for forbidding such a practice, and accordingly the committee have made a rule that no pupil during school hours shall visit any saloon or bowling alley, under penalty of being dismissed from the school. A greater watchfulness on the part of parents will make this rule almost useless,—but the necessity for it is obvious.

IV. SCHOOL HOUSES. The location of the school house in District No. 4, has long been a subject of discussion among the residents of the district, and the committee now feel bound to recommend to the town a change of location ; the present one not being, in their opinion, the best for a large majority of the district. The school house, as is well known, stands in a bleak and unsheltered lot, the nearest dwelling house and *well* being nearly a quarter of a mile distant. Since it was built, now fourteen years ago, eight new houses have been built at the Factory Village, while at the east end, not a single new home has been established. By an examination of the following abstract of the registers for the last ten terms, it will be seen how large a proportion of the scholars are from the Factory Village :

No. of scholars from the Factory Village :	No. of scholars from the Pail Factory :	No. of scholars from the East End :
29	4	5
33	3	10
32	2	6
34	3	6
36	2	4
33	4	3
33	6	7
37	4	5
31	6	9
23	5	8
321	37	63

Here is an average of more than thirty-two from the Factory Village, and of just ten from the rest of the district. There are now in that village thirty-four children between the ages of five and fifteen years,—a greater number than in any school in town outside the centre. This does not include the five children sent by Mr. Richardson to the nearer school in Acton, for which we this year pay the sum of $22,50.

We therefore recommend that the school house be removed to a lot of land, (which will be given to the town for the purpose,) near the west end of the woods lying between the railroad and the highway, and about half a mile west of its present location. This point is found by measurement to be about as near the Pail Factory as the present location is by the road. There will be but four families,— those of Messrs. Derby, Sampson, Gross and Tarbell,—seriously inconvenienced by this change, while at the west end *thirty-one* families will be half a mile nearer the school.

This is on the supposition that several families living at the extreme east end be transferred to the centre district, whose schools they have in past years occasionally attended.

An additional reason for making this change is that owing to the distance of the school house from any dwelling where the teacher can board, we have paid for the last few years an increased salary in this district.

The committee would also bring to the notice of the town, what has already been referred to,—the need of a new school room in the centre of the town. If the town should not wish to incur the expense of building, at present, it may be possible to hire such a room as is needed,—and we are informed that the school house owned by Judge Hoar can be obtained.

V. Superintendent's Report. Since the new organization of the committee, three years ago, the town has had the services of a Superintendent of Schools, whose zeal, ability and devotion have proved his eminent fitness for the office. He has brought to his work extraordinary endowments and long experience, and he has doubled or trebled the labor required of him by the terms of his office. He has worked, too, not only for the town, but for the State and the world; for his annual reports, widely circulated and received with appreciation, have done much to advance true ideas of education in other towns, and throughout the land. The town's liberality in publishing such reports has been well bestowed; but this year it has not been thought best to occupy so much space in this way. We continue, however, to print the names of the pupils in each school, and have added a list of the books actually used by each teacher. Under the High School list we have also printed the names of books authorized in any of the schools.

The school regulations are re-printed with some alterations.

The usual tables are annexed to our report.

J. S. Keyes, Chairman,	District
F. B. Sanborn, Secretary,	No. 1.
G. Reynolds,	
E. W. Bull,	No. 2.
F. A. Wheeler,	No. 3.
E. C. Damon,	No. 4.
J. B. Farmer,	No. 5.
J. D. Brown,	No. 6.
Nathan Barrett,	No. 7.

Concord, March 17th, 1862.

FINANCIAL STATEMENT.

The amount placed at the disposal of the Committee by vote of the town was:—

Appropriation for Schools,	$3300 00	
Income Cuming and Beaton Fund,	94 00	
Income Massachusetts School Fund,	95 55	
Unexpended balance of last year,	221 83	
		$3711 38

Which has been expended as follows:—

Mr. Shepard, teaching High School, to date,	$900 00	
Miss Hosmer, teaching female department of do.,	124 00	
Proportion of fuel and care of rooms,	80 88	
Books, chalk and incidentals,	19 32	
Total cost of High School, 40 weeks,		$1124 20
Miss Dillingham, teaching Intermediate School,	$246 00	
Proportion of fuel and care of room,	80 88	
Books, chalk and incidentals,	14 36	
Total cost of Intermediate School, 40 weeks,		$341 24
Miss Goodall, teaching North Primary School,	$195 00	
Fuel, care, books, chalk, &c.,	42 65	
Total cost of North Primary School, 39 weeks,		$237 65
Miss Hosmer, teaching East Primary School,	$195 00	
Fuel, care, books, chalk, &c.,	40 78	
Total cost of East Primary School, 39 weeks,		$245 78
Miss Richardson, teaching West Primary School,	$195 00	
Fuel, care, books, chalk, &c.,	44 46	
Total cost of West Primary School, 39 weeks,		$239 46
Miss Hubbard, teaching East Quarter School,	$190 00	
Fuel, care, books, chalk, &c.,	49 54	
Total cost of East Quarter School, 38 weeks,		$239 54
Miss Stearns, teaching Nine Acre Corner School,	$195 00	
Fuel, care, books, chalk, &c.,	42 57	
Total cost of Nine Acre Corner School, 39 weeks,		$237 57
Miss Moore, teaching Factory Village School,	$202 00	
Cash paid Acton for scholars from the district,	22 50	
Fuel, care, books, chalk, &c.,	60 55	
Total cost of Factory Village School, 39 weeks,		$285 05
Misses Prescott and Buttrick, teaching Barrett's Mill School,	$195 00	
Fuel care, books, chalk, &c.,	38 64	
Total cost of Barrett's Mill School, 39 weeks,		$233 64
Misses Bean and Brown, teaching Bateman's Pond School,	$195 00	
Fuel, care, books, chalk, &c.,	36 77	
Total cost of Bateman's Pond School, 39 weeks,		$231 77
Miss Brown, teaching North Quarter School,	$195 00	
Fuel, care, books, chalk, &c.,	24 98	
Total cost of North Quarter School, 39 weeks,		$219 98
Total cost of Schools, teaching,	$3049 50	
Fuel, care, books and incidentals,	566 38	
Total cost of Schools,	$3615 88	
Unexpended balance,		$95 50
		$3711 38

SCHOOLS.	TEACHERS.	SUMMER.		WINTER.		No. over 15.	No. under 5.	Wages per month.	Length in weeks.	SUB-COMMITTEE.
		Whole No. of Scholars.	Average Attendance.	Whole No. of Scholars.	Average Attendance.					
High School,	Edw'd O. Shepard, Miss A. P. Hosmer,*	51	46	52	48	39	0	$800‡ $20†	40	J. S. Keyes, G. Reynolds,
Intermediate,	Miss M. A. Dillingham, Miss E. C. Hunt,*	62	44	60	45	2	0	24	40	F. B. Sanborn.
North Primary,	Miss Susan Goodall,	68	39	44	31	0	2	20	39	J. S. Keyes, Nathan Barrett.
East Primary,	Miss Jane Hosmer,	55	45	41	38	0	0	20	39	F. B. Sanborn, E. W. Bull.
West Primary,	Miss S. Richardson,	57	45	59	48	0	3	20	39	G. Reynolds, E. C. Damon.
East Quarter,	Miss A. F. Hubbard,	22†	20	30	27	3	0	20	38	E. W. Bull, G. Reynolds.
Nine Acre Corner,	Miss R. M. Stearns,	22	20	25	20	12	0	20	39	F. A. Wheeler, E. C. Damon.
Factory Village,	Miss Emma Moore, Miss M. E. Prescott,	46	34 1-2	36	28 2-3	1	3	21	39	E. C. Damon, F. A. Wheeler.
Barrett's Mill,	Miss A. Buttrick,	31	23	25	21	2	4	20	39	J. B. Farmer, J. D. Brown.
Bateman's Pond,	Miss L. Brown, Miss S. P. Bean,	21	15	19	15 2-3	2	2	20	39	J. D. Brown, J. B. Farmer.
North Quarter,	Miss S. A. Brown,	10	8	15	12 1-2	0	3	20	39	Nathan Barrett, J. S. Keyes.
	Total,	445	339 1-2	406	329 1-3	62	14			

*Miss Hunt preceded Miss Hosmer. Both were assistants in the two schools, High and Intermediate.

† Estimated.—Register not received. ‡ Wages per year.

REGULATIONS.

SECT. 1.—All the Schools in town shall commence at 9 o'clock, A. M., and 1 o'clock, P. M , and close at 12, M., and at 4, P. M., except the Centre Schools, which may commence in the afternoon at half-past 1, and close at half-past 4. The Teachers are required to observe *punctually* the hours of closing as well as opening the schools, and to be present ten minutes before the opening of the school in the morning.

SECT. 2.—The government of the Schools is entrusted by law to the Teachers, and they are expected to preserve strict order and discipline, and to pay constant attention to the language, the manners, and the conduct of the scholars in and about the schools.

SECT. 3.—The schools shall be opened in the morning by reading the Scriptures, and it is recommended that the Lord's Prayer, or a short written or extempore prayer, be offered.

SECT. 4.—No book shall be used in the schools without the sanction of the Committee.

SECT. 5.—If a scholar be absent from school, he or she shall bring a written excuse from the parent or guardian.

SECT. 6.—It shall be the duty of the Teachers to see that no injury is done to the school houses or the premises belonging to them ; and if there is, to give immediate notice to the Committee. Also, to see that their school rooms are properly swept, warmed and ventilated.

SECT. 7.—The schools shall keep five days in a week,—the High School giving Saturday for a holiday,—the Intermediate and Primary Schools Wednesday and Saturday afternoons, and the other schools adopting either course as the resident member of the Committee may decide. The following shall be holidays also : Fast and Thanksgiving, the 19th of April, May Day, Fourth of July, Agricultural Fair, Christmas, New Year, and the 22d February.

239

SECT. 8.—Teachers will be allowed to visit each school in town once during the year, and for this purpose only, to devote one afternoon in a month, making in all cases the appointment therefor beforehand, and also will be allowed one afternoon in each month, if the Sub-committee do not object, for an excursion with the pupils, or a visit with them to other schools.

SECT. 9.—Candidates for the Intermediate School shall be able to read correctly in Hillard's Second Class Reader, and to spell and define common words. They shall pass a satisfactory examination in Colburn's Primary Arithmetic, in the four ground rules of Written Arithmetic, and in Cornell's Intermediate Geography as far as the 19th page ; and be able to point out and define the parts of speech and the marks of punctuation, and to write their names legibly.

SECT. 10.—Candidates for the High School shall be able to pass a satisfactory examination in Reading, Spelling, and Grammar, and be able to parse, analyse, and write correctly common sentences in prose. They must be familiar with the sounds of the letters, with accent and punctuation, and pass a good examination in Greenleaf's Common School Arithmetic as far as Proportion ; in Cornell's Geography and Maps, and in the History of the United States, and be able to write a fair hand.

SECT. 11.—Scholars may be admitted into these schools twice in the year, but in no case without the written permission of the Committee.

SECT. 12.   No pupil shall be allowed to visit any saloon or bowling alley between the hours of 9, A. M., and half-past 4, P. M., under penalty of being dismissed from the school.

Per order of the Committee.

F. B. SANBORN, Secretary.

Revised, March 17th, 1862.

REVISED LIST OF BOOKS.

Sanctioned by the Committee.

For the Teachers' Use.

Picture Testament.
Pilgrim's Progress.
Krummacher's Parables.
Shakspeare, Milton and Thompson.
Gleanings from the Poets.
Plutarch's Lives.
Bailey's Etymological Dictionary.
Webster's Dictionary.
Williams' Book of the Constitutions.

Primary, Intermediate, and other Schools.

Philbrick's Tablets.   Worcester's Primer.
Mrs. Barbauld's Lessons and Hymns.
Miss Edgeworth's Early Lessons.
Sargent's Readers.
Town's Progressive Speller.
Emerson's Primary Arithmetic.
Colburn's First Lessons.
Greenleaf's Common School Arithmetic.
Hawthorne's Parley's History of United States.
Weld's Grammar.
Fowler's Manual of Conversation.
Fowler's Book of Synonyms.
Lovell's Young Speaker.
Sharpes' Diamond Dictionary.
Payson and Dunton's Writing Books.
The School Bell Singing Book.
Letter Books and Diaries.

HIGH SCHOOL.

Classical and French Books.

Andrews' Latin Series.
Arnold's Latin and Greek Series.
Moore's Virgil.
Johnson's Cicero.
Sophocles' Greek Grammar.
Xenophon's Anabasis.
Homer's Iliad.
Fasquelle's French Grammar.
Fasquelle's Reader.
Chouquet's French Lessons.
Nouvelles Genevoises.

ENGLISH BOOKS.

Sargent's Fifth Reader.
Eaton's Arithmetics.
Loomis' Geometry.
Sherwin's Algebra.
Hill's First Lessons in Geometry.
Olmstead's Astronomy.
Well's Natural Philosophy.
Well's Chemistry.
Cornell's Geographies.
Fitch's Physical Geography.
Tenney's Geology.
Smellie's Natural History.
Gray's Elementary Botany.
Quackenboss U. S. History.
Manual of Agriculture.
Manual of English Pronunciation and Spelling.
Worcester's Comprehensive Dictionary.
Hanaford and Payson's Book-keeping.
Letter Books and Diaries.

The Books authorised in the High School may be used in the other schools of the town.

Pursuant to law a sufficient supply of the above books has been procured, and the same can be obtained at A. Stacy's Bookstore, at cost.

REPORT

ON THE

CONCORD SCHOOLS,

TO THE

SCHOOL COMMITTEE,

FOR THE YEAR 1861-'62.

BY A. BRONSON ALCOTT,

SUPERINTENDENT.

SCHOOL COMMITTEE OF CONCORD FOR 1861, '62.

THE VILLAGE OR CENTRE,
INCLUDES THE

NORTH PRIMARY SCHOOL,   EAST PRIMARY,

HIGH SCHOOL,

WEST PRIMARY,   and   INTERMEDIATE.

District
No. 1.
{ JOHN S. KEYES, Chairman,
  F. B. SANBORN, Secretary,
  GRINDALL REYNOLDS,

No. 2.	EPHRAIM W. BULL,	The East Quarter.
No. 3.	FRANCIS A. WHEELER,	Nine Acre Corner,
No. 4.	EDWARD C. DAMON,	The Factory Village.
No. 5.	JACOB B. FARMER,	Barrett's Mill.
No. 6.	JOSEPH D. BROWN,	Bateman's Pond.
No. 7.	NATHAN BARRETT,	The North Quarter.

A. BRONSON ALCOTT, Superintendent.

DUTIES OF SUPERINTENDENT OF THE SCHOOLS.

I. VISITS.—The Superintendent shall make all the visits required by law, and such others as shall be necessary from time to time.

II. REPORTS.—He shall make a report to the committee at their regular monthly meetings of the condition and wants of the several schools, and shall attend said meetings for the purpose of affording the committee information ; and he shall also at the end of the school year make to them in writing a detailed report of the condition and operation of the several schools, with suggestions for their improvement.

III. POWERS.—He shall have and exercise in concert with the sub-committee for each school all the powers and duties of the general committee over the admission, classification, and discipline of the scholars in said schools.

IV. GENERAL OVERSIGHT.—The aim and object of the Superintendent shall be to elevate the standard of the schools, increase the average attendance and awaken the interest of the pupils, improve the methods of teaching, and promote a better understanding between the different teachers, and between the teachers and the parents of the pupils.

SUPERINTENDENT'S REPORT.

Gentlemen of the School Committee :

I conceive this year has been an advance on the past in the general prosperity of our schools. The attendance has been better generally, and they have been managed with greater ease to the several teachers. There has been nothing, so far as I know, to break the harmony heretofore existing in the districts and neighborhoods throughout the town ; the relation between families and the schools, between these and the teachers, has been every way agreeable. There has been but one change of teachers since the school year came in.

MONTHLY VISITS. Your Superintendent has established very pleasant relations with the children and their teachers. Thus far, I have walked mostly on my monthly rounds, visiting two schools a day in the outer districts, seldom more in the centre. Half a day affords time for observing how the schools are taught and managed ; more were desirable to give to each school if one had it at command, and could devote himself to this good service. It is my practice to take the schools as I find them, follow the classes as they come up before their teacher, whose manners and methods I am to note, without causing interruptions of her usual course of exercises : asking sometimes the privilege of making remarks, or of reading, or of conversing, towards the close. I wish my visits to be seasons of enjoyment and associated with scholarship, with behavior, and the mind ; seasons to be thought of afterwards and remembered with interest and delight. I believe in the efficacy of accosting children as children, and persuasively ; esteeming such supervision of the schools as most becoming their monthly visitor and Superintendent.

I know of no readier means of varying the routine of a school than in offering lectures, readings, and conversations occasionally. It seems a graceful way for parents, and persons of the learned class particularly, for all lovers of children, to give pleasure to them and their teachers ; and one of the best ways in which the town should

3

claim the use of its best men and women. Owing to the civil troubles of the country, I have not asked attendance at the school houses, for discussing the general subject of schools, as on former seasons.

PILGRIM'S PROGRESS. The children, from the Intermediate to the Primaries, have now heard the first and second parts of Pilgrim's Progress read to them, and have expressed their unqualified interest in it, the smaller ones especially ; nor have they been displeased with the running conversation on the images and incidents as we read ; the playful sallies and applications, the paraphrased renderings, and comments on the text, to suit their moods and dispositions at the moment. There has been no lack of hands raised for more; dream on longer being the general vote ; and, at the several interviews, they have had a glimpse of pleasures in reserve in the show of leaves still to be read, but now turned to the very last one, and the story closed. I have thought their parents would not have been out of place had they been sitting occasionally beside their children, for a single reading at least, if no more, and tasting at the springs of innocency and delight also.

Books like this, and the hour for enjoying them, are a need of every family, every school, and of every day spent in them. Nor have we good right to children's attentions, save by the complaisance that attractive lessons and influences shall win. If ours, they are ours, by lively baits mostly, and for moral ends and uses altogether.

> " You see the ways the fisherman doth take
> To catch the fish; what engines doth he make?
> Behold how he engageth all his wits,
> Also his snares, lines, angles, hooks, and nets,
> Yet fish there be that neither hook nor line,
> Nor snare, nor net, nor engine can make thine;
> They must be groped for, and be tickled too,
> Or they will not be caught whate'er you do."

The English people are about raising a monument to Bunyan's memory. 'Tis a late, but fitting, token of respect, shown to the genius that has insinuated a livlier spirit than the schools had to give into the fancy and heart of the nation for these two hundred years past, and has interpreted the Christian faith, to old and young, as even the church, with every advantage of learning and ritual, could not. And here, in Bulkley's town, for a season, our children have enjoyed the lights of his pleasing allegory, and cherish his Pilgrim's Progress with an affection scarcely second to that they have for any volume in the library of the family or Sunday schools.

THE NEW TESTAMENT. The New Testament has been used as a class book from the foundation of our schools, but not always in the best manner. Read in course, and without regard paid to its fitness to the ages of the classes, it neither answers the ends of learning or religion, but becomes a pretence and a hindrance. It should be so used as to be fresh ever and attractive to the youngest listeners as to the readers, and secure the reverence it deserves from all. Its narratives and parables have a charm for all ages, and the memorable sentences in which it abounds, the divine life it portrays, cannot be impressed on the memory too early, or laid too soon to heart. Read simply, and by a teacher imbued with its spirit, it must enkindle the spark of piety, latent, if not glowing, in every young heart; thus aiding the ends of life, of religion, and serving the interests of the family and Sunday schools in ways most useful and becoming. There is preparatory work to be done for every child, for fitting him to make the most of his advantages while in school, and after he leaves it. The morals nurse the mind, and with these education properly opens.

THE PICTURE TESTAMENT, including the Sacred Narratives, is the best selection for morning readings of any that I know of, and should have the preference as a class book in our schools. An American edition of this attractive volume is much needed for them, and for private use in families.

I trust we retain something of the Puritan besides the name we praise. Certainly we cannot have too many helps to genuine piety; nor can we spare the young any advantages of religious culture which our times afford. They ask all the nurture and supervision school and family can give them, all the church and State can render; nor is their virtue safe, nor our institutions fast planted, till these are freed from the dominion of the worst in them by assistances from the best above them : the spirit of goodness that alone succors and saves. All history shows that man is an animal, and no more, till he reasons, and worships something better and higher than himself.

RURAL CULTURE. The State has anticipated and done something towards supplying a prime want of education for the people, in preparing a Manual of Agriculture, for using in our schools, and by farmers and housekeepers. And her proposed endowment of the College of Technology, including, as it does, a school of natural history (and we trust of rural affairs), proves her sympathies in the means of providing a wholesome system of popular culture. The publication of the Rustic Authors, beginning perhaps with "Columella's Husbandry," would add other claims on her munificence, and serve the people in the best way of any within the State's power to confer on the community.

It should be the State's first aim to ensure a homestead to every citizen ; and of the church the duty to see that this be kept in a wholesome condition ; since without those advantages man has neither self-respect nor a country. And if a like enthusiasm could spread amongst the towns generally, for improving the human population, especially the children, that is already kindled in our farmers for improving the soil and the better breeds of cattle, we might speak with the greater consistency and pride of something that might properly claim to be human culture ; the growing of man, as the best crop our acres and families could harvest, for the State and the country.

An agricultural town like ours has many advantages for the training of youth that a city has not. It permits a freedom not allowable there, and promotes health and good morals. Then its opportunities for labor and recreation, so conducive to these, are friendly to every other accomplishment. Education, indeed, in the large and comprehensive sense, is scarcely possible elsewhere than in the country, and amidst the social advantages which a rural population affords.

SHADE TREES. With our shaded walks along the village already planted, the school yards may now claim their share of the town's bounty ; a liberal allowance of which, I doubt not, will go for their ornament, as for the comfort of the children, who like the shady side of things sometimes as well as their elders. A school house is an orphan without trees and shrubbery ; and some of ours, standing in their loneliness apart, appear motherless and deserted to your Superintendent, till he finds himself fairly past their horrors, and inside of them.

In conformity with our former practice, we now give some notices of the several schools, in their order ; of their management by the respective teachers ; the books used ; interspersing occasional observations on methods and defects of teaching ; the wants of the districts ; along with the committee's examinations, and the children's names. Some account of the Annual Exhibition of the schools, in the Town Hall, follows in a supplement.

SCHOOL PORTRAITS.

THE GOOD TEACHER plays the double part by the mind, combining in due proportions the requisite sensibility and intelligence. Perhaps nothing has wrought a more beneficent change in our schools than the entrance into them, of late years, of young women as teachers. For, as the perfect Mind is of both sexes,· finely conjoined in disposition and sympathy, woman brings the better half and best, if we may not have both abreast and conspiring in the art of instructing. There is a brute vigor proper to animals, a savage intelligence, repulsive always and the dread of children, ill-suited to mould the manners and the mind. "Knowledge," says Plato, "is not easily implanted by force and violence; but by gentleness, accompanied with art, and by every kind of invitation."

PRIMARY SCHOOLS.

EAST PRIMARY SCHOOL.—MISS JANE HOSMER, Teacher.

Pupils.	Ages.	Pupils.	Ages.	Pupils.	Ages
L. Gertrude Bowers,	9	Elizabeth O'Brien,	10	Joseph Dean,	5
Jane Bartlett,	6	Martha Pierce,	9	Harrison Fay,	9
Jessie Barrett,	5	Ida Pierce,	6	Martin Gannon,	7
Mary Brennan,	13	Mary Ryan,	7	John Gannon,	5
Frances Burke,	8	Catherine Shannon,	7	Edward Howard,	6
Margaret Battles,	7	Alice Watts,	7	Francis Lacey,	4
Kate Bulger,	10			James McManus,	8
Lillah Cotton,	8	George Adkins,	9	Thomas McManus,	5
Lizzie Cary,	9	George Bartlett,	8	Martin Nolan,	12
Kate Cary,	6	Edward Burke,	8	James Nolan,	7
Caroline Dean,	8	James Burke,	6	John Nolan,	6
Lillah Downing,	5	James Battles,	9	Thomas O'Brien,	9
Mary Gillooly,	6	John Battles,	7	Michael O'Brien,	5
Catherine Gannon,	9	James Bulger,	10	Patsie Pinders,	6
Elizabeth Howell,	9	John Bulger,	5	Everett Reynolds,	10
Margaret Lacey,	10	Charles Bulger,	7	Frank Reynolds,	5
Louise Melvin,	9	Michael Craig,	6	John Shannon,	10
Catherine McManus,	10	Bartholomew Downing,	8	William Watts,	10
Mary Murphy,	4	Robert Downing,	10	Horace Watts,	5
Julia O'Brien,	7	Frank Derby,	5	George Walcott,	7

BOOKS.

FOR THE TEACHERS' USE IN THE PRIMARY SCHOOLS.

New Testament, | Krummacher's Parables,
Pilgrim's Progress, | Webster's Dictionary.

Philbrick's Tablets,
Tower's Gradual Primer,
Tower's Introduction to Gradual Reader,
Miss Edgeworth's Easy Lessons,
Hillard's Second Class Reader,

Colburn's First Lessons,
Cornell's Primary Geography,
Cornell's Intermediate Geography,
Payson and Dunton's Writing Books.

EXAMINATION. Of the thirty-six on the present list for the term,
thirty-two were present. The committee listened with great interest
to the exercises of the several classes, and bestowed much praise on
the general good reading and spelling. The singing, too, was sweet
and simple. A large number of the parents came to the examination.
I am sure nobody else could have done what Miss Hosmer has for
this school, considering its peculiarities of race and condition; and it
is pleasant to find that every family owns its indebtedness to her extraordinary and successful endeavors for its prosperity.

WEST CENTRE PRIMARY SCHOOL. — MISS SARAH E. RICHARDSON, Teacher.

Pupils.	Ages.	Pupils.	Ages.	Pupils.	Ages.
Jane S. Barrett,	9	Margarette Lacy,	12	Orra Foss,	12
Lizzie Bean,	8	Francis Lacy,	5	John Garrity,	
Kate Byron,	10	Mary McManus,	6	William Garty,	7
Mary Jane Byron,	8	Lucy G. Reynolds,	10	Horace George,	11
Lizzie Carey,	10	Eliza Ryan,	15	Frank George,	5
Joanna Carey,	11	Alice Reynolds,	6	Ambrose Gorman,	5
Kate Carey,	6	Ida Smith,	8	George Haggerty,	10
Adelia M. Dennis,	9	Alice Stowell,	5	James Haggerty,	9
Mary Edson,	10	Mary Ann Wall,	14	John Haggerty,	14
Hannah Edson,	6	Annie Wetherbee,	11	Charles Hobson,	8
Sarah Farrar,	9			George Hubbard,	10
Jane Garty,	5	Le Baron Austin,	9	Philip McManus,	7
Joanna Gleason,	4	Frank W. Barrett,	7	Arthur Meehan,	8
Ella Gorman,	9	Henry S. Damon,	10	Cornelius Murphy,	5
Julia Haggerty,	8	Michael Dempsy,	8	Martin Nolan,	12
Ellen Haggerty,	6	Edward Dempsy,	6	John Nolan,	7
Elizabeth Hoar,	7	John M. Dennie,	8	James Nolan,	5
Ida Hobson,	10	James Edson,	12	James Russell,	5
Lily Hobson,	6	Frank Edson,	8	Edwin Warren,	10
Fannie E. Hubbard,	8	Patrick Flanery,			

Philbrick's Tablets,
Hillard's Second Class Reader,
Edgeworth's Early Lessons,
Tower's Second Reader,
Colburn's Arithmetic,

Emerson's First Part,
Cornell's Intermediate Geography,
Cornell's Primary Geography,
Payson and Dunton's Writing Books.

EXAMINATION. Here are fifty-eight children, and of these forty-
seven were present. The exercises were exceedingly good, particularly those in writing on the black-board — a large number of the
children writing a flowing and even clerkly hand, and that too with a
speed of execution surprising to the committee. The reading was
sprightly, and their voices sweet and cultivated. The variety of
speaking and singing was unusually spirited and pleasing.

Here, little Frank and Rosamond are books next popular to
Pilgrim's Progress, and have done much to improve the reading, as

they have in all the schools, and interest the children as no others on our list ; showing that the best books for children are simplest in their language and conception, and that only good persons can prepare good books for the most cordial wants of the schools.

Perhaps no school in town has undergone more improvement, whether in learning or behavior, than this, since it came under the good management of Miss Richardson ; the committee awarding their unqualified commendation of its excellence.

NORTH PRIMARY SCHOOL.—MISS SUSAN GOODALL, Teacher.

Pupils.	Ages.	Pupils.	Ages.	Pupils.	Ages.
Maggie Battles,	7	Ella Todd,	8	Daniel King,	6
Mary Carson,	6	Agnes Edna Tolman,	10	Edward Keating,	6
Harriet Garfield,	8	Ella Warren,	6	Michael Moore,	9
Abby Garfield,	7	Elizabeth Wood,	12	Charles Mullett,	7
Emma Goodnow,	10	Jenny Wood,	10	Thomas Murray,	5
Francis Hall,	10			Benjamin Nealey,	12
Alice Hartshorn,	9	James Battles,	11	Charles Nealey,	7
Mary Hosmer,	9	John Battles,	8	Eddie Nealey,	6
Annie Hosmer,	6	Philip Carson,	8	Charles Newton,	10
Elizabeth Howell,	10	Nicholas Coclin,	5	Everett Reynolds,	10
Katie Keating,	8	Ward Davidson,	6	Willie Sexton,	6
Lillie Keyes,	7	John Dowd,	9	Edward Simmons,	9
Mary Melvin,	6	John Dowd,	5	Evarts Smith,	9
Sarah Murray,	11	Frank Dowd,	8	Louis Surette,	7
Ellen Murray,	7	Thomas Foley,	8	Daniel Surette,	5
Alice Prescott,	8	Frederic Hartshorn,	7	George Tulis,	9
Caroline Rhoades,	9	Densmore Hosmer,	12	John Tulis,	7
Ellen Sexton,	8	Charles Hosmer,	8	Batty Tulis,	8
Minnie Stearns,	6	Herbert Hosmer,	7		

CLASS BOOKS USED.

Philbrick's Tablets,	Colburn's Arithmetic,
Worcester's Primer,	Greenleaf's Common School Arithmetic,
Tower's Gradual Primer,	Cornell's Primary Geography,
Tower's Introduction to Gradual Reader,	Cornell's Intermediate Geography,
Edgeworth's Early Lessons,	The Progressive Speller,
Hillard's Second Class Reader,	Payson and Dunton's Writing Books.
Emerson's Arithmetic,	

EXAMINATION.   Thirty-six pupils of the forty-four attending during the winter term, were present.   The exercises were very satisfactory to the committee, and the simple and natural behavior of the children gave them great pleasure.   Pleasant faces, whether of mistress or of pupils, usually win favor even under some blemishes, and make any school attractive and deserving of praise.   Nothing need be added to our last year's picture of this little company.

OUTER DISTRICTS.

EAST QUARTER SCHOOL.—MISS A. F. HUBBARD, Teacher.

Pupils.	Ages.	Pupils.	Ages.	Pupils.	Ages.
Susan E. Adams,	16	Sarah J. Tibbets,	14	S. Douglas Mason,	13
Lucy Balcom,	6	Ida M. Tibbets,	11	Carlton W. Mills,	10
Fannie Eaton,	7	Alice A. Wheeler,	13	John H. Moore,	8
Libbie Everett,	7	Kattie E. Wright,	12	Horace S. H. Paine,	12
Fannie A. Hall,	8			James H. Wright,	17
Angie Hall,	15	Ephraim W. Bull,	12	George A. Wright,	15
Emma Hatch,	10	John C. Bull,	10	Eddie L. Wright,	9
Alice E. Noyes,	13	Edward Connor,	12	Frank K. Wheeler,	8
Ida G. Paine,	7	William Connor,	14	Henry N. Wheeler,	11
Elma Russell,	10	George A. Everett,	10		
Mary J. Tibbets,	15	Earl H. Gowing,	9		

FOR THE TEACHERS' USE IN THE OUTER DISTRICTS.

New Testament,
Pilgrim's Progress,
Krummacher's Parables,
Book of the Constitutions,
Gleanings from the Poets,

Plutarch's Lives,
Fowler's Manual of Conversation,
Fowler's Book of Synonyms,
Manual of Agriculture,
Webster's Dictionary.

CLASS BOOKS USED.

Philbrick's Tablets,
Sargent's Fifth Reader,
Hillard's Second Class Reader,
Edgeworth's Early Lessons,
Tower's Introduction to Grad. Reader,
Smellie's Natural History,
Andrew's & Stoddard's Latin Grammar,
Weld's English Grammar,
Cowper's Task, for Analysis,

Fowler's Book of Synonyms,
Worcester's Dictionary,
Greenleaf's Common School Arithmetic,
Colburn's Arithmetic,
Cornell's High School Geography,
Cornell's Intermediate Geography,
Cornell's Primary Geography,
Lovell's Young Speaker,
Payson and Dunton's Writing Books.

EXAMINATION.   Twenty-five of the thirty in this school took part in the examination.   The recitations were very faithful, and some of the speaking especially praiseworthy.   A little less dependence on the memory, and something more of explanation on the part of the teacher, would have better pleased some of the committee, but all were gratified by the general excellency of the exercises.

We have spoken heretofore of Miss Hubbard's good knowledge of the branches she teaches, and of her familiarity with the books she uses.   If her order is subjective, and not at once apparent to the superficial observer, there is nevertheless work despatched, and this too without anxiety or fret — a grace of the first importance in a teacher, and the best course for securing the general love and confidence of the school and of the neighborhood.   The examination was largely attended by the parents and friends of the teacher.

NINE ACRE CORNER SCHOOL. — MISS R. M. STEARNS, Teacher.

Pupils.	Ages.	Pupils.	Ages.	Pupils.	Ages.
Annie Blaisdell,	7	Henry A. Blaisdell,	13	George Stacy,	13
Lizzie M. Garfield,	11	Hiram Blaisdell,	10	Elbert Wheeler,	12
Sarah F. Lee,	12	Daniel Callagan,	7	Harvie Wheeler,	14
Henrietta F. Miles,	14	Alfred Dakin,	13	Alvah G. Wheeler,	13
Mary Mullay,	6	Joseph Fitzpatrick,	12	Willie Wheeler,	10
Adelaide Tozier,	8	Almado Garfield,		Cyrus Wheeler,	9
M. Lizzie Wheeler,	11	Hubert Haynes,		Frank Wheeler,	6
Mary Williams,	10	Francis Mahan,		David Williams,	7
		Granville Miles,	16		

CLASS BOOKS USED.

Philbrick's Tablets,
Sargent's Fifth Reader,
Edgeworth's Early Lessons,
Tower's First Reader,
The Progressive Speller,
Tower's Speller,
Greenleaf's National Arithmetic,
Greenleaf's Com. School Arithmetic,
Greenleaf's Primary Arithmetic,
Colburn's Mental Arithmetic,

Cornell's High School Geography,
Cornell's Intermediate Geography,
Cornell's Primary Geography,
Tate's Philosophy,
Quackenboss' History of United States,
Hawthorne's Parley's History of United States,
Green's Analysis,
Tower's Algebra,
Payson and Dunton's Writing Books.

Examination. The examination of this school was well attended by pupils and parents ; twenty-three of the twenty-four pupils being present. The recitations in arithmetic and philosophy were particularly noted as showing great familiarity with the subject. In geography and reading, the classes did not appear so well, and the prevalence of a bad tone in all the reading classes was remarked upon. In this respect an entire change should be made, and it cannot be begun too soon, for this school, in which there is excellent material, and plenty of sound sense and information, now compares unfavorably with most of the schools, in point of animation and the manner of displaying the knowledge it has acquired.

FACTORY VILLAGE SCHOOL. — Miss Emma F. Moore, Teacher.

Pupils.	Ages.	Pupils.	Ages.	Pupils.	Ages.
Elizabeth Auty,	10	Mattie Leonard,	10	Frank Munroe,	9
Hannah Auty,	7	Elsie Leonard,	15	Edward Nolan,	11
Ella Casley,	10	Charlotte Nolan,	10	Henri Priest,	11
Maria Cass,	11	Bridget Ryan,	10	Hiram Pierce,	10
Mary A. Doherty,	9	Agnes Ryan,	8	William Priest,	13
Hattie Gross,	5	Ella A. Sampson,	14	John Ryan,	11
Esther Gross,	11	Angeline Tarbell,	17	Franklin Stone,	12
Emma A. Hosmer,	13			Michael Wall,	15
Lilla Hayward,	13	Jonas Auty,	9	Nelson Wood,	15
Laura Hayward,	13	John H. Cass,	14	Gilman Willis,	13
Clara Hoar,	11	Augustus Gross,	15	Howard Willis,	11
Emma Hayward,	8	James McMahan,	10	Samuel Willis,	5

CLASS BOOKS USED.

Philbrick's Tablets,
Greenleaf's Com. School Arithmetic,
Colburn's First Lessons in Intellectual Arithmetic,
Cornell's High School Geography,
Cornell's Intermediate Geography,
Cornell's Primary Geography,
Greene's Analysis,

Tower's Gradual Primer, and Introduction to the Gradual Reader,
Edgeworth's Early Lessons,
Hillard's Second Class Reader,
Quackenboss' History of United States,
Worcester's Pronouncing Spelling Book,
Tower's Gradual Speller.

Examination. Numbers thirty-five, and thirty-two of these were present. This school showed the effects of very faithful and stimulating instruction at its examination. The committee noticed especially the excellence in reading and spelling. An air of vivacity and intelligence prevailed in the school room, one of the best evidences of the success of the teacher.

It has been a difficult school to manage hitherto, being the largest of any in the outer districts and composed of mixed samples, some requiring the bit of restraint, and much given formerly to kicking against the pricks of authority. But Miss Moore has shown great good sense and firmness in the use of hers, as did her predecessor, and raised the school to be among the best behaved and most advanced of any of them.

4

BARRETT'S MILL SCHOOL. — Misses Prescott and Buttrick, Teachers.

Pupils.	Ages.	Pupils.	Ages.	Pupils.	Ages.
Lizzie Brooks,	10	Sarah Winn,	13	Lewis George,	18
Ellen Carter,	13	Laura Winn,	11	Charles H. Meek,	9
Mary Carter,	10			George L. Meek,	11
Eliza Dakin,	12	Charles Barrett,	5	Andrew Rhoades,	12
Mary Dakin,	10	George P. Barrett,	11	Charles F. Smith,	5
Carrie Hildreth,	12	Stephen G. Brooks,	11	William A. Shaw,	6
Adaline Robbins,	8	Nathan H. Brooks,	8	Nathan B. Smith,	12
Ella A. Shaw,	10	John L. Carter,	6	Horace E. Winn,	15
Mary G. Shaw,	16	Alfred B. Dakin,	13		

CLASS BOOKS USED.

Philbrick's Tablets,
Sargent's Fifth Reader,
Hillard's Second Class Reader,
Edgeworth's Early Lessons,
Tower's First and Second Reader,
Greenleaf's National Arithmetic,
Greenleaf's Com. School Arithmetic,
Colburn's Mental Arithmetic,
Quackenboss' History of United States,

Hawthorne's Parley's First Book of History,
Greene's Analysis,
Weld's Grammar,
Cornell's Geography,
Tower's Progressive Speller,
Tate's Philosophy,
Payson and Dunton's Writing Books.

EXAMINATION. Twenty-five whole number, twenty-four present. Much gratification was expressed by the committee at the readings and general proficiency of the scholars. Some problems, in rapid combinations of numbers were surprising, and a composition read by one of the young ladies, gave great pleasure.

An unusual number of the parents of the neighborhood came in to the examination.

Miss Prescott did much to interest and instruct her scholars while the school was under her exceedingly judicious and praiseworthy management. We were sorry to lose her services, for the time, but fortunate in finding a lively and spirited successor in Miss Buttrick, under whose care the school seems prospering, and likely to maintain its good name while she has charge of it.

BATEMAN'S POND SCHOOL. — Miss S. P. Bean, Teacher.

Pupils.	Ages.	Pupils.	Ages.	Pupils.	Ages.
Lottie Adams,	7	Augusta Penniman,	15	James Melvin,	15
Ella Adams,	11	Lottie Stowe,	10	James C. Melvin,	14
Lizzie Brown,	14			Otis Penniman,	8
Amelia C. Brown,	12	J. D. Brown,	12	George Penniman,	11
Charlotte Brown,	10	Dennis Keefe,	22	Henry Wetherbee,	11
Mary Brown,	8	James W. Jones,	7	Frank Wadley,	14
Lucy Jane Melvin,	13	Charles Melvin,	17		

CLASS BOOKS USED.

Philbrick's Tablets,
Wilson's First Reader,
Town's Second Reader,
Edgeworth's Early Lessons,
Sargent's Standard Reader,
Emerson's Arithmetic,
Colburn's Arithmetic,
Greenleaf's Arithmetic,
Day's Algebra,

Cornell's Geography,
Berard's History of United States,
Worcester's History,
Comstock's Philosophy,
Tower's Progressive Speller,
Andrews' and Stoddard's Latin Grammar,
Payson and Dunton's Writing Books.

EXAMINATION. Of the nineteen on the register, seventeen were in attendance, and the ease and excellency of every thing exhibited won, as it has uniformly before, the praise of all members of the committee present. The variety of methods of questioning on the part of the teacher ; her care to have the sense of the text rendered in words of the pupil, was especially noticed and commended ; as was an exercise heretofore new to most of our schools, and well suited to supply a want beginning to be felt in all of them. Last summer, some of the oldest scholars here, and in Miss Prescott's school, began writing diaries ; the two schools united also for spelling together once a fortnight, and they corresponded by letter as often, their letters being sent by chance post, and read before the schools by the mistresses, as exercises in composition. I suggest that these exercises be adopted in all the schools.

Every thing had the air of a family circle at the examination, and the only regret the committee had to express was, that this district and the town, were to lose the services of one who may be named as a model for general imitation by teachers every where. It must take some time for the worst of teachers even to spoil this fine school. One never leaves it without wishing to speak pleasant words to it, and taking sunny memories away with him. Nor did it suffer, while for a month or two, it was under the genial management of Miss Brown ; whose services may well be secured whenever a vacancy occurs in any of our districts.

NORTH QUARTER SCHOOL. — MISS SARAH A. BROWN, Teacher.

Pupils.	Ages.	Pupils.	Ages.	Pupils.	Ages.
M. Lizzie Dakin,	13	George F. Flagg,	13	Alfred B. Jenkins,	14
Lizzie Flagg,	11	Charles Green,	9	Abbot Lawrence,	9
Ellen F. Green,	10	Alvin S. Green,	7	Henry M. Pratt,	8
Fannie Holden,	8	George H. Hunt,	13	John P. Willis,	5
Emeline A. Stacy,	13	David B. Holden,	4	Abner B. Willis,	4

CLASS BOOKS USED.

Philbrick's Tablets,	Intermediate Geography,
Introduction to Gradual Reader,	Cornell's High School Geography,
Edgeworth's Early Lessons,	Weld's Grammar,
Hillard's Second Class Reader,	Greene's Analysis,
Sargent's Fifth Reader,	Tower's Algebra,
Colburn's Arithmetic,	Andrews' and Stoddard's Latin Grammar,
Greenleaf's Com. School Arithmetic,	mar,
Greenleaf's National Arithmetic,	Jarvis' Physiology,
Emerson's Arithmetic,	Fowler's Synonyms,
Primary Geography,	Payson and Dunton's Writing Books.

EXAMINATION. Fifteen is the whole number here, and fourteen were present. Some exercises in algebra, reading, and Latin were excellent. The writing books were kept exceedingly neat, and some of the writing was very graceful.

This, the smallest of our eleven schools, Miss Brown has continued to manage, under the past disadvantages of irregular attendance, and other impediments, to the satisfaction of the district generally, as far as I am informed, and in the best manner that could be expected under the circumstances.

INTERMEDIATE SCHOOL. — Miss M. A. DILLINGHAM, Teacher.

Pupils.	Ages.	Pupils.	Ages.	Pupils.	Ages.
William T. Adkins,	14	Thomas W. Mallard,	13	Mary S. Eaton,	12
Edward F. Adkins,	12	Norman L. Meek,	13	Susan E. Farwell,	14
Frank H. Bigelow,	10	Michael McManus,	13	Mary Garrity,	
Charles E. Brown,	11	Daniel Marley,	14	M. A. M. Goodnow,	12
Thomas Bulger,	16	Bryan McDonough,	14	Adelia M. Hobson,	12
Edmond Burke,	10	Frank Pierce,	12	Francis L. Hosmer,	11
John Dempsey,	13	Michael Ryan,	14	Mary F. Kelly,	13
Fred. M. Dennie,		William Shannon,	15	Mary A. Lynch,	14
John B. Dodd,	14	Fred. F. Skinner,	12	Annie F. Reynolds,	
John Downing,	11	Charles F. Watts,	15	Elizabeth S. Rhoades,	
Orlando W. Fay,		Frank W. Wilson,	14	Mary E. Rhoades,	
John Flannery,	13	Horace Walcott,	10	Emma F. Smith,	10
Willard F. Farrar,	11			Abbie A. Staples,	12
James Garrity,		Jennie M. Barrett,	11	Mary A. Todd,	14
Daniel Haynes,	14	Josephine Bartlett,	12	Emma A. Todd,	12
Fred. H. Harlow,	11	Nellie F. Bigelow,	11	Caroline E. Tozier,	15
John A. Hartshorn,	14	Emma F. Collier,	13	Elizabeth M. Warren,	11
Frank W. Holden,	13	Edith D. Davidson,	9	Mary L. Watts,	14
Fred. W. Hosmer,	11	Harriet A. Dean,	13	Amelia F. White,	
Cyrus Hubbard,	11	Mary Dowd.	12	Martha Walcott,	10
William H. Ingram,	14	Sarah Downing,	13		

FOR THE TEACHER'S USE.

New Testament,
Gleanings from the Poets,
Plutarch's Lives,
Pilgrim's Progress,

Krummacher's Parables,
Webster's Dictionary,
Fowler's Manual of Conversation,
Fowler's Book of Synonyms.

CLASS BOOKS USED.

Quackenbos' History of United States,
Greenleaf's Com. School Arithmetic,
Colburn's Mental Arithmetic,
Weld's English Grammar,
Cornell's High School Geography,

Cornell's Intermediate Geography,
Hillard's Second Class Reader,
Worcester's Spelling Book,
Andrews' Latin Lessons,
Payson and Dunton's Writing Books.

EXAMINATION. Of the sixty scholars, fifty-two came to the examination, which was also largely attended by the parents and friends of the scholars, and testified to the teacher's admirable discipline and good management. The recitations were prompt and correct, and the general appearance of the school highly pleasing. The classes in grammar and reading attracted particular attention. At the close of the exercises, the chairman of the committee spoke in their behalf, thanking the teacher for what she had done in this school, formerly so difficult, and regretting that she was so soon to leave it. The town will be indeed fortunate to find a successor so devoted, kind, and efficient as Miss Dillingham has been.

The classes in geography and reading, which have been under the charge of Miss Abbie P. Hosmer for a part of the year, gave evidence of her superior gifts as a teacher. She promises to be an acquisition to our company of teachers.

HIGH SCHOOL.—Mr. E. O. SHEPARD, Teacher.

MISS ABBIE P. HOSMER, Assistant.

Pupils.	Pupils.	Pupils.
Addie E. Adams,	Laura P. Meek,	Hersey Brown,
Jennie M. Adams,	Mary H. Moore,	Benjamin W. Brown,
Hattie A. Adkins,	Ellen J. Nealey,	William H. Brown,
Sarah E. Benjamin,	Mary Neagle,	Charles J. Dakin,
M. Augusta Bowers,	Ella Pierce,	M. Joseph Gleason,
Kate I. Bowers,	Eliza P. Potter,	Ephraim M. Hatch,
Nellie Brown,	Amelia Russell,	Confucius Hayden,
Abbie Brown,	Georgiana Russell,	J. Galen Hoar,
Alice M. Brigham,	Mary D. Wheeler,	J. Willard Hobson,
Mary E. Bull,	Mary C. Wheeler,	Charles T. Holbrook,
Maggie Byron,	Mattie M. Wheeler,	S. Albertus Hosmer,
Hattie L. Eaton,	Ida A. Wilson.	Charles F. Monroe,
Annie E. Gregory,		Edward G. Reynolds,
Hattie A. Hoar,	Frank A. Adams,	Reuben Rice. Jr.,
Ella S. Hosmer,	Richard F. Barrett,	Charles H. Walcott,
Susan D. Hosmer,	Joseph Barrett,	Charles H. Wetherbee,
Susan H. Hubbard,	Charles H. Bartlett,	Edwin M. Wheeler.
Hannah R. Hudson,	Henry T. Brown,	

Of these, thirty-nine are between the ages of 15 and 18, inclusive; thirteen are between the ages of 12 and 14, inclusive.

FOR THE TEACHERS' USE.

New Testament,	Long's Classical Atlas,
Pilgrim's Progress,	Zumpt's Latin Grammar,
Krummacher's Parables,	Doederlein's Latin Synonyms,
Shakspeare, Milton and Thompson,	Miss Peabody's Universal History,
Gleanings from the Poets,	Fowler's Manual of Conversation,
Plutarch's Lives,	Fowler's Book of Synonyms.
Anthon's Classical Dictionary,	

BOOKS RECOMMENDED.

Eschenburg's Manual of Classical Literature,	Brande's Encyclopedia,
	Crabbe's English Synonyms,
Lippincott's Pronouncing Gazetteer,	Dana's Selections from the Poets,
Bailey's Etymological Dictionary,	Roget's Thesaurus.

CLASSICAL AND FRENCH BOOKS.

Andrews' Latin Series,	Fasquelle's Reader,
Arnold's Latin and Greek Series,	Chouquet's French Lessons,
Moore's Virgil,	Nouvelles Genevoises,
Johnson's Cicero,	Le Roman d'un Jeune Homme Pauvre,
Sophocles' Greek Grammar,	Spier & Lureimes' French Dictionary,
Xenophon's Anabasis,	Andrews' Latin Lexicon,
Homer's Iliad,	Liddell and Scott's Greek Lexicon.
Fasquelle's French Grammar,	

ENGLISH CLASS BOOKS USED.

Worcester's Comprehensive Dictionary,	Loomis' Geometry,
	Smellie's Philosophy of Natural History,
Webster's Quarto (Unabridged),	Sargent's Fifth Reader,
Sherwin's Algebra,	Plutarch's Lives,
Eaton's Arithmetic,	Gleanings from the Poets.
Stockhardt's Chemistry,	

Early in the autumn, in consequence of the increase in number of the pupils, it was decided to appoint an assistant in the High School. Miss Emma C. Hunt filled this place for a month, and was succeeded by Miss Abbie P. Hosmer, whose services, it is to be hoped, the town may retain. She has taught with great assiduity, spirit, and efficiency. By her assistance, Mr. Shepard has been enabled to devote himself more entirely to the higher studies, and has taught Latin, French, algebra, and geometry with great success.

EXAMINATION. At the examination the classes specially noticed were the Latin and arithmetic classes of Miss Hosmer, and those of Mr. Shepard in French, algebra, and natural history. The French pronunciation was much improved since the last examination ; and the Latin classes, though small, recited well. The committee noticed with pleasure that at least two-thirds of the school studied either Latin or French, and nearly that proportion studied Latin. There is a single pupil in Greek.

The exercises in spelling and defining were specially commendable, the words having been written from dictation, and Mr. Shepard giving the derivations and such other information as the dictionary and his learning afforded at the time of hearing these lessons. The committee were pleased to find the good progress which the school has undergone, both in learning and behavior, since it came under his supervision.

A new feature of our examinations this year, it will be perceived, has been the large attendance of parents and families in the several districts, and of the teachers. They have been pleasant occasions, alike for the children in the neighborhoods, for parents, teachers, and committee. We have succeeded in putting something of color and sprightliness into these exercises, taking out most of the terror, the depression, the dullness, so disastrous to the interests of a virtuous ambition and true manliness.

THE MOTHER TONGUE. Most of you, Gentlemen of the Committee, I believe, agree with me in thinking that we should urge upon all our teachers, from the Primaries up to the High School, the importance of giving more time to spelling and defining the words most used in the common affairs of life, as the readiest means of attaining the arts of conversation and of composition ; in all of which there is at present a shameful deficiency — more time being spent upon every other branch of study than of the English tongue.

SPELLING AND DEFINING. The deficiency in spelling and defining is almost universal, and the present methods are in some measure accountable for the general defect. I find there was room for complaint in this respect years ago. Mr. Frost, who had charge of our schools for many years, does not conceal his views of the state of things in his day. In his report of 1846, he says : —

"Spelling is a branch that has been neglected of late years. The older classes have felt above spelling, except guessing at a few hard words out of their reading books. This is a great mistake. Spelling depends greatly, almost entirely, on the memory. Unless its endless details are impressed early on the memory by frequent repetition, and become a habit, they can never be retained. The committee recommend that all the scholars should be put in the spelling book, and kept there until every word in it is fixed in their memories."

Poor spelling is an attainment in which the rising generation bid fair to outstrip all preceding ones, and leave their elders in hopeless despair of ever being able to overtake them. I fear there is small chance for mending the spelling or defining much till we have a book adapted to the uses of the scholar as he comes up to the common occasions and necessities of life. All our spelling books and dictionaries are deficient in this respect. The nearest approach to what is wanted is to be found in the Manual of English Pronunciation and Spelling, containing a full alphabetical vocabulary of the language, with a preliminary exposition of English orthoepy and orthography, designed as a work of reference for general use, and as a text-book in our schools, by Messrs. Soule and Wheeler. The book seems well adapted to these purposes, and is included in our list.

WORD BOOK. A simpler book is wanted, containing only the roots of our tongue, omitting the derivations and giving apt illustrations from the best authors ; the words arranged as they come into common use, and for ease of attainment ; these to be spelled, written, and conversed about from the smallest classes to the highest, and combined in exercises of composition. It should embrace the current vocabulary of the practical man and the scholar — the terms of art, of science, and of mythology, being given in an appendix or separate volume — thus leaving the body of our language to be acquired in the course of common education ; the teacher dismissing his scholars with a fair command of their native tongue, both in speaking and writing it.

Conversation, speaking, spelling, reading, writing, and composition, are the essence and exercise of language, and, next to life and thinking — which are primary to all else — should have the first care of the teacher. I believe experience has proved that there is no better method for securing proficiency and accuracy in these attainments than by frequent practice ; and that spelling and writing are best taught together ; the scholar first writing the words of his lesson, from the columns of the spelling book, sometimes from dictation, and defining them also.

BAILEY'S ETYMOLOGICAL DICTIONARY. The best book I know for our purpose is the dictionary compiled by Bailey, much used by the scholars of the last century, and by the best of this, for tracing the etymologies of words, and for its simple and clear definitions, suited to the minds of children. The book is arranged on the plan of making the language of easy attainment, and on the principle, as the author informs us in his introduction, that : —

" It should be the special care and study of every teacher who would furnish the minds of his pupils with the useful knowledge of things of any kind, to give them true and distinct ideas, — something more than vague notions — of the proper sense and meaning of the words they speak and write ; the terms of art, in which they are expressed, and without which no real progress is ever made in any study."

WORD–LESSONS. Word-lessons thus given out for spelling and writing, for conversation on their meanings and derivations, would be exercises admirably suited to facilitate the acquisition of our language, and in ways delightful alike to teacher and classes. A Book of Proverbs might be used, in a similar way, to great advantage for the younger classes. Sharpe's Diamond Dictionary appears to be better suited to this end than any other that has fallen under the eye of the Superintendent.

CONCORD BOOK. Our Book of Selections for the use of the reading classes, from the works of Concord authors, comprising some names well known to literature, and intended for family reading also, has been delayed for the present ; some progress has been made, however, in the compilation, and the work will appear whenever the state of the country shall warrant its publication. We hope to have it accompanied with proper illustrations and a good map of the districts, the location of the families, with the antiquities of education from the first settlement.

LOCAL PREJUDICES. Perhaps as few prejudices remain with us, as any where, of the penny wisdom that spares any expense for refining the mind and morals, to spend the amount in the baser ends of existence ; any project for improving the condition of the schools, having been heretofore entertained with respect, and, if reasonable and necessary, carried out ungrudgingly for the good of all.   It is not wise to propose too much at once, and impatiently.   Let us deal generously with prejudices, if any there be, by showing the better methods to be the cheapest in the end.   Our people are of the primitive type, and perhaps slower than some to accept any changes till they are proved to be for the better, and a profitable recasting of the ancient manners and ways.*

We do well to respect the local feelings and wants of the several neighborhoods, since, by doing so, we give real unity and permanence to the State's designs, along with theirs, and secure the advantages of such co-operation where it can be effected without variance.   Proper adaptation of one to the other is desirable, indispensable often, to meet the demands of localities and the spirit of improvement.

And though our schools doubtless compare favorably with those of most towns in our Commonwealth, it needs no extraordinary perception to discover many deficiencies and blemishes, that, when made apparent to the larger number of our people, and at the proper time, will be removed from their otherwise fair frame and countenance.   If it were the best way to blazon these defects — whether of discipline, teaching, teachers, parents, children — about our village and the districts, they were too personal to be named here, or dwelt upon, by your Superintendent.   We think it best to speak of what is praiseworthy, and so intimate what is not, by contrast, rather than to fall into the habit of open blame, which seldom helps reform, whether of persons or States.

SCHOOL REPORTS.   I have heard that School Reports were sometimes very dull, and mostly unreadable.   It must be the ill-natured satire of some morose old gentleman of the past generation, on the learning and good name of worthy and wise men like ourselves ; for

---

* A pamphlet entitled Plans and Illustrations of a new Public School System, by Rev. W. B. Wait, teacher of a seminary at Greenwood, in Reading, Mass., has been sent us by the author. It contains a natural system for bringing all the schools of a town under the charge of professors and assistants, in one central building, and of cheapening very much the cost of instruction, while it gives efficiency and greater variety to the course of studies. The plan seems excellent for a village institution, and a practicable one for the adoption of the towns, where a system has not become so rooted in the traditions of the people as to render a change not easy, nor, perhaps, desirable. But there is no reason why it might not be adopted in a new settlement, and comprehend several schools in its general economies. The book deserves a reading by school committees and all interested in education.

5

certainly there can be nothing more tempting, to a scholar and citizen, for trying his pen, than the schools offer him. I see no good reason why reports should not be made as attractive as other writings, and as well worth preserving, while children and youth are ornaments of our houses, and their education the prime interest of the towns in our Commonwealth. Nor why they may not properly reflect some personal features, and come as near, as delicacy permits, to being a portraiture of their social and religious life — next only to profiles of the family heads, and general history; if, indeed, even these can be omitted wholly, while the schools are their liveliest looking-glasses, exhibiting their personal traits in the children; the characteristics of past times being again epitomized in the several families and neighborhoods; the first settlers, surviving, under slight disguises, in their descendants. Still, with this broad opportunity before me, I cannot hope to have done more, within the small space I have taken, than to have intimated, what, I trust, the town will gladly encourage their School Committees following into fuller details, hereafter making their annual messages as good reading for the children as for their parents, the tax-payers, selectmen, and assessors.

Again thanking you, Gentlemen, for your confidence and co-operation, the children and teachers for theirs; with the wish that I could have served them, and the town generally, more to their advantage, and agreeably to my sense of the proper duties of my office, I submit this, my third annual report.

A. BRONSON ALCOTT, SUPERINTENDENT.

CONCORD, April 1, 1862.

SCHOOL EXHIBITION.

The third annual Exhibition of the public schools took place on the 15th of March. Although the weather was stormy, the number of pupils present was 320, and there were at least as many spectators. After some delay in seating the large number of children, Mr. Alcott, the Superintendent, called the assembly to order at a quarter before two o'clock, and spoke as follows :

" *Parents and townspeople,*—

Believing the annual Exhibition of the schools has been adopted into the list of holidays for the pleasure of every one in our town, the school committee have again assembled them here before you, to-day, to show you some choice samples of the fruits of the last year's endeavors of children, youth and their teachers, and,—as they take pride in believing,—of their own well meant exertions for promoting the interests of education during this period.

They have desired their Superintendent to introduce the schools to you, one by one ; and ask you to excuse them from taking anything from the pleasure or fitness of this occasion by obtruding any words of their own, being persuaded that these groups of sprightliness and beauty, as they shall come successively before you, can speak a more significant speech than they have either wit or grace to deliver. And, following out their wishes, our services will now open with some acknowledgment of the Fountain of life and light, that kindles alike all minds, and from which all good learning and high aspirations proceed."

After prayer by the Reverend C. B. Smith, the exercises of the schools began. The following song was sung by a choir under the direction of Messrs. Stacy and Winch, the children joining in the well known chorus.

SONG.

Air :—"THE JOHN BROWN SONG."

Welcome Fathers! here's welcome to you all!
Welcome Mothers! right welcome to the Hall!
Sisters, Brothers! we welcome one and all!
    The children's day has come.

    Chorus.—Glory, Glory Hallelujah,
          Glory, Glory Hallelujah,
          Glory, Glory Hallelujah!
          The children's day has come.

Slow goes Winter in icy armor forth,
Spring comes slowly to thaw the frosty North,—
Sing till birds come, ye children of the North!
    Until the blue birds come.

    Chorus.—Glory, Glory Hallelujah, &c.,
          The blue birds soon shall come.

Northward flying a little bird I hear,
Blue birds singing not half so loud and clear,—
All ye children his sounding voice may hear,
    When to the North he's come.

    Chorus.—Glory, Glory Hallelujah, &c.,
          To counsel us he's come.

" Raise loud anthems to Him who reigns above,
Sing His praises, His mighty power and love,—
Oft your fathers have known His power and love,
    And seen His judgments come.

    Chorus.—Glory, Glory Hallelujah, &c.,
          His jubilee has come!

" Drums shall echo the Lord's high decree,
Cannons thunder, and then declareth He,
Bugles blowing, His heavenly decree—
    TO ALL SHALL FREEDOM COME!

    Chorus.—Glory, Glory Hallelujah, &c.,
          To all shall Freedom come.

" Sing ye children, ye children of the North!
Freedom's banner shall lead your army forth,
Victory's coming to meet the marching North,
    And Liberty shall come!

    Chorus.—Glory, Glory Hallelujah, &c.,
          Fair Liberty has come! "

The schools came on the platform in the order given below :—

MISS HOSMER'S SCHOOL.

EAST PRIMARY.—34 Pupils Present.

Song.—" Happy are we to-day friends."
Scenes from our School Room, with Reading, by Miss O'Brien.
" Ida's Address."
Song.

———

MISS RICHARDSON'S SCHOOL.
WEST PRIMARY.—48 Present.
Song.—" We love the land of the Stars and Stripes."
Recitation.
Dialogue.—" What is most beautiful? "
Recitation.—" The Fairies."
Recitation.—" Lift up the banner high! "

MISS GOODALL'S SCHOOL.

NORTH PRIMARY.—34 Present.

Song.—" The Bright Rosy Morning."
Recitation.—" Lord Ullin's Daughter."
Song.—" See the Stars are coming."
Recitation.—" Robinson Crusoe."
Song.—" Kind Words can never die."

MISS BROWN'S SCHOOL.

NORTH QUARTER.—9 Present.

Recitation.—" Life Clock."
Exercise in Grammar.
Declamation.
Recitation.—" Io Triumphe."

MISS BEAN'S SCHOOL.

BATEMAN'S POND.—14 Present.

" Voyage of the Good Ship Union."
" The Angels."

MISS STEARNS' SCHOOL.

NINE ACRE CORNER.—15 Present.

Declamation.
Singing.—" The Revolutionary Tea."
Recitation.—" Death of Little Nell."
Dialogue.—" The Gridiron."
Song.—" The Child's Wish."

RECESS.

MISS MOORE'S SCHOOL.

FACTORY VILLAGE.—24 Present.

Dialogue.—" The Model School."

MISS BUTTRICK'S SCHOOL.

BARRETT'S MILL.—20 Present.

Song.—" Marching Along."
Recitation.—" Hohenlinden."
Song.—" Maiden Fair."
Song.—" The Flag of our Union."

MISS HUBBARD'S SCHOOL.

EAST QUARTER.—30 Present.

Dialogue.—" King Alfred."
Oratorical Gestures.
Declamation.—" The Rescued Child."
Concert Recitation.—" The Battle."

MISS DILLINGHAM'S SCHOOL.

INTERMEDIATE.—47 Present.

FAIRY SCENE.

King of Elves.—All ye sprites of Elfin land,
Light of heart and strong of hand,
Queen of Fairies.—All ye fairies, radiant, bright,
Sporting merrily all the night,

Both.—All that own our peaceful sway,
Seek the fairies' court to day.
Now in our regal hall
Loud ring our merry call.
All ye sprites of Elfin land,
Light of heart and strong of hand,
Elves and fairies one and all,
Hearken to our merry call.

SEMI-CHORUS.

Fairies.—We are here, we are here!
Sprites from the mountain,
From grove and clear fountain
And under the sea.

Gipsies.—A gipsy band we fondly stray
'Neath mild Italia's richest sun,
Where olive orchards blossom wild
And braided streamlets swiftly run.
While chanting fancy's roundelays,
We watch the pale and dimpling light
That on the soft Etruscan rose
With gilding rays falls soft and bright.

The opal glows with ceaseless fire,
As on the Arno's banks we roam,
Companions of the gipsy band,
Unknown the bliss of settled home.
The Contadina's songs we hear
While bells at vespers chime and ring;
The glens resound with minstrelsy,
And all in chorus gaily sing.

When wavelets murmur in the breeze,
And winds are stealing gently by,
And twinkling stars their vigils keep
Along the arches of the sky;
Then gipsy maidens seek the dance
With measure unrestrained and free;
As sunbeams on the waters fall
They lightly step and trip wtth glee.

Queen of the Zephyrs.—Come, come pretty birds!
And sing a song for me,
I'll listen with pleasure
To your sweet melody;
Come, come and begin!
I'll learn your happy strain
And warble so sweetly
O'er hill and flowery plain.

Sing, sing pretty birds!
Your songs I love to hear,
They tremble so sweetly
Upon the listening ear;
Come, come and begin!
Don't droop your pretty wings,
But turn your eyes on me
And sweetly, sweetly sing.

Elfin King.—I'm king in the Elfin land,
And my palace towers white and tall,
With a stately grace, do stand,
Keeping watch o'er my audience hall;
And there doth my council brave
Ponder many a weighty plan,
For the glory of Elfin-land
And the good of the world and man,

Queen of Fairies.—I'm queen of the Elfin land,
And my subjects good and true
Swiftly on our fair designs
Day by day our toils renew.
For man's best good we toil,
And treasures vast and fine
We store in the depths of the earth,
In the veins of the gleaming mine.

CHORUS.

Hail! Hail! Fairy Queen,
Hail! Hail! Fairy King,
True hearts around you, bright planets above,–
Long, long may your power
Reign o'er grove and bower,
Bright be your glory wher'er you roam.

Two fairies on their way to the festival are supposed
to arrive at the track of a railroad. They stop the train.

The Conductor sings.—Pay your fare my little maids!
I cannot long delay,
I must rush the lightning train
A thousand miles to-day.
Ring the bell, blow the whistle,
Shrilly, clear and strong;
Blow the whistle, ring the bell,
Rush the train along.

Fairies.—We cannot pay, we wish we could,
We've left our purse at home.
For we have come from fairy land,
Around the world to roam.

Conductor.—You cannot go, my pretty maids,
To carry you were wrong,
Ring the bell, blow the whistle;
Rush the train along.

An Elf in disguise.—Pray don't refuse the little maids,
I'll pay their fare with pleasure;
Jump on, my dears, and when you 're there,
Repay me at your leisure.

CHORUS.

Away, away, the morning freshly breaking
Shines o'er the deep our lingering steps to chide;
And light with sport and song our labor making,
We cheerily haste to stem the tide.
The gentle zephyrs o'er the waters playing
Invite us forth unto the foaming main;
Our willing steps our cheerful hearts obeying,
Unfurl our fairy wings again!

MR. SHEPARD'S SCHOOL.

HIGH.—42 Present.

Recitation.—" Cœur de Lion at the Bier of his Father."—Addie E. Adams.
Declamation.—" The Spirit of the War."—C. F. Wetherbee.
Recitation.—" Iphigenia and Agamemnon."—Mary C. Wheeler.
Dialogue. { Concord Bridge,   { C. H. Bartlett,
{ Bunker Hill Monument. { Hersey Brown.
Chorus.—" Hail Columbia."

Miss Hosmer's school, though smaller than usual, appeared with its accustomed grace and liveliness. The present of a ring and basket of flowers to the teacher by one of the children was a compliment well deserved, and a testimony to the affection with which Miss Hosmer is regarded by her pupils and their parents.

Miss Richardson brought more scholars to the platform than any of the teachers, and her exercises were well chosen and given with great spirit. She has nothing to fear from a comparison with any of our teachers.

Miss Goodall's school showed good training in singing and declamation,—the spoken parts being delivered with much force and courage by the young orators.

Miss Brown's school is the smallest in the town, and owing to the storm, some of her small number were absent from the Exhibition. One or two pupils therefore were made to represent the whole, and these gave their exercises in a very creditable manner.

Miss Bean's school also was smaller than usual this year, making up in patriotism what they lacked in numbers. No one can see this docile little band, with their gentle, wise and painstaking teacher, without recognising her great fitness for the position, and their entire confidence in her.

Miss Stearns brought with her to the platform more boys than girls, and her exercises were of a more decided character, suited to the fancy of boys, than those of most of the schools. Force and readiness mark all that this school undertakes, and for strength and good will it is unsurpassed by any.

Miss Moore's school was both less in numbers and in the age of the pupils than for the last two years. It has lost, too, one of its ornaments in the sweet singer who has been listened to with so much pleasure at our former Exhibitions, and whose death was so touchingly alluded to by one of her schoolmates. But the appearance of the school was still excellent, and in no other respect inferior to former years. The dramatic piece was well sustained and a good satire on schools and committee-men as we are informed they were in former times.

Miss Buttrick's scholars with their waving flags and choral singing gave an agreeable diversity to the Exhibition. Nothing is more pleasant than to see the various characters of the several schools brought out in this way. The little orator who recited Hohenlinden with so much courage won great applause, as did Miss Moore's youngest declaimer.

Miss Hubbard's scholars showed much readiness and careful training. Their dramatic piece was well performed and gave great satisfaction to young and old.

Miss Dillingham's school, being the largest present except Miss Richardson's, and mostly dressed in .fanciful costumes, made a very striking appearance. Perhaps a little more indulgence of the fancy on such occasions would add to the interest of the performances, and be no little advantage to the children. The text of the miniature opera performed by this school so well, is printed on a previous page.

The High School did not appear on the platform but was well represented by those who spoke for it, and at the close united with great effect in singing our earliest national hymn. The scenic representation of Hosea Biglow's patriotic verses was admirable, and called down great applause.

The audience owe much to the volunteer choir, not connected with the schools, who added so much to the pleasure of the afternoon by their agreeable music.

Half an hour was spent in serving the battalion of school children with the ample refreshments provided, and at five o'clock nearly all had left the hall; the whole performances continuing less than three hours and a half. This promptness and punctuality much added to the comfort of the occasion, and though the room was too small to seat or even contain all who came, we believe all went away with a hearty delight in what they had seen and heard.